THE DIFFICULT TRIANGLE

Other PACCA Books
from Westview Press

From Confrontation to Negotiation: U.S. Relations with Cuba, Philip Brenner

The Dangerous Doctrine: National Security and U.S. Foreign Policy, Saul Landau

Crisis in Central America: Regional Dynamics and U.S. Policy in the 1980s, edited by Nora Hamilton, Jeffry A. Frieden, Linda Fuller, and Manuel Pastor, Jr.

In the Shadows of the Sun: Caribbean Development Alternatives and U.S. Policy, Carmen Diana Deere (coordinator), Peggy Antrobus, Lynn Bolles, Edwin Melendez, Peter Phillips, Marcia Rivera, Helen Safa

This book is a project of
Policy Alternatives for the Caribbean and Central America
(PACCA)
in cooperation with

Centro de Investigación y Docencia Económicas (CIDE)

Coordinadora Regional de Investigaciones
Económicas y Sociales (CRIES)

THE DIFFICULT TRIANGLE

Mexico, Central America, and the United States

H. Rodrigo Jauberth, Gilberto Castañeda,
Jesús Hernández, and Pedro Vuskovic

A PACCA BOOK

WESTVIEW PRESS

BOULDER • SAN FRANCISCO • OXFORD

Translator's Note: This volume cites many English-language sources, the majority of which are filtered through Spanish-language media. "Quotations" from such sources are therefore an approximation of the original, faithful to the spirit—but not the letter.

Copyright © 1992 by Policy Alternatives for the Caribbean and Central America

Published in 1992 in the United States of America by Westview Press, Inc., 5500 Central Avenue, Boulder, Colorado 80301-2847, and in the United Kingdom by Westview Press, 36 Lonsdale Road, Summertown, Oxford OX2 7EW

Published in Spanish in 1991 as *La Triangulación Centroamérica-México-EUA*

Library of Congress Cataloging-in-Publication Data
Triangulación Centroamérica-México-EUA. English.
    The difficult triangle : Mexico, Central America, and the United
States / H. Rodrigo Jauberth . . . [et al.]
        p.   cm.
    Translation of: La triangulación Centroamérica-México-EUA.
    "A PACCA book."
    Includes index.
    ISBN 0-8133-8203-3. ISBN 0-8133-8204-1 (pbk.).
    1. United States—Foreign relations—Mexico.   2. Mexico—Foreign
relations—United States.   3. Central America—Foreign relations—
United States.   4. United States—Foreign relations—Central
America.   5. Central America—Foreign relations—Mexico.   6. Mexico—
Foreign relations—Central America.   I. Jauberth, H. Rodrigo.
II. Title.
E183.8.M6T6513   1992
327.73072—dc20   91-38079
                                                                            CIP

Printed and bound in the United States of America

The paper used in this publication meets the requirements
of the American National Standard for Permanence of Paper
for Printed Library Materials Z39.48-1984.

10   9   8   7   6   5   4   3   2   1

Contents

Tables

Prologue

This prologue contributes a Central American perspective to this important book, complementing the commentaries from Mexico and the United States contained in the Epilogue. We thus hope to reinforce the triangular analysis of political and economic relations among Mexico, Central America, and the United States undertaken by CIDE, PACCA, and CRIES.

This is a time of rapid change in the region. As manifested in recent initiatives, Washington clearly has a policy to reshape regional ties. Examples are the planned Free Trade Agreement with Mexico, President Bush's "Enterprise for the Americas" initiative toward Latin America, and continuing U.S. efforts to reshape Central American economies, now under the aegis of the "Program for Democracy and Development."

From a Central American perspective these changes, and the attitude Mexico has recently shown toward Central America on the political-diplomatic level, raise the prospect of fundamental alterations in the triangular relationship. Is Mexico being pulled away from its traditional role of standing with other Latin American countries when they confronted the United States? Will its economic relations with Central America be determined by its trade pact with the United States?

These dilemmas and changes require a Latin American response, an agenda for reshaping hemispheric relations based on a regional perspective, rather than bilateral relations or a simple acquiescence in the Bush administration's plans. There are significant opportunities to be grasped, particularly in the end of the cold war and the global tensions and local polarizations produced by the East-West conflict. We must also broaden the range of actors who participate in and shape these hemispheric relations, especially including previously disenfranchised social sectors that have emerged and found voices in recent years.

The growing formal democratization in Central America is to be welcomed, even considering the high rates of voter abstention and continuing violations of human rights in El Salvador and Guatemala. But the apparent political homogenization is artificial, reducing the opportunities for participating in power and attenuating political pluralism. The possibility of extending and deepening democracy into broader spheres of civil society has become more remote.

In the Epilogue, Primitivo Rodriguez and David Brooks point out efforts by U.S. and Mexican trade unions to play a role in determining the shape of the Free Trade Agreement. It is not just that unions and other affected social sectors should play, for democratic reasons, a role in determining their own countries' policies. Given the transnationalization of capital, labor movements must also reach across borders and cooperate, or be placed at a serious disadvantage.

The argument of this book, that a multilateral relationship allows the weaker parties greater opportunity to exercise sovereignty than do bilateral relations that maximize the advantage of the most powerful country, applies to economic relations just as to political-diplomatic ties. If rather than forging closer trade links among themselves and making economic policy that responds to local needs, Latin American countries synchronize policies according to the formulas advocated by Washington, the asymmetries of wealth and economic power will put each country at a disadvantage with respect to the United States. Latin nations will end up competing on the basis of low wages and lax regulation—the comparative advantage of misery—while much of their already-poor populations becomes beggars and delinquents. The results will be increasing social polarization, violence, drug trafficking, and migration.

Diversified economic relations are also less risky. If Latin American countries trade extensively with Europe, Asia, and Africa as well as the United States, they will be less vulnerable to a U.S. recession. This applies especially to the small Central American economies. Nor is the U.S. economy helped if a domestic recession produces crisis in Latin America and weakens demand for U.S. exports.

The regulatory roles played by the International Monetary Fund (IMF), World Bank, and, increasingly, the Inter-American Development Bank must be redefined around goals of fair trade and equitable competition and sustainable and renewable growth, all of which are to be found in their charters but which have been subordinated to their present roles of inspector and keeper of monopolistic and asymmetrical market power for the wealthier countries. The protectionism practiced by the Group of Seven (G7) is not subject to this inspection, nor is the United States forced into "structural adjustment" on account of its gigantic foreign debt and fiscal deficit. The democratization of these multilateral bodies, now controlled by the G7 countries, is a fundamental item on the new agenda.

In Central America, the role of the U.S. Agency for International Development in economic policy making further complicates the conditionalities of the multilateral institutions. Under these conditions, a further opening of the Central American markets cannot create the conditions for a more competitive market; instead, it will create even more asymmetric and subordinated economic relations.

At this historic crossroads, with Mexico and Central America occupying structurally subordinated positions as much in the economic sphere as in the political and military sphere, an alternative vision, based on broad social participation and stressing many-sided relations rather than inequitable bilateral ties, is necessary to transform current threats into future possibilities. This book is commended to the reader as a means of refreshing our historical consciousness and making that alternative vision more concrete.

Xabier Gorostiaga

Acknowledgments

This book is a synthesis of the shared academic interest of three institutions: the Centro de Investigación y Docencia Económicas (CIDE), the Coordinadora Regional de Investigaciones Económicas y Sociales (CRIES), and Policy Alternatives for the Caribbean and Central America (PACCA), whom we wish to thank for their support, especially Carlos Bazdrech, Xabier Gorostiaga, and Robert Stark, respectively. We thank David Ayon, Ricardo Anzaldua, and Miguel Garcia y Griego for their help in getting this project started. We gratefully acknowledge the generous support of the John D. and Catherine T. MacArthur Foundation for this project.

Similarly, we would like to extend our gratitude to those who enriched this work and shared their concerns with us, reading and commenting on our efforts, offering suggestions, facilitating materials and interviews, and so forth, without which it would have been difficult to meet our objectives during the course of our labors. Our thanks go chiefly to those with whom we held our workshop at CIDE on July 8, 1989: Juan Arancibia (Universidad Nacional Autónoma de México—UNAM), Lucrecia Lozano (Centro de Estudios Latino Americanas [CELA]–UNAM), Luis González Souza (UNAM), Fernando Carmona (UNAM), Jorge O. Guzmán (Investigaciones Socioeconómicas de Honduras—INSEH), and Cheryl Esback (University of Virginia).

In addition, we are grateful to the following individuals who read our work and gave us their salient comments: Guadalupe González (CIDE), Manuel Pastor, Jr. (Occidental College), Rafael Guido Bejar (Facultad Latinoamericana de Ciencias Sociales de México—FLACSO MEX), Adolfo Aguilar Zinser (UNAM), Colin Danby (PACCA), Raul Hinojosa (University of California at Berkeley), Cameron Duncan (Greenpeace International), Evelyn Jacir Lobo (Programa de Estudios Centroamericanos, Centro de Investigación y Docencia Económicas—PECA-CIDE), Johnny

Fox (Massachusetts Institute of Technology), Giancarlo Soler Torrijos (Maestría en Economía Política Internacional–CIDE—MEPI-CIDE), and Sergio Aguayo (Colegio de México—COLMEX). We would also like to thank Rosa L. Aguilar, secretary of CIDE's Central American Studies area, for her laborious effort and Maxine Kligerman Siri for her commendable professionalism in translating the entire work. We thank Colin Danby for all his work in editing this English edition, as well as Maryanne DePresco, Elizabeth O'Connor, and Megan Crowley for their valuable assistance in preparing it for publication. Thanks also to Barbara Ellington of Westview Press for her help in bringing this book to a North American audience.

H. Rodrigo Jauberth
Gilberto Castañeda
Jesús Hernández
Pedro Vuskovic

Introduction

H. RODRIGO JAUBERTH

The historical process is a unit in time . . . the present contains all of the past and in the present, what is essential in the past comes to fruition.

            —Antonio Gramsci

HISTORICALLY, MEXICO, CENTRAL AMERICA, and the United States have been linked together in a triangular relationship. When the national interests of Central America and Mexico have coincided in confronting U.S. influence, their national autonomy has benefitted.[1]

Recently, however, there has been a visible modification in this triangle, springing largely from the erosion in ties between Central America and Mexico. Central America has been placed on the back burner in the diplomatic agendas of Mexico and the United States, while these two countries have sought rapprochement. Despite this, the underlying factors that shape the triangular relationship have not changed.

There is always a conflict on the horizon in Central America, because the grave social crisis that provoked the revolutionary outburst of the 1970s has yet to be resolved. Thus there is a continuing need for the involvement of players like Mexico that can advocate formulas for easing tensions and nourishing development and peace in the area.

Viewed from Central America, Mexico is also being buffeted by the winds of history—domestic and foreign—and today is confronted with the challenge of remaking its international economic relations and, consequently, its foreign policy. On the one hand, Mexico is driven toward the formation of an economic bloc with the United States and Canada. At the same time, it is constrained by the need to maintain and strengthen its historic ties with Latin America.

The policy issues are more complex than these simple dichotomies, but one undeniable fact is that "Mexico maintains some 80 percent of its tourism and over two-thirds of its trade with the United States, with

1

more than 200 million crossings over a common border more than 3,000 km. long."[2] What is regrettable, in contrast, is that Mexico's trade with Latin America is rather limited, roughly 4 percent of its total foreign commerce.

The debate in Mexico over the prospects for a future Free Trade Agreement with the United States and its anticipated domestic and external impact has intensified recently; the how and the when of it captures the interest of Mexicans and other Latin Americans, especially Central Americans. This decision by Mexico, plus the challenge of consolidating a new relationship with the United States, demonstrates that this process of commercial rapprochement is more far reaching than it appears. Its unforeseeable impact will transcend domestic decision making, involving not only Mexico's future as an independent and sovereign nation, but the autonomy and sovereignty of Latin America.

Mexico's challenge of forging a new type of relationship with the countries of Latin America and the United States is the same one that (either singly or, ideally, jointly) the countries south of the Rio Grande and from the Caribbean to Patagonia will have to face in their relations with the United States. The framework will be the current reorganization of the world economy and the course of U.S. economic policy toward Latin America.

In January 1989, in a little-known statement, Henry Kissinger outlined the policy that, in his view, the Bush administration should pursue in Latin America. He said, "It makes no sense for state capitalism to continue to reign supreme south of the Rio Grande. . . . Privatization, the free flow of capital, and a reduced state burden should be key elements in this program." (Actually, there is a neoliberal consensus on this today throughout Latin America.) Kissinger went on:

> Historical timing and geographical proximity have combined to make Mexico a test case. The United States and Latin America have been lucky in that the first governmental changeover within the massive transformations on the horizon for the entire Continent has brought President Salinas to power in Mexico. No other leader in Latin America shares the U.S. preference for market economies, private capital, and cooperative solutions to such an extent. . . . Mexican-U.S. relations could serve as a model for negotiations with the other countries. . . . In practice, this means that greater priority should be granted to real progress with Mexico during the first six months of the Bush administration; there is much at stake in the Western Hemisphere. . . . The Bush administration faces no challenge as urgent as revitalizing its relations with our southern neighbors.[3]

These statements call at least two questions to mind: Is Mexico the first U.S. "experiment" that will lead to subsequent commercial and political dealings with Latin America? Or is it simply a U.S. launching pad toward this vast market? If the latter is true, how will it be accomplished and what will costs and benefits be for Mexico and Latin America? Furthermore, we must anticipate the pace and the extent of Mexican–U.S.–Canadian integration with respect to other integration and cooperation processes already under way between Mexico and Latin America.

The possibility of a recession in the United States and President Salinas's Latin American tour in October 1990 are links in the chain of events involved in the Mexican debate that has sparked the interest of Latin America. Paraphrasing Sergio de la Peña in a recent analysis, the question is whether these presidential tours constitute Mexico's traditional foreign policy paradigm of "international equilibrium." Are they an expression of the country's aspirations for an improved relationship with the United States and respect for the sovereignty of peoples and nonintervention in their internal affairs, or will they serve as the launching pad that we have just mentioned? This traditional paradigm, de la Peña notes, "would explain Mexico's sudden rush to rebuild ties with Latin America, offended by more than a decade of neglect, to offset the sudden and enormous increase in Mexican-U.S. relations that the promise of integration holds. Another traditional game of 'international equilibrium' has been to pit European against U.S. interests."[4]

These questions are not merely theoretical; they spring from very concrete dynamics and U.S. demands on the Mexican government with respect to economic relations. Actually, this new interest—first in Mexico and next in Latin America—is not for nothing; one explanation for it is the fact that the United States is seeking to solve the problem of the already stiff worldwide economic competition that it will have to face with the integration of Europe in 1992. For the United States, access to broader markets and cheap labor has become an urgent necessity, in view of the fierce competition emanating from the Pacific Rim countries.

We must now situate this problem, which involves Mexico, Central America, and all of Latin America, within a context of increasing interdependence of the world economy, which restricts states' freedom of action. The challenge is even greater now, at the end of the millennium, owing to the acceleration of history—a geometric explosion, where the progress of years takes place in a matter of days, impelled by a dizzying torrent of events that has caused a bipolar world to crumble before our very eyes. We are moving toward an easing of international tensions, the end of the cold war, and the emergence of a multipolar world insofar as international relations are concerned.

The European Economic Community (EEC), scheduled to operate as an economic bloc as of 1992, and Japan, the dominant pole in Asia, have speeded up their development and bolstered their international roles. The Soviet Union has diluted its presence worldwide, as a result of its domestic crisis, the breakup of its system of alliances, and its loss of influence over the countries of Eastern Europe. The United States, with its structural weaknesses and its enormous financial difficulties, appears to have lost economic clout, relatively speaking, in this reaccommodation of forces, though the same cannot be said of its indisputable military might and its political and ideological role. Thus, in the medium term, it will be obliged to negotiate its international policy with Japan, Europe, and probably other nations as well.

Latin America in general—and Central America in particular—faces the challenge of determining how they will fit into this changing international environment. Unfortunately, these countries are not dealing from a position of economic strength, nor are they able to overcome their isolation and take concerted action in negotiating their participation in the new world scenario.

Both the emergence of economic blocs and Bush's "Enterprise for the Americas" initiative have intensified debate in all circles on the future of Latin America. Discussions include the nature of Mexican-U.S. and U.S.-Latin American relations, as well as Mexican-Latin American and Mexican-Central American relations in such areas as free trade, integration, and interdependence; they also include political reflections on principles like national sovereignty, autonomy, and self-determination.

In Central America in recent years, there has been an ongoing discussion about the changes that have been taking place in the region's relationship with Mexico, and there is concern as to whether the high priority Mexico has granted to economic integration with the United States (despite the national debate that it has sparked, Mexico's vast historical and cultural reserves, and its traditionally independent and progressive foreign policy) will also accentuate some of the trends toward a political entente with the United States—an understanding that could diminish and/or alter Mexico's political and diplomatic activism, though not its economic and commercial role in the area.

How these matters are resolved will be crucial for Central America and Latin America. Historically, Mexico, Central America, and the United States make up a triangular system that is extremely important for the isthmus. Although this system has been neither uniform nor constant over the years and is dominated by the United States, it has occasionally permitted modifications in Mexican-Central American relations, thus reducing U.S. control to the advantage of regional processes of peace and self-determination, democracy and development. Examples of this triangularity of relations can be found from as early as the independence of Mexico (1810) and Central America (1821) up to the present day, and especially since 1978.

The analytical point of departure in this volume is the dialectic between the historically different patterns of behavior of Mexico, Central America, and the United States and the specific actions, decisions, and attitudes of Mexican and U.S. foreign policy toward Central America—"foreign policy" being defined in the broadest sense of the term.[5]

The triangular methodological perspective allows us to highlight some important differences between Mexican and U.S. conduct toward Central America. Mexico's policies, behavior, and attitudes toward the region have always respected the autonomous decisions of each of the countries and has been a positive influence in terms of their national goals, even though Central America has not been Mexico's number one priority and Mexico does not have the power or influence that the United States has in the region.

For some reason, this triangular relationship has never been subjected to an academic analysis like the one that we are undertaking. There have been bilateral studies of Mexican–Central American, Mexican-U.S., and Central American–U.S. relations, but never an examination of this triangularity in and of itself.

We believe that in examining the Mexico–Central America–United States triangle, it is essential to capture and appreciate the differences among the parties, particularly the presence, features, nature, and weight of the United States within the relationship. Mexico and Central America, the other two angles of the triangle, have their own dynamic, their own players, their own timetable, but the United States has been a dominant force—in some situations hegemonic—in the unfolding of regional events. Therefore, while each country develops its foreign policy on the basis of its own political system and self-interest, the policies of Mexico and the Central American countries possess a duality. Each country has a foreign policy in and of itself, pursuing national principles and interests. But each also has a foreign policy defined in terms of its response to an external player: the United States.[6]

Face to face with each other and the United States, Central America and Mexico share the challenge of achieving self-determination and a richer democracy and development accompanied by national independence. To ensure this, we must identify the strategic elements, past and present, of both parties' bilateral relationship with the United States and understand how they have evolved throughout the course of Mexican–Central American, Central American–U.S., and Mexican-U.S. bilateral relations, as well as within the triangular relationship.

The United States occupies a privileged angle of influence over Mexico and Central America, because of its position as a world power and its historical inclusion of Central America and Mexico within what it considers its sphere of influence.[7] We are thus dealing with a power that judges its independence and ability to control its own destiny largely on the basis of its capacity to control and influence the destiny of others, to keep them dependent. For small countries or regions, the objective is not to be one of those "others."[8]

Even so, the United States has lacked a concrete policy toward Latin America. In Central America, Ronald Reagan's administration followed its own course in dealing with the challenges to its hegemony, seeking to achieve an East-West balance in what in its judgment was a key area for U.S. strategic security. Reagan's thesis was that the alien enemy (Cuba and the Soviet Union) had infiltrated Nicaragua and, little by little, would extend its tentacles throughout the region until it reached as far north as Mexico, gaining control of strategically important resources: the Panama Canal, the oil fields of Mexico, and so forth. The Reagan strategy reached its pinnacle in the doctrine of low-intensity conflict, a more flexible approach combining economic, political, social, and military measures that, over a protracted period, is intended to represent a relatively low-cost involvement for the United States. For the nations that fall victim to this strategy, however, the costs are terrible.

Within this context, the United States also undertook a variety of initiatives in Central America at odds with Mexico's activities, widening its angle of the triangle and increasing its influence and control over the region. The United States' characterization of the crisis in Central America and strategies to deal with it are diametrically opposed to those of Mexico.

Mexico's relations with Central America were strongly affected by its relationship with the United States, which has always considered Mexico part of its "sphere of influence." Nevertheless, an examination of Mexican history discloses that Mexico has never been a strategic ally of the United States where Central America is concerned; neither has it enjoyed complete autonomy nor truly defied the U.S. presence in the region. To understand how and how much the U.S. presence permeates relations between Mexico and Central America requires a search for an answer whose roots are in the past and the present, and which will therefore be a constant in the future.

Mexico came into direct confrontation with the United States in Central America starting in 1978 because of its support for the anti-Somoza struggle in Nicaragua. This confrontation was the result of Mexico's foreign policy thesis that stability in the area would be impossible without the conditions for sociopolitical change, implying commitments for Mexico that transcended the Estrada Doctrine.[9]

Two years later, from 1981 to 1982, for reasons noted in the chapters that follow, Mexico moved from activism in Central America toward a policy of achieving needed stability through a regional easing of tensions. It contributed in this fashion to the Nicaraguan-U.S. dialogue in Manzanillo and to the signing of the French-Mexican Declaration on El Salvador, the earliest forerunner of the current dialogue between the Salvadoran government and the Farabundo Martí Front for National Liberation (FMLN).

By 1982, with the deepening of Mexico's economic crisis and the pressure from the Reagan administration over the country's position on Central America, Mexico multilateralized its policy toward the region through the Contadora Group, confronting U.S. belligerence and political and diplomatic initiatives from another angle.

Mexico and Contadora (1983) offset the U.S. presence in Central America and opened up some room for the exercise of national autonomy. But within the region, relations shifted quickly. For example, while Costa Rica joined Mexico in openly aiding Nicaragua's revolutionary movement in 1979, during the Contadora period Costa Rica closely allied itself with the United States, Honduras, and El Salvador to block the Mexican–Latin American peace initiative.

From 1987 on, under the Esquipulas II negotiations process, Mexico lost its leadership role in the area and turned inward, emphasizing economic priorities, especially its trade relations with the United States. At the same time, the domestic affairs of the Central American countries began to take on relevance within the negotiations process as a key to pacification of the region. Among the main issues were the lack of democracy, human rights abuses, and the urgent need for national reconciliation. Mexico, with its attachment to the principle of nonintervention and also out of self-interest, began to distance itself from the region.

For Central America, whether in terms of government, movements for change, or society as a whole, Mexico is of fundamental importance. Generally speaking, its presence in the region has implied only significant political gains, such as those resulting from its participation in Contadora, or economic advantages, like the San José Pact, which provided Mexican petroleum to Central America on generous terms. In the last few years, Central American–Mexican relations, as we have known them, have eroded and are no longer as important as they were in the late 1970s and early 1980s.

Recent Mexican gestures toward Central America that we consider to be important go back to the search for a new but different kind of rapprochement—for example, the renewal and broadening of the San José Pact, with improved terms of payment, the reconversion of Central America's debt with Mexico through investment in production (exemplified in the prospect of allowing Petróleos Mexicanos [PEMEX] to drill for oil in Costa Rica), and Mexican support for broadening economic, financial, and technical cooperation agreements.

In Mexico, Central America perceives the potential for diversifying its foreign relations—with all the risks and costs that this implies. Mexico's role in the Río Group and in international forums to keep interest in Central America alive is highly valued. Also of note today is the call by Mexico and "all the countries of Latin America and the Caribbean to have the region sign an agreement on arms limitation and a reduction in militarism and the arms buildup in Central America to free these resources for development."[10]

Structure of the Book

This triangular approach permits us to examine little-explored facets of the current Central American situation within the dynamic of its international relations. Thus, the main object of this book is to analyze some of the content and extensions of Mexican–Central American–U.S. relations, their implications, and their consequences for the region. This work is a team effort, although final responsibility for chapters rests with their authors.

The first chapter, by Jesús Hernández, takes a historical approach to Mexican and U.S. relations with Central America, revealing conflict, encounters, and breakdowns in their bilateral relationships. In addition, Hernández analyzes some regional events that have had repercussions at some point on bilateral relations between Mexico and the United States. This first chapter, then, is a historical examination of the hypothesis of the Mexican–Central America–United States triangle. It attempts to show how Mexico and the United States, from their very origins as nations, have evolved historical, cultural, and national differences that have crystallized in a common area of interest and influence: Central America.

In line with this first chapter, the second, by H. Rodrigo Jauberth, analyzes the negotiations process and the peace alternatives in Central America within the framework of the Mexico–Central America–United States triangle. Jauberth opens his chapter with a presentation of some basic concepts necessary for an analysis of this political/diplomatic dynamic: peace, development, democracy, and national independence. In his view, these concepts—within a more general analytical framework—are essential for an understanding of the Central American situation and its crisis and conflict and the Mexican and U.S. regional roles.

This second chapter harks back to the very origins of the negotiations process: that is, Contadora in 1983, and within it, Mexico's leadership role. Contadora was the main predecessor of the subsequent negotiations process that began to unfold in 1987 in the town of Esquipulas, Guatemala—a process that is still evolving. In both the Contadora and Esquipulas initiatives, Mexico and the United States pursued a foreign policy based on different analyses and visions of the crisis and conflict in Central America, with openly different, if not confrontational, objectives, actions, attitudes, and strategies. This tug-of-war persisted until the Esquipulas III Summit in 1988, when the negotiations were "Central Americanized"; that is, Mexico and Contadora withdrew (or were excluded) from the negotiations process, indicating a return of U.S. hegemony and control in the region. The eight presidential summits, together with Nicaragua's elections in 1990, sparked a debate about the challenges and prospects for peace in Central America within the framework of the region's relations with Mexico and the United States.

This second chapter leaves open a number of questions and concerns: Is it possible to speak of a reformulation of Mexico's foreign policy from a Central American standpoint? How will the Contadora and/or Esquipulas negotiations model work to bring about the much-needed peace in El Salvador and Guatemala in the 1990s? What repercussions will Mexican-U.S. relations have on Central America, with the rapprochement of Presidents Salinas and Bush? There is a great deal of discussion currently going on to the effect that the governments of Mexico and the United States have agreed to bilateralize their relations with the Central American countries without altering their particular stances on the underlying problems that have divided them. The basis for this agreement is said to be an understanding that cooperation is possible in spite of their differences. The question is, Is this really possible and can this possibility be generalized to all of Latin America?

The third chapter, by Pedro Vuskovic, describes the features, nature, and significance of the regional crisis, the protagonists and interests in play (both domestic and foreign), and the role of these foreign interests in terms of the national and regional goals that are beginning to emerge. In addition, it highlights relevant economic and political aspects related to the significance for Central America of a greater Mexican-U.S. integration and/or the establishment of a North American common market that includes Canada.

The fourth chapter, by Gilberto Castañeda, discusses Central American–Mexican–U.S. relations as a whole and their outlook, emphasizing the international context and the current implications of Mexican-U.S.

relations for Central America. Castañeda highlights the major changes occurring worldwide and their impact on Latin America in general and Central America in particular, tracing the main parameters of Mexican-U.S. relations in order to project their evolution. From this, he appraises the limitations and possibilities of this interaction for Central America and proceeds to issues connected with the triangular relationship; among them the war on drugs, the payment of the external debt, and the migration of undocumented Central Americans to Mexico and from there to the United States. Castañeda concludes with some considerations on the possibilities of strengthening Central American–Mexican ties.

The fifth chapter is a team effort. Here we summarize the authors' conclusions and discuss the scenarios likely to emerge from the triangular relationship. This section seeks to generalize, project, and summarize the contents of the book; however, it also incorporates elements that came out of the discussions, interviews, round tables, and dialogues with academics from other Mexican, Central American, and U.S. institutions.

Notes

1. There is sufficient reason, grounded in a common national history and a multiplicity of other factors, to deal with Central America as a region. The relevant events in the area have become regionalized: In this century alone, we need only mention the Central American Common Market (CACM), the Contadora and Esquipulas II initiatives, plus U.S. handling of the conflicts in the isthmus. All this permits us to consider Central America a unit—one angle in a triangular relationship with Mexico and the United States. It is not our wish to gloss over or deny the uniqueness of each of the Central American countries; however, this approach allows us to analyze the areas of greatest relevance to the triangle, without going into specifics.

2. Fernando Solana, "Sección Internacional. México-EU una Relación Dinámica," *Excélsior,* 5 October 1990, pp. 1, 19.

3. Margarita García C., "Desmedido interés de EUA por un mercado común," *Excélsior,* 20 April 1990, p. 10.

4. Sergio de la Peña, "Estamos con el Imperio," *Excélsior,* 16 October 1990, p. 16-A.

5. See Guadalupe González, "Tradiciones y premisas de la política exterior de México," in *La política exterior y la agenda México–Estados Unidos,* ed. Rosario Green and Peter H. Smith (Mexico: Fondo de Cultura Económica, 1989), p. 35. See also Baghat Korany, *How Foreign Policy Decisions Are Made in the Third World: A Comparative Analysis* (Boulder: Westview Press, 1986).

6. This affirmation that an exploration of the international relations of the Latin American countries should start out with the relations between their national political systems and the processes that dominate the international picture is shared by Santiago Escobar in his article, "Sistema político nacional

y relaciones internacionales," *Nueva Sociedad* (Venezuela), No. 104, December 1989. Escobar notes, moreover, that this proposition implicitly includes the hypothesis that both the behavior and trends of Latin America's political systems, plus the key features of the international processes under way, de-statify the international politics of the region. One theoretical discussion that has been very useful to us in the elaboration of this book concerning the perspectives and different analytical frameworks employed to reflect on the nature of relationships in foreign policy that are so unequal is in Green and Smith, *La política exterior,* p. 16. Among those analytical frameworks, see: the presidential personalities; the elements of continuity rather than change in foreign policy (historical, cultural, and structural): Mexico's dependence on the United States due to a peripheral status on a par with that of Central America; the concept of Mexican-U.S. asymmetry; the notion of interdependence and/or asymmetrical interdependence; the diversified decision-making process in the United States. These are analytical perspectives whose features are often complementary. It is not the purpose of this book to spark an academic debate over the different analytical approaches to foreign policy contained in the various works cited here, but it is possible to acknowledge a creative effort in all of them to integrate the separate elements.

7. The declaration by Undersecretary of State Robert Olds in 1927 summarizes decades of Central American–U.S. relations: "The Central American area down to and including the Isthmus of Panama constitutes a legitimate sphere of influence for the United States. . . . We do control the destinies of Central America, and we do so for the simple reason that national interest absolutely dictates such a course." Cited by Richard Millett, *Guardians of the Dynasty: A History of the U.S.-Created Guardia Nacional de Nicaragua and the Somoza Family* (Maryknoll, NY: Orbis Books, 1977), p. 52.

8. To expand on this topic, see Cristina Eguizabal, "Determinantes internos y perspectiva de una política exterior autónoma para CA," University of Costa Rica, May 1985, mimeo. See in addition José Juan Olloqui, "La no dependencia como una política exterior alternativa para México, marco analítico," in Green and Smith, *La política exterior.* This latter work says that dependence should be understood as a situation where the economy of a country or group of countries is influenced by the development and growth of other nations. Dependence implies a subordination that tends to be self-perpetuating, owing to the unequal strength of the countries. In this regard, in his book *Alcances y límites de la política exterior de México* (Mexico: Colegio de México, 1984), p. 9, Mario Ojeda opines that for analytical clarity, dependence assumes the character of a series of formal and informal economic and political ties that serve as direct conduits for hegemonic power to exert more discreet and effective pressure, thus restricting the freedom of action of the governments involved. This notion can be applied to countries in both the U.S. and the Soviet orbit independently, in the final analysis, of their economic system and their political orientation.

9. The Estrada Doctrine (named for Mexico's minister of foreign relations during the 1930s) states that no country has the authority to make value

judgments as to the legitimacy of a government (that is, to recognize it), for that is a degrading practice. It therefore indicates that Mexico will limit itself to establishing diplomatic relations or not with a particular country, with the understanding that it may break relations, or downgrade or upgrade its permanent or temporary delegation in that country.

   10. *Excélsior,* 14 October 1990, pp. 1 and 27A.

CHAPTER 1

Mexican and U.S. Policy Toward Central America

JESÚS HERNÁNDEZ

THIS CHAPTER TRACES THE HISTORY of the Mexico–United States–Central America triangle, attempts to explain why Mexican and U.S. policies toward Central America have sometimes differed, and describes how these differences have hindered efforts to find lasting solutions to the region's problems. The analysis suggests that these differences, more out in the open during the 1980s, have been present throughout the history of inter-American relations. Moreover, the divergent approaches of Mexico and the United States toward Central America can be traced to the history of their relations with each other.

The first part of this chapter is devoted to an exploration of the roots of the two countries' foreign policies on two levels. First, the historical world context at the start of their relations, and each country's particular development, is examined, with an emphasis on U.S. expansionism, the creation of the inter-American system, and their historical significance for Mexico. Second, the formation of a national consciousness that has evolved throughout the history of these two countries is looked at, with an attempt to determine its influence on the ongoing development of foreign policy.

The second part explores the evolution of the Central American foreign policy of each country since the nineteenth century, when the political geography of the region had scarcely been mapped, but when there were already signs of the problems that would induce both Mexico and the United States to adopt specific postures and conduct in line with their emerging foreign policies. This part also highlights the importance of the Pan American movement that developed under U.S. leadership and the nature of Mexican and U.S. foreign policy measures in response to the various Central American problems, from the early nineteenth century to the postwar era. In particular, it examines the foreign policies of these countries and their actions with respect to

13

attempts at Central American union, the demarcation of the Guatemalan-Mexican border, the construction of the Panama Canal, and the conflicts of the twentieth century up to the 1970s.

The third part deals with the 1980s, discussing the historical significance of a century of underdevelopment and dependence for the triangular relationship. It examines the evolution of Mexican-U.S. relations in response to the Central American situation of the 1980s and discusses the Contadora process, though analysis of the Contadora and Esquipulas negotiations is covered more fully in Chapter 2. Finally, it analyzes the regional problem in light of recent events.

We have attempted to employ the triangular methodology of the book, understanding the triangularity to be part of the historical processes involved. Here, a grasp of the structural nature and features of the relationship of dominance and subordination between the United States and the other two parties to the triangle is essential for an understanding of the topic at hand.

Whatever modest advances we may have made, our handling of this subject is still inadequate because the topic is inexhaustible, owing to its breadth and its profound implications for the wide assortment of national, regional, inter-American, Latin American, and world problems. Our intent, therefore, is simply to stimulate debate over the current reality of the relationship between Mexico, the United States, and Central America.[1]

Historic Roots of Foreign Policy Differences
Between Mexico and the United States

A variety of historical events set the stage for the development of foreign policy in the individual countries of the triangle. Each nation's need to define its borders and forge relations with others, and the historical point when its material and spiritual foundations and real development possibilities began to converge, must be taken into account if its positions and conduct in the world context are to be understood.

Also critical over the passage of time is a nation's collective consciousness of problems, dangers, and the outlook for the future, which help determine a people's unique way of thinking. While this consciousness comes from a people's aspirations and concerns, it also reflects a determination among the groups in power to preserve and extend their rule.

An understanding of the historical underpinnings of the national consciousness created by events over time, as well as the subsequent foreign policies developed by both Mexico and the United States, permits a keener insight into the positions of each with respect to Central America.[2]

Origins of Mexican and U.S. Foreign Policy

Mexico and the United States discovered each other as neighbors at the dawn of the nineteenth century, just when the world was radically changing—when Spanish and French power was on the wane in the Americas and free-trade relations, championed by England, already played a dominant role in the international picture. The conflict between Spain and England, with its roots in the fourteenth and fifteenth centuries, was a contest between crumbling feudalism and burgeoning capitalism. Spain was forced to seek new maritime routes to expand its markets, leading to the discovery of a new continent in 1492. There, the country encountered well-established societies that resisted conquest, but were in the end subjugated and annihilated both militarily and culturally.

From then on, Spain, losing ground to England and overwhelmed by financial need, exported little to the new continent but the mercantilism it had mastered so well. Imbued with a tremendous desire to acquire wealth that would allow it to compete, it plundered the precious metals and other riches of its colonies. England, for its part, needed to expand its capital throughout the world and sought to accomplish this through the colonization of North America, beginning in the seventeenth century. In contrast to Spain, which impoverished its colonies, England encouraged capital accumulation in its colonies in order to reap the benefits.

Thus, the role of the Thirteen Colonies in the subsequent development of North America was determined not just by the progressive spirit of the European colonists but also by the objective needs of an expanding free market in the New World, under specific historical conditions. The simple growth of the population in the colonies encouraged territorial expansion unanticipated by the English themselves, who witnessed the development of an economy far more self-reliant than the simple supplier of raw materials they had planned, an economy that was instrumental in helping the new nation achieve independence. From that point on, a vigorous social structure evolved in the United States with the labor of its people, within a free market whose distinguishing characteristic was the ambitious search for new territories to fuel the necessary expansion.

The market that was also beginning to emerge in other countries of the continent in the nineteenth century did so in the context of this North American situation, although the peculiarities of Spanish rule stamped different features on the local accumulation process, highly influenced by mercantilism. Thus, the Spanish American nations developed under the plundering legacy of the Conquest, with inadequate local investment and internal wars that sapped national potential.

Here, there was no sudden emergence of the market as a mere outgrowth of economic development in North America or the rest of the world. Instead, the market developed in a restrictive setting, shaped by European and U.S. investment. Because of these peculiar conditions, the countries of the region turned out to be underdeveloped, lacking industry of their own, subject to and dependent upon other industrialized nations, and dominated from the first by the monopoly power of foreign enterprises that was to become the overriding feature of economic relations.

In fact, it is during the era when the free market began to emerge in many Latin American countries that the system on a worldwide scale began to move toward the monopolistic phase of development. According to some experts, this is why the region's market emerged as "a crippled capitalism, lacking its own engine of growth, lacking an organic capacity to make use of . . . the productive potential that it generated. . . . It was a counterfeit and subordinate capitalism that henceforth would develop both as an integral part and yet on the tail of an unstable world market."[3]

This is the context in which the initial relations between Mexico and the United States evolved, promising many decades of silent and open conflict.

The History of Mexican-U.S. Relations

After centuries of Spanish rule, Mexico obtained its independence through a bloody civil war—a reflection of the conditions that demanded the liberation of all America from the yoke of colonialism. Mexico's libertarian ideals, like those of others in Central and South America, were also Ibero-American: hemispheric, not simply national.

Mexico determined its constitutional path and became a unified nation only after what are acknowledged as the three greatest moments in its history: Independence from Spain in the second decade of the nineteenth century; the Reform, which nourished local capital accumulation during the 1850s, and the Revolution of 1910–1917, which established the legal and political foundations for modern Mexico.

The Independence of 1810–1821 was a very complex phenomenon, with origins in the Spanish conquest and the colonial era. At the root of the independence movement was the emergence of a new society of native-born Spaniards (Creoles) and people of mixed blood (mestizos), which clashed with the colonial regime.

When the armed conflict was over, Mexico was defenseless, with only fragile institutions, at a time when it had to confront other powers— chiefly the United States, which was advancing south and west in the quest for new territories.[4] At the same time, Mexico had to deal with the designs of France, which, in an attempt to exploit the country's weakness in 1862, intervened militarily and imposed the rule of Emperor Maximilian of Hapsburg.

The Reform of the 1850s was the culmination of a long stage in the development of an independent Mexico. During this time, in the apparent chaos of incessant coups and internal power struggles, a complex and paradoxical social and economic process was evolving against the backdrop of a changing international picture, in which the Industrial Revolution in England, the French Revolution, and U.S. independence acted as stimuli to the world market.[5] English capital advanced inexorably in the form of investment and the search for raw materials toward an independent Latin America endowed with enormous resources and an important potential market for manufactures that began to clash with U.S. interests.

During the three decades prior to the promulgation of the Reform Laws and the Constitution of 1857, an incipient domestic market evolved in spite of serious domestic difficulties—for example, the armed intervention of France, British trade (which literally invaded all the new markets), and U.S. expansionism that by midcentury had already stripped Mexico of over half its territory. From then on, the weak and unstable Mexican economy developed in the suffocating presence of these great powers, under conditions that gave rise to the structural dependence and underdevelopment that characterize it to this day.[6] Nonetheless, the country developed a growing capacity to defend itself, which Benito Juarez did with singular patriotism, after which new governmental institutions took shape, based on the Reform Laws that Juarez himself had promoted several years previously, and which established the legal foundations for the country's development.

The Mexican Revolution of 1910–1917 was an outgrowth of the need for greater national development arising from the social, economic, and even cultural changes of the mid- to late nineteenth century. These changes created unsalvageable political differences and at the same time stimulated long-cherished popular aspirations, unrealized after a century of independence. The armed phase of the Mexican Revolution culminated in the drawing up and ratification of the Constitution of 1917. At that point, Mexico entered a new phase in which the state was transformed into the most important guarantor of national development, albeit within the country's underdeveloped state.

Subsequently, until the mid-1920s, Mexico was caught up in a variety of struggles with local or national factions that were attempting to gain power. Nevertheless, following the creation of the National Revolutionary Party in 1928 (the earliest ancestor of the current PRI, later reformed by Lázaro Cárdenas in 1938, when its name was changed to the Mexican Revolutionary Party), the country began to enjoy a long period of political calm, except for some minor conflicts.

From here until the 1970s, development in Mexico occurred within the context of a worldwide market boom, particularly in the United States. Specifically, the Mexican and Latin American economies evolved under conditions that led to a slight growth during the first half of the century. After World War II, however, there was considerable development of the productive forces, plus major changes in social relations—the result of a rise in U.S. investment during the expansive postwar period and the development strategies applied in the region.

We turn now to the United States; its need for territorial expansion began with the independence of the Thirteen Colonies. A new nation was formed whose people, imbued with Puritan doctrines, subscribed to myths that they had a divine mission in the world. Under the mantle of a constitution influenced by the European currents of the day but derived from collective popular needs and with ideals that encouraged a belief in a new type of man in a promised land for the colonizer, it was a nation that created expectations for itself that were unusual for that era. From that moment on it steadfastly began to expand.

After the Louisiana Purchase, and with the Atlantic border secured and the boundaries with Canada defined, the only avenues for expansion open were to the west and the south, to regions formerly belonging to Spain and now to an independent Mexico.

According to a number of U.S. historians, expansionism was spurred on by the same colonizing population, motivated among other things by the attractiveness of the lands to the west.[7] In this respect, the important thing to remember is not, of course, the legitimate aspirations of the colonizers to seek better living conditions for their families, much less an awareness of the need to forge a new nation with ever-better prospects for guaranteeing its own identity and the common good. Rather, it is the specific responsibility of the dominant governing classes in these processes—above all the slave-owners of the South and the successive U.S. administrations—who collaborated in the sweeping takeovers that characterized U.S. expansion, at the cost of other nations like Spain, and eventually, Mexico.

The two Floridas are an example of the expansionist pattern: North American colonists settled on these lands, consolidating themselves socially and economically until they formed a government and demanded independence from Spain. This created a conflict in which the U.S. government, in alleged defense of its own citizenry, ended up annexing the new territory. This pattern was repeated in Texas, but this time it was used against an independent Mexico whose viability as a nation was still precarious; thus, the annexation served as the gateway to the takeover of a much vaster territory, with the declaration and prosecution of a war in which the disparities in economic and military might were evident.

This was a nation in the middle of unstoppable development. Reaching the Pacific, acquiring the greatest possible geographical extension to the west and south, and exploiting the natural potential of these territories was an enterprise of the very first order, vital to those who governed, if a great world power was to be built.

With territorial expansion complete and its national boundaries virtually fixed, the United States entered a boom comparable only to that of the Industrial Revolution, but with the added economic potential of the markets of the newly independent nations of the hemisphere. Throughout the early twentieth century, with the inter-American system already formed, the United States began to traverse Latin America under the banner of "dollar diplomacy," competing with English, German, French, and other capital for investment and interest in the various continental regions.[8] However, it was not until after 1945, with Europe devastated, that Latin America became almost the exclusive hunting ground of the United States, with no competition to speak of for the next three decades.

Mexico Versus U.S. Expansion

If one thing left a profound imprint on the spirit of nationalism and the nature of Mexico's international policy, it was U.S. territorial expansion. Even before it gained its independence, Mexico anticipated the course that events would take, since U.S. leaders were already showing signs of an expansionist attitude commensurate with the ambitions of this vigorous young nation.[9] Because of this, the war and eventual annexation of Texas in 1846 was merely the culmination of a process whereby the legitimate aspirations of colonists in a practically virgin land were entwined with the expansionist ambitions of the southern states.[10]

For Mexico, U.S. expansion meant the loss of over half its original territory, an unavoidable historical fact in inter-American relations that signified that territorial annexation was a possibility that could be repeated at any time, to the detriment of Mexico or other nations of the hemisphere. This was subsequently confirmed when the United States attempted to invade Mexico at the height of the Revolution, in 1916.

The decades that followed the ratification of the Constitution of 1917 did not witness any more disastrous U.S. territorial expansion. However, at that point, another type of expansion was underway that was less noticeable but far more effective in the long run in consolidating underdevelopment: that of international capital. Mexico faced—and still faces—the designs and decisions of the "Colossus of the North," which causes the country's still heavy dependence. This is why the country persists in maintaining its firm foreign policy stance with respect to the United States.

Mexico's history provided sufficient cause for anti-imperialist and sometimes even anti-U.S. sentiments among many of its thinkers and patriots who, reflecting popular attitudes, supported positions that in time would influence the country's foreign policy. Mexico's international posture is not an impulsive one—the result of rancor over the past or even the resentment of the weak when confronted with the strong, as some U.S. authors have so casually stated. The country's foreign policy is clearly internationalist in scope, the consequence of a history of humiliation, but also of just aspirations and firm positions—a foreign policy that defends the right of peoples to self-determination, peaceful international coexistence, equality among nations, and the right to asylum, just as it condemns the arrogance of any powerful nation that lords its position over a small one. Thus, the essence of the nationalistic and profoundly Latin Americanist thought of many Mexicans has been clearly retained in the principles that have guided Mexico's foreign policy over the decades—principles that have made themselves felt throughout the Central American conflict, especially when more active participation by Mexico became necessary.

Unquestionably, its long history of domestic conflict and U.S. aggression had a profound impact on the Mexican consciousness. Over the years, the need for peace at home, peace with its neighbors, and the freedom to decide its own destiny grew out of the need to survive and develop. Thus, during the period of insurrection, the first stages of Mexican independence, and on through the era of the Reform, the foundations for foreign policy were laid. Venustiano Carranza first articulated Mexican foreign policy as we know it today in response to the U.S. aggression of 1914 and the new incursion by U.S. troops into northern Mexico in search of guerrilla leader Francisco (Pancho) Villa.

Henceforth, up to the era of Lázaro Cárdenas, Mexico's foreign policy continued to define itself, taking on more permanent features. During this time, the juridical and political frameworks that lent more consistency to it were established in the form of doctrines (the Estrada Doctrine, the Carranza Doctrine, or the Cárdenas Doctrine).[11] These policy lines constitute the solid moral underpinnings for one of the most consistent modern-day foreign policies in Latin America—a policy whose strength lies more in its political and ideological nature than its economic and military might, and which in Central America has managed to curb some U.S. activities that run counter to regional interests.

History of Mexican and U.S. Foreign Policy
Toward Central America

Several developments in Spanish American history in the early nineteenth century would subsequently influence inter-American events. The purpose of the 1824 proposal by Simón Bolívar to convoke the Panama Congress was to establish a confederation of nations that would unite the former Spanish colonies.[12] The Congress, which opened in 1826 in Panama and closed in Tacubaya, Mexico, in October 1828, had to be suspended because of domestic problems in some of the countries represented. This marked the end of the earliest forerunner of the idea of uniting these republics and all the nations with Spanish roots that would later constitute Latin America.[13]

Among the countries not invited to the Congress was the United States, since its incorporation into the Confederate Powers of America to be established was not contemplated, perhaps because by that time the U.S. presence was already beginning to be felt with more pain than pleasure, and the United States had shown little solidarity with the Congress.[14] Reservations about the Panama Congress in the United States were part of the expansionist logic whose prevailing idea was that all the American nations should be one big happy family, but headed by the United States.[15] This no doubt was the main goal of the United States from then on and an excellent reason for it to exploit the virtual collapse of Spanish-Americanism. After this, Washington promoted the so-called American Conferences that began in 1889–1890 and finally ended in 1936 with the establishment of the inter-American system under U.S. hegemony.[16]

From the very first winds of independence, there were warnings about the future nature of the triangular relationship between Mexico, the United States, and Central America. The 1810 movement for independence in Mexico, for example, reached the Captaincy General of

Guatemala (i.e., Spanish Central America) almost immediately, where it provided the impetus for the struggle to emancipate the Central American provinces.[17] Miguel Hidalgo's attempts to obtain U.S. support in the struggle for independence were frustrated when Mexican envoy Bernardo N. Gutiérrez de Lara, after an important interview with then-Secretary of State James Monroe, reached the conclusion that the United States was not disposed to lend assistance for nothing.[18] This attitude was also noted by José Manuel Zozaya, named Mexico's first independent representative to Washington in 1822.[19]

In this context, Mexico itself faced new challenges with respect to its triangular relationship with the Central American isthmus. With the arrival of Joel Poinsett as ambassador in 1822, the U.S. government adopted a strong position from the very outset, with the object of making Mexico's interests coincide with those it had already begun to regard as fundamental to the United States in the region.

Time would confirm the fears of those early Mexican diplomats about U.S. conduct in Latin America and the vital need for Ibero-American union as the only means of curbing U.S. ambitions, when Mexico lost over half its original territory to its powerful neighbor to the north. It is largely for this reason that the country would reset its sights on the republics to the south, in search of a common Ibero-American defense.[20]

Mexican and U.S. Reaction to Changes
in the Central American Political Map
During the Nineteenth Century

Central American unity was but a historical glimmer during this period. Circumstances conspired against any real federalism, and the confrontation between the Guatemalans and the inhabitants of the other provinces, with the thousand jealousies and resentments that had built up over the years, was far from over. Moreover, with the Spanish withdrawal, the British presence increased. Commercial and strategic interests, like the question of the interoceanic canal, came into play that ended up involving and even subtly pitting the peoples of the isthmus against one another.

In November 1824, the Federal Republic of Central America was established under the aegis of the Liberal Party, which led a protracted armed struggle against the conservative aristocracy located chiefly in Guatemala City. This conflict between different social groups was the basic obstacle to the success of this endeavor.[21] The outcome was that the Creole oligarchy confined itself to Guatemalan territory, while the liberal bourgeoisie of the other territories abandoned their goal of organizing the federation under a single flag.[22] In 1829, there was a new attempt to unify the isthmus under the Honduran general Francisco Morazán, who in addition to defeating the conservative Guatemalans militarily, tried to reimpose federal authority. For a time, Morazán's military strength kept the five territories united, but in 1838, following a series of uprisings instigated by the Conservative Party, the federal government fell apart.[23]

Confronted with its own domestic difficulties, Mexico could devote itself only to passive observation and to learn about the new political geography through the course of events; some time later the United States, having determined its hegemonic interests in the isthmus at this point, promoted the 1907 Central American Peace Conference which consolidated the disunity and set the new terms for the triangular relationship. This gathering undoubtedly ensured greater political stability in the region, but it also banished indefinitely the ideal of unity promoted mainly by the liberal sectors.

The new Central America, literally divided into five separate republics, came into being at a time when Latin America was already darkened by the shadow of foreign capital (especially U.S. capital), while its leading economic sectors were unable to meet the economic development needs of the new nations. Central America was born just as the so-called inter-American system was being defined in favor of the "Colossus of the North." With the construction of an interoceanic canal in the offing, the United States made the security of this geographical area a key and permanent objective of its policy in the region.[24]

Central America was considered a marginal region—often turbulent and unstable—to be "pacified" at any price, given its strategic proximity. The 1907 congress held in Washington and the establishment of the Central American Tribunal of Justice—both the work of Secretary of State Elihu Root and Theodore Roosevelt—sought to achieve this objective. Secretary of State Philander Knox devised a simple formula that opened a new era in dollar diplomacy in the isthmus: The newly pacified republics of the isthmus would be induced to contract loans with U.S. bankers in order to liquidate European claims and normalize their treasury balances, while U.S. investors would be encouraged to obtain concessions and set up businesses in the region.[25]

After the Congress of 1907, whose sequel was held in 1923 under U.S. auspices, other attempts at unification were undertaken in Central America.[26] Little by little, however, they were blocked by the economic interests of the most influential groups in these republics, ever more entwined with foreign interests.

The 1929 stock market crash and subsequent depression, which struck Central America hard during the next decade, revealed very clearly the need for economic integration treaties to boost the region's industrial capacity.[27] Nevertheless, integration was subordinated from the very start to the foreign presence—so much so, that in the case of the Central American Common Market in the 1960s, the project of the Economic Commission for Latin America (ECLA) had to be scrapped, owing to the alliance between the national monopolies and U.S. companies, who opposed it.[28]

Such was the context of U.S. actions in Central America, as well as Mexico's position with respect to this contiguous zone. Both had their origins in the expansionist U.S. attitudes and the defensive posture that Mexico was forced to assume in light of its disastrous history as the next-door neighbor of the United States. From then on, an increasingly well-defined pattern of U.S. conduct in Latin America began to emerge—a pattern that moved from crude gunboat intervention to the doctrine of national security in the second half of the twentieth century, enforced by the Central Intelligence Agency (CIA).[29]

Since the nineteenth century, throughout Central and Latin America's conflicts, Mexico has maintained a position of open solidarity, as a natural response to both its historic fraternal bonds with these regions and the real possibility that U.S. interventionist policy would once more eventually be used against it.

Nineteenth-Century Regional Conflicts

Before the era when the national security doctrine dominated the Latin American scene, but after the time of the troubled independence of the new Ibero-American republics, several events began to outline the nature of the Mexico–United States–Central America triangle: the rise of filibusterism and the Central American national war, the Mexican-Guatemalan border dispute, and the construction of the Panama Canal.

Filibusterism and the Central American National War. From the time of the territorial expansion, U.S. filibusterism affected not only Central America but the Caribbean and even Mexico. Mexican territory was understandably the favorite target of U.S. adventurers, since the country shared such a long border with the United States. Several states in northern Mexico were hence the focus of ambitions by diverse filibusterist expeditions. Mexico vigorously protested these incursions on a number of occasions, but, given the deep-rooted expansionist spirit of the era, the United States always responded with a refusal to apply the Neutrality Act of 1818.[30]

Mesmerized by proslavery and Puritan ideas and following in the footsteps of Boulbon, a Frenchman who had unsuccessfully attempted to organize an independent republic on Mexican soil, William Walker organized an expedition to that country. Failing, he departed, and in 1855, liberal Nicaraguan sectors came to his aid. Under the promise of land concessions in this Central American country, Walker armed a mercenary expedition, eventually imposing his schemes and forming a government under the control of his mercenaries.[31] This government was recognized by the U.S. Department of State in May 1856, to the consternation of the other Central American countries and the British government.

The governments of the isthmus banded together against Walker, and an army commanded by Costa Rican president Juan Rafael Mora and equipped by the British managed to overthrow him in May 1857, after over a year of fighting. This war, justly called "the national war," ensured the independence of Central America and at the same time represented the height of conservative power in the isthmus.

Nicaragua next ran afoul of U.S. interests in 1912, when Washington intervened to oust its liberal president José Santos Zelaya, described by U.S. Secretary of State Philander Knox as a "dictator who attempted to impose a liberal hegemony and reunify Central America by force." In fact, Zelaya's main offense was his interest in negotiating a canal treaty with other foreign powers.

The Mexican-Guatemalan Border Dispute. Even the problem of demarcating Mexico's southern border following Central America's separation from the Mexican empire—which should have remained a strictly Mexican and Guatemalan affair—revealed the interventionist nature of the United States within the nineteenth century triangular relationship.[32] Guatemala, it should be recalled, was part of the Mexican empire until 1823. When Augustín de Iturbide abdicated, Mexico was on the brink of disintegration, with several regions declaring independence and the Central American provinces favoring separation. When the Constitution of 1825 was adopted, Chiapas voluntarily rejoined Mexico; not so the rest of Central America, which began to splinter in several directions.[33] Guatemala's bourgeoisie never accepted Chiapas's decision, which gave rise to a protracted struggle that nearly led to war.[34]

In 1881 Guatemala's leader, Justo Rufino Barrios, requested U.S. support to reduce the inequalities between Guatemala's and Mexico's forces, even suggesting the possibility of ceding the Mexican region of Soconusco in Chiapas (or whatever it gained from Mexico) to the United States in exchange for protection in the event of war. The United States did not take this offer seriously, but Secretary of State James Blaine attempted to take advantage of it to promote the construction of a canal through Nicaragua; to this end, he instructed his representative in Mexico to inform the government of that country of his willingness to serve as a mediator with Guatemala. Mexico mobilized troops along its southern border, which led Blaine to alter his attitude. In a threatening note, he warned that any aggression against Guatemala would be considered contrary to U.S. interests.

The Mexican government rejected the offer of mediation, but its minister of foreign relations sent the U.S. government several volumes of documentation that supported Mexico's claim to Chiapas. The United States insisted that a tripartite commission review the case to determine the exact demarcation. Mexico accepted, on condition that Guatemala accept Mexico's claims to Chiapas outright.[35] The death of President Garfield on September 19, 1881, altered the game by removing Blaine as secretary of state. Guatemala offered the new U.S. secretary of state, Frederick Frelinghuysen, a different treaty that granted the United States the right to station troops on Central American soil in exchange for protection. In the end, Mexico managed to get Barrios to acknowledge its rights over Chiapas, signing a treaty in 1882 that in essence ratified the Mexican position on direct negotiations between the two countries.[36]

In reality, despite the outwardly conciliatory conduct of the United States, behind the scenes were the economic interests of U.S. companies who sought to retain advantageous conditions for their operations in the border zone. This grew evident at the height of the border dispute, when in 1892, the man in charge of the Border Commission for Guatemala, U.S. engineer Miles Rock, together with some soldiers, an official from police headquarters in El Petén and an employee from Jamet, a logging company that had won concessions from Guatemala in the area under litigation, crossed into Mexican territory and set fire to a number of game preserves. Fortunately, in April 1895 the De León-Mariscal Convention was finally signed, wherein Guatemala agreed to pay for the damages incurred in this flagrant assault.[37]

The Panama Canal. By the late nineteenth century, after its various expansionist advances, the United States had already decided that the possession of an interoceanic canal was its main objective in Central America. The country therefore channeled its efforts toward removing the obstacles to the canal's construction. In 1899, the U.S. government launched an investigation into the advantages of promoting this project in Panama versus Nicaragua—an investigation that actually concerned issues connected with the interests of the investors involved in the potential business. The New Panama Canal Company, founded in Paris in October 1894 and composed of an assortment of European and U.S. businessmen, lobbied to win U.S. congressional approval for their final project, with the aim of having Panama chosen over Nicaragua.[38]

Once this problem was solved, the government of the United States opened negotiations with the government of Colombia—the country to which Panama belonged in this era—but a variety of reasons prevented

Colombia's final acceptance of the accord (the Hay-Herrán Convention).[39] The United States then began to pressure Colombia to change its mind. Exploiting the discontent with the central government among various sectors of Panamanian society, it fomented and militarily supported the rebellion that led to the separation of Panama from Colombia—in exchange for the new government's concession of the canal to the United States.[40]

The Panamanian revolt triumphed on November 3, 1903, and the new government was recognized by the United States on the 6th. That same day, French citizen Felipe Bunau-Varilla, representing the New Panama Canal Company, was named special envoy and minister plenipotentiary of the new Republic of Panama to Washington, with the authority to negotiate the canal treaty. On the 11th, Bunau-Varilla presented his credentials to Secretary of State Hay, and five days later a treaty was signed, granting the United States the right to construct an interoceanic canal on Panamanian territory. We will not comment on U.S. actions, both with respect to the way the canal was built and the manner in which the United States continues to retain possession of it by military force; suffice it to say that commentaries abound.[41]

Twentieth-Century Regional Conflicts

In the twentieth century tensions between the United States and Mexico were heightened as a result of a number of regional conflicts, which included Sandino's war in Nicaragua, the 1932 insurrection and consequent repression in El Salvador, the civil war of 1948 in Costa Rica, the October 1944 revolution in Guatemala as well as a number of other conflicts in South America and the Caribbean.

Sandino's War in Nicaragua. Because of its domestic conflicts, Nicaragua was the country where the United States most needed to apply the principle of "peace and security" in the isthmus. However, the progressive plans of Nicaragua's liberal bourgeoisie represented a stumbling block. For this reason, the United States, claiming "just cause," attempted to help the more conservative agro-exporting sectors, who would guarantee support for its interests.

From 1913 to 1924, there were more than ten armed uprisings against the conservative government. However, it was not until 1926 that the Constitutionalist War began, leading to the organization of Augusto Sandino's people's army. This conflict ended in May 1927, but from then until his assassination in 1934, Nicaraguans under Sandino fought U.S. marines. This conflict excited interest and admiration among many of Latin America's peoples and governments, for besides legitimately defending Nicaragua's national sovereignty against the armed occupation, it demonstrated the need to create a unified Spanish American front to halt the advance of the United States in Latin America.[42] Because of this, Sandino's name was respected in Mexico, and the support that he received from the country was cause for concern in some U.S. circles, which pressured to influence even the extent of solidarity with this effort.[43]

Furthermore, Mexico's foreign policy during the 1920s began to be one of solidarity with all of Central America.[44] Various cultural support activities for the region, the elevation of Mexico's minister plenipotentiary in Guatemala, Alfonso Cravioto, to the post of ambassador in 1926, and the manifestations of sympathy with the defense of Nicaraguan sovereignty led to real concern on the part of some sectors in the United States.[45] The United States tried to influence Mexican diplomacy, particularly where solidarity with Sandino's struggle was concerned.[46]

From the Insurrection of 1932 to the Civil War of 1948. The deep recession of 1929 produced unemployment, hunger, and misery in El Salvador. In 1930 and 1931, agricultural workers went on strike and were violently suppressed. The political crisis reached its climax in a coup d'etat in December 1931, in which General Maximiliano Hernández Martínez overthrew President Arturo Araujo. In the context of an important electoral period and as a reaction to the repressive measures, the economic crisis, the electoral fraud, the absence of real solutions to the growing social problems and widespread discontent, a popular insurrection was unleashed in 1932, led by semiarmed campesinos who were virtually massacred by a well-equipped army.

The U.S. government did not officially recognize General Hernández Martínez at this time, given the doubts that the Salvadoran oligarchy itself had about a de facto president in the country. The repression was formally condemned by the United States, therefore, though it is obvious that the country took advantage of the situation to consolidate its own alliances.[47]

In time, the Salvadoran people reorganized and a popular movement began to sprout, much to the alarm of the military and the oligarchy. Thus, a new coup was delivered in 1944 that imposed Castaneda Castro as president. Running for reelection in 1948, he was overthrown by midranking army officers, who then installed a Revolutionary Government Council.[48] Some university students declared the date of the takeover by this new body a day of national rejoicing (December 14, 1948), an action that began to be called "the Salvadoran revolution of 1948." This period coincided with the events known as the "civil war" in Costa Rica, which opened a new chapter for that nation.[49]

The October Revolution of 1944 and U.S. Intervention in Guatemala in 1954. When Juan José Arévalo took office as president in October

1944, a significant period in Guatemalan history known as the "October revolution" began, spanning the administrations of Arévalo himself (1944–1950) and Jacobo Arbenz Guzmán (1950–1954) and laying the groundwork for the political structures necessary to modernize and democratize the country.[50] On taking office in 1951, Arbenz said:

> Our government proposes to set out on a path of economic development in Guatemala, with the following three basic objectives: to transform our country from a dependent and semi-colonial nation to an economically independent one; to transform Guatemala from a backward country and a predominantly feudal economy to a modern, capitalist country; and to carry out this transformation in a manner that will lead to the greatest possible elevation in the living of the great mass of the people.[51]

For the large U.S. companies, however, the main problem with Arbenz was his national program, which even in a free market context threatened their interests; hence, for them, this government was a cause for concern and even hostility.[52] The encouragement of unions in the countryside and the city, the enactment of social legislation, the expansion of the educational system, the adoption of an independent foreign policy, the ending of the U.S. monopoly over the communications media, and the agrarian reform were elements that would inevitably check the power of the oligarchy and the banana growers of the United Fruit Company.[53]

This is why the U.S. government took a firm stand against the government of Arbenz, which it toppled by means of the anticommunist Carlos Castillo Armas and a precarious army backed by CIA-contracted mercenaries.[54] Thus, the possibility of Guatemalan independence, even through a free market approach, was foreclosed for many decades.

The U.S. government, it should be recalled, sought to legitimize its intervention through a condemnatory resolution introduced at the 1954 meeting of the Organization of American States (OAS) in Caracas. In Guatemala's case, Mexico was unable to undertake broader diplomatic action to uphold the principles of nonintervention and the self-determination of peoples, but it made its position clear when, together with the government of Argentina, it opposed the resolution and other later moves against the constitutional government of Arbenz. This was highly significant and brought its profound differences with the United States concerning events in both Central America and Latin America into focus. Mexico, moreover, made extensive use of its traditional policy of the right to asylum, welcoming dozens of its Guatemalan brothers fleeing from the new dictatorship after the bloody events that brought Castillo Armas to power.[55]

The Impact of Other Latin American Conflicts. The natural context of the Mexico–United States–Central America triangle has been influenced by the other Latin American players. The attempts by the peoples of Cuba, Chile, Argentina, Uruguay, Peru, and Panama to liberate themselves from historical domination had an inevitably different impact on each of the three parties: on the United States, by inducing it to respond with arms to preserve its hegemony; on Mexico, by forcing it to take a stand while seeking an equilibrium between its racial brethren and its unwanted ally; on Central America, by fanning the flames of its people's rightful liberty.

Thus, the Cuban Revolution, which came to power in 1959, and U.S. attempts to prevent its consolidation, the overthrow of Juan Bosch and the subsequent invasion of Santo Domingo by U.S. marines in 1965, and the coup d'etat and assassination of Chile's constitutionally elected president, Salvador Allende, in 1973 were notable events for the triangular relationship. Likewise, the rise of the various South American dictatorships in response to popular uprisings, with U.S. complaisance, and even the sad conflict sparked by legitimate Panamanian nationalism against the illegitimate military enclave in the Panama Canal Zone also were important moments for the triangular relationship in the second half of the twentieth century.

Worried about the spread of Cuba's revolution to the rest of Latin America, the U.S. government in the 1960s began a broader and more systematic program of espionage and destabilization in a number of countries, intervening either directly or indirectly and hardening the political climate.[56] Mexico, for its part, could do practically nothing to stop these interventionist activities. It did voice its opposition to them however, both in the OAS and the United Nations and through express declarations by its government; there were even popular demonstrations of solidarity with the aggrieved peoples. At the same time, as in other cases before and after, Mexico's humanistic policy of the right to asylum provided an opportunity for many Chileans to seek exile there, where they found a second homeland to start a family or prepare for an eventual return to their humiliated country.

Thus, with the passage of time, it became more than evident that U.S. rhetoric of forming one big inter-American family would be accompanied by the use of force to ensure U.S. hegemony, at the cost of other countries' dreams of real independence leading to fuller development. With the exception of Cuba, Latin America's nations found themselves subject to U.S. designs; however, they held fast to the hope of some day attaining well-being, seeking to find new formulas for self-defense in their race and in their language, without foreign interference.

Mexican and U.S. Foreign Policy Toward
Central America: Present and Future

As we have stated, Central America's situation is a product of its history. At the same time, however, it exists within the broader context of a continent in a concrete stage of historical development. To a large extent, therefore, Central America's crisis is part of Latin America's larger crisis. This has forced governments like Mexico's into an active role to prevent that crisis from spreading to neighboring countries—this at a time when the rising discontent stemming from the social costs of a so-far unresolvable economic crisis could prove fertile ground for a political destabilization with untold consequences.

In Central America, however, it is not simply military or even geopolitical implications that have been in play, as demonstrated by Contadora, which at one point became Mexico's primary foreign policy tool in the region. Contadora sought formulas to reconcile the different countries involved and to find economic cooperation mechanisms for solving the problems of decades of underdevelopment. Thus, from day one, the Contadora Group attempted to find political, juridical, and diplomatic solutions, as well as the resources to guarantee international and regional stability, by instituting a dialogue on the principles of sovereignty and respect.

In a broader sense, though, Contadora was just one more expression of the crisis in Latin America, its economic and political paradoxes, and the relative erosion of the inter-American system under U.S. domination. At the same time, this multinational effort, which the Lima Group with similar concerns would later join, would also attempt to assist in the search for better economic and structural conditions for the region and even Latin America as a whole, where a revival of economic growth and a just distribution of income would benefit those who would otherwise be left out under an unequal international economic order.

The Central American situation thus acquired a special significance for both Mexico and the United States, since it not only sharpened regional and inter-American difficulties but national problems as well, owing to the deepening of the social and economic crisis that began in the late 1970s and continues unresolved to this day.

Mexican-U.S. Relations and Central America in the 1980s

The Central American crisis began to have a profound influence on the inter-American system in the 1980s, affecting Mexican-U.S. relations. The Mexican government and diverse sectors of Mexican society voiced concern that the problems of the early 1980s would undermine Mexico's political situation in the future. It was because of this that the United States became wary about Mexico's domestic situation and even critical of its diplomatic conduct in international organizations during the bulk of the decade.[57]

In the 1970s, it should be recalled, Mexico began to confront a hard reality: The strong economic development it had enjoyed for some years, which some had boasted of as "the Mexican miracle," had come to an end. The economic and political crisis that ensued after the failure of the Alliance for Progress obliged the Mexican government to institute new reforms grounded in the new world scenario, in order to extract the country from its difficult domestic situation and broaden its relative margin for autonomy.

For this project to achieve consensus and consistency, it required a more active foreign policy, which was not difficult in view of Mexico's traditional diplomatic posture. Without abandoning the principles of international law and, at the same time, without taking a radical turn, the changes in Mexican foreign policy in the 1970s marked the beginning of a more open relationship with the world. The government began to participate more actively in international forums, where it strengthened old ties or established new ones, for example with the Socialist bloc, and began to identify with other Third World countries, with which it had many problems in common. The economic resurgence of other powers and even the advance of the Socialist economies generated high expectations of trade in the eyes of Mexico.

The country thus began to promote a variety of multilateral actions in international forums, such as the creation of the Latin American Economic System (LAES), the Charter of the Economic Rights and Duties of States, and a generally pro–Third World policy sustained out of a profound conviction that "Pan-Americanism has not vanished as something to aspire to." Mexico's transformation into an oil-producing nation was a key element that lent clout to its new diplomatic posture, not just in the multilateral arena, but in its relations with its northern neighbor as well. Turmoil in the Middle East, which threatened U.S. oil supplies and magnified the advantage of having an energy-rich ally as a next-door neighbor, somewhat improved Mexico's position in relations with the United States.[58]

With the resurgence of the revolutionary struggles in Central America and renewed U.S. aggression against Cuba throughout the 1970s, Mexico was forced to fall back on its traditional principles. It broke diplomatic relations with Somoza in May 1979 and backed the Sandinista revolution. It also reaffirmed its ties with Cuba. At the same time, in an attempt to promote the peace process by averting the spread of the armed conflict and seeking to broaden Central America's margin for autonomy in the face of U.S. policy, the Mexican government issued a joint declaration with France in August 1981 recognizing the Farabundo Martí Front for National Liberation (FMLN) and the Democratic Revolutionary Front (FDR) as political forces representative of the Salvadoran people.[59]

The Reagan administration's reaction to Mexican policy in Central America during the 1982 Mexican crisis was framed in terms of East-West confrontation. Officials like Ambassador Jeane Kirkpatrick called the Mexican government "irresponsible" for taking this position, without taking the supposed threat that "the revolutionary movements represent for its own national security" into account.[60] From this point on, Mexican security became an important preoccupation for U.S. national security planners, on a par with the so-called "Soviet-Cuban-Sandinista penetration of Latin America."[61]

Within this context, the Contadora Group emerged in January 1983 as a possibility for achieving a peaceful solution to the Central American conflict that had been worsening since 1981, due to the Reagan administration's determination to overthrow the Sandinistas. As one of Nicaragua's principal backers, the Mexican government received a harsh response from the U.S. administration. Meetings between Presidents de la Madrid and Reagan were more or less permeated with differences over Central America. Referring to the fourth meeting, which took place on January 2, 1986, Elliot Abrams, assistant secretary of state for inter-American affairs, said this question was asked at the summit: "Why hasn't Mexico backed the United States during U.N. votes on Central America?"[62] At times, it even seemed that U.S. pressure (which at one point was interpreted as "a campaign against Mexico") was aimed at coercing fundamental changes in Mexican foreign policy, especially with respect to Cuba or Nicaragua.

At the time there was no real consensus in the United States as to the true nature of Mexico's foreign policy. While a variety of conservative sectors claimed to see "irresponsibility" on the part of the Mexican government in the face of "threats to hemispheric security," more liberal sectors justified it, suggesting that these positions had helped achieve domestic political stability. The truth is that U.S. diplomacy with regard to Mexico during the 1980s had a far broader frame of reference than merely that country's international position. Bilateral relations between the two nations continued to be defined along the lines and constraints imposed by Mexico's dependence and underdevelopment with respect to its powerful neighbor, with the essential ingredient being the U.S. desire to prolong indefinitely the same relationship of domination.

The Future of the Mexico–United States–
Central America Triangle

For nearly two centuries, the triangular relationship has implied the preeminence of the United States, which because of its economic and, hence, political and military might, has made use of virtual police powers to make its interests prevail. It has imposed the inter-American system to legitimize its hegemony and used many means, including direct intervention, to guarantee its control.

In contrast, Mexican policy developed its own dynamic over decades as a politically independent but economically dependent and under-developed nation. Though wary of its powerful neighbor to the north, Mexico's relationship of solidarity with its brethren to the south has remained constant over the decades. Central America found itself in a similar situation but with fewer development possibilities owing to a larger foreign presence and a weaker economic base; nonetheless it, too, aspired to autonomy and development. With the passage of time, these precarious circumstances would inexorably plunge the region into the social and political conflicts that have marked the twentieth century.

The most recent changes in the international scene, amply dealt with in Chapter 3, do not alter this essential reality. With regard to Mexico, not even the turmoil surrounding the presidential election of 1988 implied any real threat of changing its traditional subordination to the United States. On the contrary, with impressive political control, the new government of Carlos Salinas de Gortari has been able to institute a number of reforms begun under the administration of Miguel de la Madrid and, under the pretext of modernization, has promoted the greatest economic openness that an underdeveloped nation has ever had to endure, through measures that will ultimately lay the groundwork for economic integration with the United States.[63]

Such changes have had a particular effect on U.S. strategies for the 1990s, strategies that respond to the needs of giant multinational corporations to reproduce their capital, compelling them to seek terms and conditions that allow them to maximize profit through the glob-alization of the economy, the integration of regional markets, and eventually a single world economy. For the countries of Latin America, this translates into the need to prepare themselves to play efficiently the subordinate role that will inevitably fall to them in the new international division of labor.[64]

The modification of these economic conditions already created in Mexico by U.S. action and the presence of additional players like Japan or Europe will have irrevocable repercussions for the country's political situation, since they imply an inexorable denationalization and, hence, a loss of sovereignty. Therefore, a modification in the terms of the triangular relationship that existed until the 1980s, when Mexico took a firmer posture against U.S. activities in Central America, is hardly surprising. Its position on Panama, for example, is in sharp contrast to its former stance: After inconsistently endorsing its expulsion from the Group of Eight and manifesting a patently pro-U.S. attitude in a condemnation of Noriega, Mexico issued just a single diplomatic statement of little political note concerning the bloody U.S. military invasion.[65]

Hence, there is the need for a precise definition of the outlook for U.S. foreign policy in this new international context. Hence, there is also the need for Mexico to remember its historic reasons for adopting foreign policy principles like those of the past, which have lately undergone a modification in response to new structural conditions.

It must be reiterated that the foreign policy of nations has its roots in their experiences; that is, different conditions throughout their history have served as the foundations for their international positions. These positions are also the product of a national awareness of the country's circumstances and of the perspectives that help create a people's unique way of thinking, which, in the final analysis, expresses its aspirations and concerns.

In light of the country's continuing underdevelopment and dependence, Mexico's history supports the government's traditional international stance. This position is by no means one of reflexive rancor over the past or even the resentment by a weak country of a stronger neighbor. It is a clear and consistent internationalist position with just aspirations and firm postures in its dealings with the rest of the American and world community. Mexico's foreign policy attempts to identify what is just and what is unjust and defends the right of peoples to self-determination, as well as peaceful international coexistence, equality among nations, and the right to asylum, while condemning powerful nations that abuse their position.

The essence of this policy, so fundamental to the course of Mexican–U.S.–Central American relations, is a nationalist and profoundly Latin American viewpoint, clearly incorporated as principles into Mexico's foreign policy. These principles have sustained the country's international position over the decades and have been present throughout the Central American conflict—even more so when active participation has become necessary, as in the past decade.

These have been the firm moral underpinnings for a consistent foreign policy, whose strength is political and ideological, rather than economic or military. Over the nearly two hundred years of this triangular relationship, Mexico has endeavored to make Latin Americans and even North Americans who believe in peace and democracy and international cooperation—instead of the arrogant use of brute force—aware of the urgent need to redouble efforts to defend the sovereignty and the right of nations to determine their own destiny. This is the only condition that will permit a true easing of tensions and real peace, which are the cornerstones of authentic development and democracy, both for the main protagonists of the triangular relationship and the rest of the Latin American and world community.

As Richard Fagen says in another PACCA publication, "The United States has no choice but to learn to live with Central American nationalism, for it is not going to go away. On the contrary, it is the most widely shared political perspective in the region, linking groups that are otherwise far apart on the political spectrum. A more mature U.S. policy would view this nationalism as something essentially constructive. . . ."[66]

Or as we Latin Americans ourselves could say: We would do well on this continent if everyone, especially the United States, would learn to live side by side, respecting the sovereignty and the decision of the people to forge a brighter future—always promised, but never delivered. Right now, many forces are mobilizing to accomplish this, and thus, we will surely manage to lay the foundations for a new relationship between Mexico, the United States, and Central America that is truly fruitful and long lasting.

Notes

1. The author wishes to acknowledge the support of the following individuals and/or institutions: Rodrigo Jauberth, Gilberto Castañeda, and Pedro Vuskovic, whose salient comments assisted in the elaboration of this chapter; the Centro de Investigaciones sobre Estados Unidos de América of the National Autonomous University of Mexico (UNAM), where preliminary versions of the first two parts were advanced; Antonio Rivera, who contributed by providing training on the computer; Lucía Chavolla, who collaborated in the initial phases of the chapter and helped compile the bibliography; and the many friends who contributed materials, support, and understanding throughout this effort. All of them are responsible, it should be understood, for whatever has been achieved in this work, while the author, on the other hand, is accountable for any defects.

2. That is, each country's stance and political conduct toward others at the regional or world level—the result of this national consciousness in response to the international situation and the interests involved at a given point in its evolution as a sovereign nation.

3. Fernando Carmona, *Latin American Capitalism* (Seminar on the Theory of Development, Mexico: IIEC-UNAM, 1975), p. 55. Carmona asserts that "the explanation for the persistence of underdevelopment, despite the fact that some nations like those of Latin America achieved political autonomy a long time

ago, must lie in the imperialist system, which in some cases forges and in all cases strengthens the bonds of dependence and subordination . . ." in *El drama de América Latina: el caso de México* (Mexico: Cuadernos Américanos, 1964), p. 36.

4. Historian Ernesto de la Torre notes how after the civil war "Foreigners were able to enter the country with greater ease, settle there, influence Mexico's customs and way of life, marry nationals and thus broaden the configuration of society. . . . Mexico perceived itself as part of a group of provinces united with its metropolis; when it separated, it would also be isolated from its sisters, and when it began its life of independence, it would be alone and defenseless in the face of many powerful enemies." Ernesto de la Torre Villar, "La Independencia," in *Historia documental de México,* ed. de la Torre Villar et al. (Universidad Nacional Autónoma de México, 1984), vol. 2, p. 13. The author continues (p. 14), "While Mexicans fought for their independence, Spain, pressured by the United States, which was beginning its expansionist policy, entered into a treaty on February 22, 1819, through [the efforts of] its Ambassador Luis de Onís and U.S. Secretary Adams. This treaty established the border of the United States and New Spain at the Sabines River and north from there to 32 degrees latitude, following the Red River, to continue west to 100 degrees longitude, from there, north to the Arkansas River, then to 42 degrees latitude and from there to the Pacific. Thus, on gaining independence, Mexico found that its previously limitless territory had been demarcated to its neighbor's advantage."

5. Alonso Aguilar says, "Opposing the declining yet still powerful interests of individuals who were attempting first, to preserve the Colony, and then, to save their enormous inheritance, were those who aspired to create a new Mexico by destroying the signs of the old society, from wealth in the hands of a privileged group of Spaniards, to the tribute, the tithes, primogeniture, the guilds, the sales tax, the exemptions, and the Holy Inquisition." Alonso Aguilar Monteverde, *Dialéctica de la economía mexicana* (Mexico: Editorial Nuestro Tiempo, 1972), p. 62.

6. As Aguilar states, "In the Mexico of the Reform—that is, the 1870s and the 1880s—capitalism was now, in our view, the dominant socioeconomic system. Far from being an engine of growth, however, Mexican capitalism operated as an engine while simultaneously putting the brakes on the growth of reproductive forces. For us, this system is the capitalism of underdevelopment, a capitalism whose most salient features are structural dependence, profound inequalities in national development, regional disintegration, industrial stagnation, and the presence of ruling and subject classes—a weak, incipient, alienated, unstable, and profoundly contradictory capitalism, incapable of multiplying its productive forces within a reasonably brief lapse of time . . ." Aguilar, *Dialéctica,* pp. 100–101.

7. Oscar Handlin says in this respect, "Unfavorable conditions in their old homes thrust them out, and the image of the golden West drew them on, while the removal of the Indian threat and favorable land laws encouraged migration." Oscar Handlin, *The History of the United States* (New York: Holt, Rinehart and Winston, Inc., 1967), p. 444.

8. That is, a series of continental alliances under U.S. leadership, which led to the founding of the Organization of American States in 1948.

9. Luis de Onís himself, Spanish ambassador to the United States in the early nineteenth century, clearly described U.S. intentions in a letter to the Spanish viceroy dated April 1, 1812, "Each day the ambitions of this Republic grow more and more, confirming its hostile designs against Spain: Your Excellency will already have learned through my correspondence that this government has set its sights no less on establishing its boundaries at the mouth of the Río Norte or Bravo, following its course to 31 degrees and from there, continuing in a direct line to the Pacific Ocean, thus appropriating for itself the provinces of Texas, Nuevo Santander, Coahuila, Nuevo México, and part of Nueva Vizcaya and Sonora. This project would seem a delirium to any sane person, but nonetheless it exists, and a plan has been drawn up by government order expressly for these provinces, with the Island of Cuba included within these boundaries, as if it were a natural possession of this Republic." Report of Luis de Onís on the territorial expansion of the United States, in de la Torre Villar, *Historia documental,* p. 33.

10. Naturally, not every North American shared this intent, and there were those who opposed the plan. In this regard, the view of Ohio Senator Corwin should be noted. Corwin said, "If I were a Mexican, I would say to you, 'Is it perhaps because you have no room in your own country? . . . If you invade ours, we will receive you with bloody hands and welcome you with hospitable tombs.'" Or that of another congressman from the same state, who called the war of 1847 "a war against a people that has given us no offense, [a war] without adequate or just cause, for the purpose of conquest. . . . I will not offer you any support. I will not soak my hands in the blood of the Mexican people, nor will I share the guilt for the murders already committed or for any that our army will commit in the future in that country." Cited by Leo Huberman, *Nosotros el pueblo—Historia de los Estados Unidos* (Mexico: Editorial Nuestro Tiempo, 1981), pp. 170–171. Huberman adds that, "A young Congressman from Illinois, Abraham Lincoln, later President of the United States, also opposed the war with Mexico. He later voted [for a resolution] declaring that this conflict had been 'unnecessarily and unconstitutionally provoked by the President.'"

11. For an explanation of the Estrada Doctrine, see Note 9, Introduction. The Carranza Doctrine (so named because it was advocated by Venustiano Carranza, first constitutional president of Mexico during the Revolution of 1910–1917), holds that all countries are equal; that they must mutually and scrupulously respect each other's institutions, laws, and sovereignty; that no country should intervene in any way or for any reason in the internal affairs of another; that no individual should aspire to a better position than that of the citizens of the country where he intends to establish himself, nor make of his alien status a title of protection and privilege. The Cárdenas Doctrine (maintained by Gen. Lázaro Cárdenas, probably Mexico's most important postrevolutionary president), similar to the Carranza Doctrine as far as its implications for the United States are concerned, establishes the obligation of citizens of other countries to rigorously respect the laws of the country that receives them, without debasing national sovereignty.

12. "When, after one hundred centuries," indicated the invitation by Bolívar, "posterity seeks to discover the origins of our public law and remembers the pacts that sealed its destiny, it will record with respect the protocols of the isthmus. In them, it will find the plan of the first alliances, which will trace the path of our relations with the universe." Francisco Pividal, *Bolívar: pensamiento precursor del antimperialismo* (Havana: Casa de las Américas, 1977), p. 161.

13. In the context of the Congress, several of the independent republics entered into the first regional diplomatic accord in memory in the Americas: On July 15, 1826, the republics of Colombia, Central America, Peru, and Mexico signed a treaty wherein "they bind together and confederate in war and peace, and to this end enter into a firm and inviolable pact of friendship and intimate union in perpetuity." "The object of this perpetual pact," says the second article of the treaty, "will be to uphold in common, defensively and offensively if necessary, the sovereignty and independence of each and every one of the Confederate Powers of America against all foreign domination, to guarantee forever the joys of an unalterable peace, and to this end, foment better harmony and good judgment among their peoples, citizens, and subjects, respectively, and with the other Powers with whom they may maintain or enter into amicable relations." Pividal, *Bolívar,* p. 161.

14. For example, in a letter to his chancery in Washington dated March 20, 1826, Herman Allen, U.S. representative to the government of Chile, precisely noted his opposition to what he called the "Famous Panama Congress," saying, "I have uniformly maintained that this assembly would be premature and that nothing good would come of it: that the Spanish would no longer endanger the independence of the new states; that there was no danger of intervention in their affairs from any foreign power, and under these circumstances they could better direct their energies toward improving their domestic situation instead of wasting part of them on futile and perhaps prejudicial enthusiasms." See Pividal, *Bolívar,* p. 172. Allen was not speaking lightly; the United States had already spun intrigues around the eminent Simón Bolívar, whom William Tudor, U.S. consul to the government of Peru, had called a "dictator" in a letter to then-Secretary of State Henry Clay, dated June 15 of that same year, once the Panama sessions were over. "His ambition may obviate the usefulness of the Congress whose author he is and whose idea justly enhanced his reputation." Pividal, *Bolívar,* pp. 173–174.

15. Such aspirations would be noted by Joel Roberts Poinsett, plenipotentiary representative at the time and later ambassador to Mexico. In a conversation held September 27, 1825, with England's Plenipotentiary Representative Ward, he said "it would be absurd to suppose that the President of the United States would sign a treaty at an eventual Congress of Panama that excluded his country from a federation that he should be leading. . . ." Pividal, *Bolívar,* p. 177.

16. See the following in this regard: Antonio Gómez Robledo, "Frustración hispanoamericana," *Idea y experiencia de América* (Mexico: Fondo de Cultura Económica, 1958). Reproduced in Secretaría de Relaciones Exteriores, *Política*

exterior de México—175 años de historia (Mexico, 1985), vol. 2, p. 187ff; Miguel Alfonso, "La creación del 'Sistema Interamericano': ¿imposición imperialista o ceguera de los círculos de poder latinoamericanos?" *Cuadernos de Nuestra América* III, 5 (January–February 1986), p. 8; and José Martí, "La Conferencia Americana," *Obras Completas* (Cuba: La Habana, 1975), vol. 6, pp. 34–116.

17. Two documents must be remembered in this regard: The first is a letter to General José María Morelos y Pavón dated May 1813 and signed by rebel Salvadorans Miguel Delgado, Juan Manuel Rodríguez, and Santiago José Celis, who declared, "our solidarity with you is identical to our solidarity with your interesting and just cause"; the other, dated September 15, 1821, from Guatemala's National Palace, is the Manifesto of the Head of Government to the Citizens of Guatemala, read on this date by Gavino Gaínza, Captain General of Guatemala, which announces the Central American proclamation of independence resulting from the Iguala Plan and the Treaties of Córdoba. The manifesto says, "Since 1810, the two Americas, North and South, have begun to move: since then, they have begun to defend their rights and uphold their sovereignty; since then, the accents and voices of liberty and independence have begun to sound. Guatemala, lodged between one America and the other, was a happy and serene spectator of each. Her children heard the voices with pleasure; they observed with joy the steps of those she had always considered her brothers; and if the feelings in her heart were not broadcast from her lips, they were nevertheless [Latin] American: they loved what was loved; they desired what was desired." See complete text of both documents in Secretaría de Relaciones Exteriores, *Política exterior de México—175 años de historia* (Mexico, 1985), vol. 1, pp. 22–25.

18. Spanish representative to the United States Luis de Onís recounts the conversation between Gutiérrez de Lara and James Monroe: "Mr. Monroe told Col. Bernardo Gutiérrez that the Government of the United States would back the revolution of the Mexican provinces with all its might, and it would do so not only with arms and ammunition but with 27,000 crack troops available for this purpose: but that Col. Bernardo and the other leaders of the revolution should try to enact a good constitution to assure the felicity of their countries. To this end, Monroe spoke very highly of the United States and gave them to understand that the American government wished them to adopt the same constitution in Mexico; that these republics would then be admitted to the Union, and the addition of the rest of the provinces of the American continent would lead to the creation of the most formidable power in the world. Col. Bernardo, who had listened rather calmly to the Secretary of State up to the part about the plan to incorporate the provinces, rose, furious, from his chair on hearing such a proposition and left Mr. Monroe's office very angry." Alberto María Carreño, *La diplomacia extraordinaria entre México y Estados Unidos* (Mexico: Editorial Jus, 1951), vol. 1, p. 105.

19. After spending some time in that country, Zozaya voiced his concern that U.S. intentions would confirm the fears already expressed about recent U.S. conduct, and he even asserted that in his judgment, that country would

eventually turn into the sworn enemy of Mexico. Concerning this, he indicated in a diplomatic note, "The arrogance of these republicans does not allow them to view us as equals but rather as inferiors; their vanity extends in my judgment to the belief that their capital should be the capital of all the Americas; they dearly love our money, but not us, and they are incapable of entering into an alliance or trade agreement unless it is to their own advantage, ignoring the concept of reciprocity. In time, they will be our sworn enemies, and we should henceforth treat them as such . . ." Secretaría de Relaciones Exteriores, *La diplomacia mexicana* (Colección del Archivo Histórico Diplomático Méxicano, primera época, No. 1, 1910), vol. 1, p. 103.

20. For Antonio Gómez Robledo, Mexican minister Lucas Alamán represented one of the best chances for a successful outcome to the Tacubaya Congress. Nevertheless, forced to resign because of pressure from Joel Poinsett, he was absent from the government during those decisive years, and thus, could not influence the path that Mexico's policy toward Latin America would take, this being one of the first instances where a U.S. diplomat would successfully attempt to steer the course of events in Latin America through intrigue. See Antonio Gómez Robledo, "Frustración hispanoamericana," p. 184.

21. A conservative and centrist sector headed by Creoles of Spanish origin in Guatemala and a liberal and federalist sector in the rest of the provinces, led mainly by mestizo landowners and intellectuals.

22. "The outcome of the civil war," says Alberto Fuentes Mohr, "was a consolidation of the localist forces, whether under the liberal flag or the conservative. Lacking a centralized political authority, torn apart by a village mentality, and confronted by divergent economic interests, the Federation could not survive. A small country was thus divided, whose inhabitants numbered less than a million and a half and whose independence was seriously threatened by imperialist designs that sought to ensure an interoceanic route through the Central American isthmus for itself." *La creación de un Mercado Común* (Buenos Aires: INTAL/BID, 1973), pp. 5–6.

23. The various states declared independence on the following dates: Nicaragua, April 30, 1838; Honduras, October 26, 1838; Costa Rica, November 14, 1838; Guatemala, April 17, 1839; El Salvador, February 18, 1841.

24. According to the geographical configuration of the continent, three sites were appropriate for the construction of an interoceanic canal: the Isthmus of Tehuantepec; the region from the San Juan River, crossing Nicaragua to Cape Gracias a Dios; and the Isthmus of Panama.

25. "The dollar would replace the gun and the cannon as the tool for pacification . . ." notes Ramiro Guerra in Ramiro Guerra y Sanchez, *La expansión territorial de los Estados Unidos* (Havana: Editorial de Ciencias Sociales, 1975), p. 434.

26. We can point to the following events. In 1920, Guatemala's Legislative Assembly issued a decree recognizing the need for a Central American Union, in the midst of the popular agitation that dealt a mortal blow to the tyranny of Estrada Cabrera. In 1921, the Central American Union Party concluded its assembly; headed by youths of a liberal and reformist orientation, the party,

which had been formed at the turn of the century, managed briefly to establish the Central American Pact of Union. The pact was subsequently suppressed by Jose María Orella, president of Guatemala at the time, who had many of the founders arrested—among them Salvadoran Agustín Farabundo Martí.

27. This was especially true for the Salvadoran entrepreneur, who up to this point had largely resisted the assault of direct foreign investment. Héctor Dada says in this regard, "Until 1985, direct foreign investment in Salvadoran industry was practically limited to the English proprietorship of about three-quarters of the shares of the only cigarette factory in El Salvador." He adds, "Until the late 1960s, the agro-exporting class with financial interests successfully opposed the establishment of a second foreign bank alongside the Banco de Londres y Montreal, which was on the decline. Up to that point, foreign investment must not have been very interested in a market that offered so few opportunities for gain, either." Héctor Dada Hirezi, *La economía de El Salvador y la integración centroaméricana 1945-1960* (San Salvador: UCA Editores, 1978).

28. In fact, with the first integration treaty (the Multilateral Free Trade and Economic Integration Treaty) signed in 1958 "thanks to a real balancing act with regard to its wording," says Héctor Dada, CEPAL's scheme for Central America was dead in the water; even before that time, a struggle led by El Salvador's bourgeoisie and the U.S. government had broken out to transform Central American integration into a more free trade-like process. "Although some U.S. businesses felt favored by the integration industries regime that gave them monopoly status," says the same author, "this was counter to the worldwide U.S. economic policy that rejected any type of planning: the kind of integration they were looking for was a market protected from the exterior, with free competition domestically where U.S. companies could compete." Dada Hirezi, *La economía de El Salvador,* pp. 95 and 96.

29. See Saul Landau, *The Dangerous Doctrine: National Security and U.S. Foreign Policy* (Boulder: Westview Press, 1988), pp. 28ff.

30. This law provided "That no person, within the territory or jurisdiction of the United States, may incite, organize, equip or prepare the means for any military expedition or enterprise directed against any foreign prince or state, colony, district, or village with whom the United States is at peace; any person who does so will be declared guilty of high treason and will be fined no more than $3,000 and incarcerated for no more than three years." Quoted by Josefina Zoraida Vázquez and Lorenzo Meyer, *México frente a Estados Unidos, un ensayo histórico (1776-1980)* (Mexico: El Colegio de México, 1982), p. 58.

31. "Because it was North American, Walker's expedition was popular in California, which made it all the more dangerous; cunning Santa Ana came to consider using Boulbon to stop it. Walker had envisioned two possible scenarios for Mexico: a war to bring about an additional annexation of territory, or the establishment of an independent republic that would later join the Union. In 1853, he turned to Baja California and after harassing the small villages of the southern peninsula, declared a new republic; he was ultimately expelled, however. Like the Frenchman Boulbon, failure fueled his ambition,

and one year later, he returned to Mexican territory and declared the foundation of the Republic of Sonora, which suffered the same fate as the first republic. Walker managed to flee and repeat his attempt in Nicaragua, where he was successful for a time." Zoraida and Meyer, *México frente a Estados Unidos,* p. 59.

32. "It is ironic," says Josefina Zoraida Vázquez, "that just when the northern border problems had begun to be resolved, the southern border turned into a new element of discord between Mexico and the United States." Zoraida and Meyer, *México frente a Estados Unidos,* p. 95.

33. "Chiapas automatically proceeded to declare its independence before Guatemala did, with the clear intention of demonstrating its freedom not only from the Spanish Crown, but from Spanish territories as well—in this case, Guatemala—adhering to the provisions of the Iguala Plan by refusing to accept dependence on Spain or any other nation." Pedro Medina Rodríguez, "Breve análisis del proceso de anexión de Chiapas a México," unpublished paper, División de Estudios de Posgrado de la Facultad de Derecho, Universidad Nacional Autónoma de México (September 1989).

34. In May 1832, for example, Guatemala sent an army of 800 men to their common border to support a Comitan and Soconusco declaration advocating incorporation into the country. Nevertheless, this was of little import. See "El conflicto de límites," in *Guatemala: crisis social, política exterior y relaciones con México 1978–1986,* ed. Gilberto Castañeda Sandoval (Mexico: Programa de Estudios Centroamericanos, Centro de Investigación y Docencia Económicas, 1987), pp. 76–79.

35. The outcome of the vote held September 12, 1824, to decide whether or not to incorporate Chiapas into Mexico or Guatemala was as follows: 96,829 in favor of incorporation into Mexico versus 60,400 in favor of Guatemala. See Medina Rodríguez, "Breve análisis."

36. Zoraida and Meyer, *México frente a Estados Unidos,* pp. 95–96.

37. See Castañeda, *Guatemala,* p. 79. In addition, see: *La anexión de Centroamérica a México documentos escritos de 1823 to 1828,* ed. Rafael Heliodoro Valle (Mexico: Archivo Histórico Diplomático Mexicano, Secretaría de Relaciones Exteriores, 1949); Jorge Lujan Muñoz, *La independencia y la anexión de Centroamérica a México* (Guatemala: Serviprensa Centroamericana, 1982); Prudencio Moscoso Pastrana, *México y Chiapas: independencia y federación de la provincia chiapaneca* (Chiapas: Instituto Chiapaneca de Cultura, San Cristóbal las Casas, 1988).

38. "On January 9, 1902, the House of Representatives approved a measure—the Hepburn Bill—by a margin of 308 votes to 2, in favor of the Nicaraguan route; but Cromwell and his friends lobbied so actively and effectively in Washington that it was not long before a contrary opinion prevailed," comments Ramiro Guerra."Theodore Roosevelt himself, who occupied the presidency as a result of McKinley's assassination, abandoned his previous leanings toward Nicaragua. The Walker Commission followed his example. A new report favoring the Panama alternative changed his mind about the advantages of Nicaragua. The Senate substituted the Spooner Bill for the Hepburn Bill on June 19. One

week later, the House changed its mind and approved the Senate bill. Sanctioned by Roosevelt, it became law on the 28th of that same month. The President found himself duly authorized to purchase the concession and properties for the new company . . . for the sum of $40 million, to acquire a 6-mile wide zone stretching from Colón to Panamá at a reasonable price, and proceed to the opening of the canal." Guerra, *La expansión territorial,* pp. 398–399.

39. "Roosevelt accused Colombia of acting through base pecuniary motives . . . but the truth is that the treaty failed because the United States took up the cause of the companies and attempted to serve their interests . . ." Guerra, *La expansión territorial,* p. 407.

40. "The Panamanian separatists may or may not have been justified in their grievances against Colombia; but the actions of the U.S. government were unspeakable and derived not from any motive of a legal or moral nature, but from the assurances offered . . . with regard to the concession to which the United States aspired" Guerra, *La expansión territorial,* p. 412.

41. "The Republic of Panama ceded the Canal Zone to the United States and authorized the New Panama Canal Company and the railroad company to transfer their properties to the United States. Panama reaped the benefits that the failed Hay-Herrán Convention had promised to Colombia. They could not have worked faster. Colombia had just received the same treatment as Spain and Mexico," Guerra, *La expansión territorial,* p. 414. Some time later, not content with having contributed directly to the virtual takeover of Colombian territory, President Roosevelt, with the peculiar arrogance that has characterized U.S. leaders on other occasions, complained outrageously about that nation, saying, "To speak of Colombia as a responsible power with whom we can deal as we were obliged to with Holland or Belgium, Switzerland or Denmark, is simply absurd. A better analogy would be with a group of Sicilian or Calabrese bandits; with Villa and Carranza at the moment. I did all I could to convince them to proceed properly. Unable to do so, I decided what had to be done without taking them into consideration. . . . The people of Panama were united in their wish to have a canal and to expel the Government of Colombia. If they hadn't rebelled, I would have proposed to Congress that we take possession of the Isthmus by force . . ." William Roscoe Thayer, *The Life and Letters of John Hay,* vol. 2, pp. 327–328, cited by Guerra, *La expansión territorial,* pp. 416–417.

42. No less a figure than eventual minister of foreign relations Isidro Fabela left a written record of the extent of his admiration for General Sandino, "You are fulfilling a two-fold duty: national and supranational; national, because you are courageously defending the independence of your country; supranational, because you are gallantly representing the dignity of our race, injured by another that is trying to dominate the entire continent." Cited in *Sandino— el rebelde de América, Antología bibliográfica* (Managua: Ediciones Monimbó, 1979), p. 39.

43. Nevertheless, Carlos Fonseca Amador, founder of the Sandinista National Liberation Front—FSLN, points out: "In 1929, Sandino traveled to Mexico in search of solidarity, but encountered only the perfidy of Mexico's bourgeoisie,

with its anti-imperialist demagoguery. It was hard to incorporate people who called themselves revolutionaries—people who even called the patriotism of Nicaragua's armed resistance into question, on the basis of absurd conjectures that grew out of an aberrant dialectic. Consider that Mexico at this time was one of the main centers of the workers' revolutionary movement in Latin America." Augusto C. Sandino et al., *Nicaragua: la estrategia de la victoria* (Mexico: Editorial Nuestro Tiempo, 1980), pp. 66–67.

44. In this regard, recalling the U.S. presence in Nicaragua and citing the need for an immediate modification of "our passive and spiritual diplomacy," Mexico's envoy extraordinary and minister plenipotentiary in Nicaragua, Costa Rica, and Panama, Eduardo Ruiz, said in March 1923, "We must . . . recognize that we bear much of the guilt for what has happened, and in view of what is going on, we should think very seriously about modifying our diplomacy with respect to Spanish America or decide to take a radical step and leave the field open to the Yankees until our dear racial brothers feel the iron boot and then turn their anguished gaze toward us and then, yes then, make a concerted and energetic effort themselves to shake off the odious tutelage." Confidential message by Eduardo Ruiz to General Alvaro Obregón, President of Mexico, Managua, March 7, 1923, cited in "Referencias en torno a la política de México hacia Centroamérica, 1923–1937," *Boletín del Archivo General de la Nación* 11 (January–March 1980), p. 5.

45. In this respect, an article published at the time, entitled "Mexico Seeks to Prevail in Central America" described these actions as "a definite announcement of Mexico's intent in Central America," alleging that "Mexico's interest in Central America and the Ibero-American cause has its roots and motives in its difficulties with the United States" and affirming that "Since the fall of Díaz, Mexico has been fighting the economic and political domination of the United States." *Current History* (September 1926), p. 9. The article in question begins with the subtitle, "Mexico Seeks Dominance in Central America," and says in its opening lines, " 'Mexico should be stopped in Central America', said Mr. X, an engineering consultant for Ferrocarriles Internacionales de Centroamérica, a man who for many years has been in intimate contact with this part of the Americas. He was referring to recent efforts by the Mexican government to foster close cultural ties with Central America and thus wage anti-American propaganda to move the five republics out of the U.S. orbit and place them within its own sphere of influence." During 1927, Undersecretary of State Robert Olds also accused Mexico of following a policy that "for many years has been progressively anti-American," adding that "Mexico has consistently attacked us by confiscation of the rights of our nationals on her own soil and is now delivering this flank attack upon us through Central America." "The Nicaraguan Crisis," U.S. National Archives Record Group 59 (January 1927); reproduced in Robert S. Leiken, *The Central American Crisis Reader* (New York: Summit Books, 1987). Also interesting is the reference by Rodrigo Jauberth to the active policy at this time of President Elias Rojas who "attempted to bolster the political liberation in the region and encouraged the idea that Mexico can play . . . an active role . . ." and had to renounce this because

of the concerns voiced by the Costa Rican government to the U.S. government. See "Algunos antecedentes de la relación," in H. Rodrigo Jauberth Rojas, *Costa Rica–México 1978–1986: de la concertación a la confrontación* (Mexico: Programa de Estudios Centroamericanos, CIDE, 1987), pp. 96–98.

46. The successes of this U.S. policy can be seen in a historic letter sent by Sandino on January 25, 1930, to Pedro José Zepeda, representative general in Mexico of the Defending Army of Nicaragua's National Sovereignty. Sandino states roundly that "our army will not ally itself with the international policy that the president-elect of this Republic, Pascual Ortiz Rubio, intends to follow, according to his latest press releases, since this man has been seen flirting with the Yankee government, the common enemy of our Indo-Hispanic peoples; and this attitude of Ortiz Rubio is unworthy of one who governs a people as manly as the Mexican people." Reproduced in "La posición del gobierno méxicano frente a la intervención norteamericana en Nicaragua y la proposición sandinista de alianza latinoamericana, 1926–1930," *Boletín del Archivo General de la Nación,* p. 48.

47. Manlio Tirado adds in this respect that "once nearly all the militants of the revolutionary opposition and their organizations were physically annihilated, a new, dark phase in the history of El Salvador began. Hernández Martínez was elected and re-elected. To prevent new rebellions and keep the leftist opposition from regrouping, he created a police state with the support of the oligarchy and the U.S. government . . ." Manlio Tirado, *La crisis política en El Salvador* (Mexico: Ediciones Quinto Sol, S.A., 1980), p. 14.

48. "Hernández Martínez managed to stay in power for more than a decade," says Sara Gordon Rapoport. "In 1944 he was forced to resign, owing to a general movement in which young military officers, as well as students, workers, public officials, and some members of the agro-exporting bourgeoisie participated. However, the military as an institution did not retire from the government. After a short interregnum from 1944 to 1948, characterized by a recomposition of forces, a group of army officers trained in Mexico, whose objectives were economic growth and industrialization, took control and stamped a new direction on the state." Sara Gordon Rapoport, *El Salvador* (Mexico: Programa de Estudios Centroamericanos, CIDE, 1987), p. 21.

49. "After the fall of the dictator Hernández Martínez (in El Salvador) in 1944, which opened the door to a new attempt at populism, the dialectic of reformist decisions emerged, backed by broad sectors of the armed forces, as well as political practices that mitigated against the people in the exercise of government. The tight constraints met by reform in the agro-export system that dominated the national economy would permanently block the implementation of a progressive policy." Héctor Dada comments on the work of Edelberto Torres-Rivas entitled "Notas para comprender la crisis política centroamericano," in *Centroamérica: crisis y política internacional,* ed. Jaime Labastida (Mexico: Editorial Siglo XXI, 1984), 2nd edition, p. 73.

50. "In June 1944 Ubico fell. The miracle had happened. After him came the flood; the repressed desire for change exploded in a powerful popular wave, and on October 20, the people, together with a sector of the army,

brought an end to an era, installing the only democratic system that Guatemala has known in this century. Anyone who wishes to understand the present in this country will have to go back again and again to the revolutionary decade and its tragic denouement in 1954." Alfredo Guerra-Borges, "Guatemala: tres tiempos de una historia inconclusa," in Lucretia Lozano, Salazar Valiente Mario, et al., *Centroamérica: una historia sin retoque* (Mexico: El Día/Instituto de Investigaciones Económicas, UNAM, 1987), p. 139.

51. Ibid., p. 141.

52. "The democratic project that involved the October revolution pursued the development of a national capitalism; it was consequently hostile to imperialist interests, with which it was at odds—particularly since the agrarian reform affected the properties of the United Fruit Company, and the foreign policy of the revolutionary governments clashed with the interests of the United States in the Cold War era." Gabriel Aguilera Peralta, "Guatemala: estado, militarismo y lucha política," in *Centroamérica más allá de la crisis,* ed. Donald Castillo Rivas (Mexico: Sociedad Interamericana de Planificación, 1983), p. 63.

53. In fact, as we have mentioned on more than one occasion, in Guatemala and other Central American countries, the United Fruit Company for decades acted as a state within a state. See Gabriel Aguilera Peralta, "El proceso de militarización en el estado guatemalteco," in Héctor Dada, Luis Maira, et al., *Centroamérica: desafíos y perspectivas* (Mexico: Universidad Nacional Autónoma de México, 1984), pp. 134ff.

54. In January 1954, at the request of President Eisenhower, the National Security Council approved the Diablo Plan to overthrow the Arbenz government. This plan was devised by Allen Dulles, with the assistance of Frank Wisner (director and deputy director of the CIA, respectively). Also participating were the head of State Department intelligence Walter B. Smith, Ambassador to Guatemala John Peurifoy, and CIA agent Joseph N. Randon. See U.S. Congress, Senate, *Hearings Before the Subcommittee to Investigate the Administration of the Internal Security Act* (Washington, D.C.: 1961), p. 13866.

55. They were, among others: teacher Ernesto Capuano, who lived out two exiles in Mexico, one in the early 1930s after opposing the Ubico dictatorship, and the other, following the above-mentioned events; Col. Carlos Paz Tejada, who after leaving his country for El Salvador, entered Mexico in 1962, where he was to remain; union leader Victor Manuel Gutiérrez Garbín, who was released from prison thanks to the solidarity of influential union leader Vicente Lombardo Toledano, beginning his exile in Mexico in October 1954; poet Carlos Illescas, who also remained in Mexico from 1954 on; Professor Julio Gómez Padilla, who arrived in Mexico in April 1967, running for his life for the second time since 1954. See Carlos Cáceres, *Aproximación a Guatemala* (Culiacán: Colección Nuestro Continente, Universidad Autónoma de Sinaloa, 1980).

56. See Gregorio Selser, "Golpes, invasiones, asesinatos . . . Una tentativa de síntesis de las operaciones más importantes de la CIA," *Cuadernos del Tercer Mundo* III, 31, (July 1979), pp. 28–31.

57. In this respect, it is important to recall a querulous report issued by the Department of State in 1985, denouncing the fact that 90 percent of Mexico's votes in the General Assembly had run counter to those of the United States—to which the Mexican chancery responded, "Mexico has never voted against any resolution, nor has it absented itself from any vote; the United States has voted against resolutions 60 percent of the time, has abstained on 36 occasions, and has absented itself on three. . . ." This same document notes that Mexico supported 145 resolutions calling for a peaceful resolution of conflicts related to disarmament, a reordering of the world economy, the promotion of social, human, and cultural rights, and decolonization, while it abstained on just seven occasions. *UnomásUno* (México), 25 March 1986.

58. See, among others: Centro de Estudios Internacionales, *México y América Latina: la nueva política exterior* (Mexico: El Colegio de México, 1974); René Herrera Zúñiga, "México: la política exterior en transición: el papel de Centroamérica y las relaciones entre México y Estados Unidos," in *México–Estados Unidos 1982,* ed. Lorenzo Meyer (Mexico: El Colegio de México, 1982); Mario Ojeda, *Alcances y límites de la política exterior de México* (Mexico: El Colegio de México, 1976); Mario Ojeda, *México: el surgimiento de una política exterior activa* (Mexico: SEP Cultura, 1986); and *La política exterior de México: desafíos en los ochenta,* ed. Olga Pellicer, (Mexico: Centro de Investigación y Docencia Económicas, 1983).

59. A little before this, the January 7, 1981, edition of the *Wall Street Journal* commented on the Reagan–López Portillo meeting in Ciudad Juarez, "López Portillo greeted Reagan cordially and both promised to maintain a close personal relationship in the future. However, the Mexican president also has a cordial relationship with Fidel Castro and the Sandinistas in Nicaragua. His government has sought to back a leftist coalition as a substitute for a government sponsored by the United States in El Salvador, which is currently the object of Cuban-Soviet expansionism, manifested in a bloody and ominous leftist guerrilla war." Quoted in *Excélsior,* 8 January 1982.

60. See Olga Pellicer, "La vecindad en los momentos difíciles: México y Estados Unidos en 1982," in *La política exterior de México: desafíos en los ochenta* (Mexico: CIDE, 1983).

61. Not for nothing did journalist James Reston say in 1983, "it is no accident that the Department of State tells President Reagan that the main problem in Latin America isn't El Salvador but Mexico. What to do if the Mexicans can't resolve an economic disaster . . ." *The New York Times,* 18 March 1983, quoted in *Excélsior,* 19 March 1983.

62. *UnomásUno,* 4 January 1986. The more recent accusations of Elliot Abrams concerning the Contadora process and the actions of countries like Peru and Mexico made it clear that the U.S. government still retained its traditional differences with Mexican foreign policy, while persisting in its attempts to alter it, either through overt or covert diplomacy. Calling Peru and Mexico "vocal left-wing elements," Abrams noted that in his view, Mexican policy in Central America did "not respond either to the interests of the United States or Mexico." Jesús Hernández Garibay, "Derechistas y vociferantes," in *El Día,* 4 February 1987.

63. "The denationalizing modernization is already taking off with the new (Foreign Investment) Regulation, promulgated May 16, 1990. Thanks to this, foreign capital may have up to a 100 percent share in highly important activities ranging from agriculture and financial services to newspaper publishing and even Mexican education. In light of this . . . 'menu of options,' so appetizing for foreign capital, it is understandable that in just the first four months of the Regulation, $2 billion in new foreign investment projects have been approved, in addition to other projects that have entered without the need for specific approval." Luis González Souza, "El México 'moderno' botín de las trasnaciónales," in *Estrategia* 89 (September–October 1989), p. 16.

64. In this regard, see Jesús Hernández Garibay, "México–Estados Unidos: la estrategia norteamericana hacia los noventa," in *Estrategia* 89, pp. 50–59.

65. Lately, the Mexican government has claimed that some of its statements or international activities, including President Salinas's recent proposals for greater Latin American integration, represent a return to its best foreign policy traditions. Nonetheless, the overwhelming avalanche of the multinational strategy (which, at the moment, is what is actually sustaining the trend toward globalization and economic integration) and the virtual absence of political and social forces with the capacity to curb it as yet, do not alter but, in fact, reinforce the likelihood of greater subordination for Mexico.

66. Richard Fagen, *Forging Peace: The Challenge of Central America* (New York: Basil Blackwell, 1987).

CHAPTER 2

The Mexico–Central America–United States Triangle and the Negotiations Process

H. RODRIGO JAUBERTH

Peace is an essential condition for economic and social progress.
—Report of the Kissinger Commission, 1984

Some Theories and Clarifications

THE CONFLICT IN CENTRAL AMERICA and the social, economic, and political crisis that engendered it are structural and have deep historical roots.[1] The crisis is the result of a widening of the economic inequity and a reinforcing of the political exclusion that have weighed down Central American societies for decades. We turn here to a discussion of peace in Central America and its prospects: not simply the absence of war, but the opposite. This aspiration is explored in the context of two other goals of equal importance that must be attained if the crisis in the area is to be overcome: self-determination and development. We understand self-determination as the enhancement of democracy in the context of national independence, and development as the facilitation of a comprehensive accumulation process accompanied by economic growth. Such growth must include economic, political, and social transformations in a dynamic interrelationship, having the capacity to eradicate the political and economic exclusion of the peoples of Central America. Development, peace, and democracy are prerequisites for national viability.

In Central America it is somewhat unrealistic to talk about "a firm and lasting peace," called for in the Esquipulas II presidential accords since 1987, without including the alternatives and strategies for development and democracy under a broad, pluralistic approach that gets to the heart of the structural causes of this regional crisis with its manifold expressions.[2]

Hence, throughout the negotiations process leading up to the agreements at the seven presidential summits since Esquipulas I, there has been an ongoing effort to resolve pressing problems like the armed domestic and regional conflicts. However, an in-depth analysis of the situation and the challenges to development has consistently been absent in these accords, although euphemistic or rhetorical variations of it have appeared in every communiqué and initiative that have come out of the summits. The urgency of the legitimate desire to bring the war in Central America to an end is understandable, for in the short term, without peace there is no possibility for development; however, in the medium and long term, without development, there is no possibility for peace—hence, the need to deal simultaneously with the issues of peace, self-determination, and development. In Central America we indeed find ourselves confronted with a situation comparable to that of the period from 1780 to 1830, whose culmination was the independence of Mexico and Central America from Spain and their emergence as new nations.[3]

In this framework, it is important to reflect that the peoples of Central America have begun the final decade of the twentieth century with some fundamental questions about the future. One is how the regional negotiations process will evolve, since with the fall of the FSLN in Nicaragua there has been a greater political homogenization in the region along conservative lines, within the larger context of an easing of international tensions, an end to the cold war (which the United States has won), and the formation of global trade blocs.

Will the 1980s model and framework for negotiations serve to "pacify" El Salvador and Guatemala in the 1990s? Will Central America's ruling sectors be inclined toward greater democratic political openness and cooperation through the electoral process or other mechanisms under international supervision? Will the relative pacification of the area already achieved permit national and regional cooperation, growth, and development in the 1990s? Is the past decade's cycle of war in Central America over or not? Will the eventual demilitarization of the area—that is, the relative dismantling of the armies and engines of war—together with international cooperation contribute to an alternative use of resources to finance development? Will the U.S. presence in the region be reinforced through economic, political, and military measures, and if so, how? What will the role of Mexico and Latin America be in these scenarios?

A historical postulate, one of the basic theses of this chapter, concerns the fact that the Central American conflict did not begin to spread throughout the region until the advent of the Reagan administration in the United States in 1981. Rather, it involved national issues, such as the presence of a revolutionary state in Nicaragua and armed popular wars in El Salvador and Guatemala. Even with their domestic crises, Costa Rica and Honduras were strangers to this dynamic; their social development would have followed another trajectory, at least in the medium term.

It was the Reagan administration's policy of intervention and its backing for Central America's traditional power sectors that lent a regional dimension to what had been local difficulties, compromising the national sovereignty and autonomous interests of all the countries of the region. Efforts to resolve it drew in its neighbors and Latin America as well. Until the victory of Violeta Chamorro in February 1990, the United States harassed Nicaragua by every means available. The Salvadoran government found its room to maneuver highly constrained by the power of the military and, moreover, subject to directives from the United States—all this in the midst of a division of power within its own territory. Honduras was virtually taken over. Guatemala's government suffered two coups in a country where institutional democracy was still but a glimmer; Costa Rica was so pressed by the United States that it nearly went to war with Nicaragua during the administration of Luis A. Monge (1982–1986), while the administration of Oscar Arias (1986–1990) was subjected to multiple pressures to bring it into line.[4]

As can be seen throughout this chapter, four of the five countries—Nicaragua excluded—were implicated to a greater or lesser degree in military and logistical acts of aggression on behalf of the counterrevolution and/or were used as bases for propaganda and ideological aggression against the Sandinistas. Even today, with the easing of tensions that the victory of Violeta Chamorro implies (from the U.S. standpoint), there are still pockets of violence in Nicaragua, as well as structural problems throughout the entire region. Nicaragua's transition with this new government, and even the transition of the area as a whole, does not augur any permanent solution for the time being.

The state of conflict created in Central America during the 1980s has been so continuous that its economic, social, and political consequences have seriously compromised the future of the countries of the region. It has also focused much of Latin America's attention on this situation, in order to reduce the likelihood of a regional war. In this framework the encounters—or absence thereof—between Mexico,

Central America, and the United States in what we conceive of as a triangular relationship are significant.

In fact, the Mexico–Central America–United States triangle has its own peculiarities, in terms of both bilateral relations and the triangularity of the entire relationship. U.S. dominance and that country's enormous influence on the Central American economies have served to dampen Mexico's natural direct interaction with Central America.

The methodology of the triangular analysis, as reflected in Chapter I, is historical in nature. In this section, we explore the reasons Mexico has unquestionably been the most important international player promoting dialogue in the search for consensus and a negotiated end to the crisis in Central America—in contrast to the United States, which has been one of the most belligerent parties to the conflict. The divergence between the foreign policies of the two countries has ample historical precedent.[5]

Since 1981, the Central American conflict has been characterized by U.S. belligerence and intervention. This stems from the fact that from its birth—from the very conception of its national goals both within its natural sphere of influence and worldwide—the United States developed a rationale and foreign policy logic that required a continuous concentration of its power and an expansion of its control to survive as a system. Thus, power was vital, hegemonic interests had global reaches, and the ideals of democracy, conceived with only the United States as a model, merged historically in a confusion of interests and expansionism.

The United States is the largest angle within the triangular system—the country with the most extensive area of influence and control and, thus, the one with the greatest power with respect to Mexico and Central America. Throughout its history, the United States has had overwhelming economic and political clout in Central America and, to a lesser but increasing degree, in Mexico and the rest of Latin America.

Because of its foreign policy tradition and its interests in Central America, Mexico, as the other angle in the triangle, has not remained aloof from the transformations that have taken place on its southern border. However, it has been checked by the dominant U.S. presence and its own domestic difficulties. In fact, the intimate geographical proximity of Mexico and Central America involves Mexican territory directly in terms of social problems (like migration and refugees) and the armed conflict in the area, which fuels U.S. pressure to ensure that events in this strategic area favor Washington's interests. This compromises Mexican autonomy and seriously jeopardizes sovereign arrangements between Mexico and the United States.

Mexico is interested in establishing a new regional order grounded in independent states with whom it can strengthen political and cultural ties—not in entities subordinated to the United States, since this would create a powerful geopolitical fence to the north and south that would damage its prospects for maintaining genuine political autonomy. Because of this, it can be said that "interests crucial to Mexico are at stake in Central America."[6] Similarly, Latin America has made its presence felt in the region through Contadora, the Río Group, and other means.

Another thesis of this chapter is that, despite the complexity of their differences, Mexico and the United States, both as governments and societies, have met and parted and collided in their foreign policy throughout history in this space beyond their borders and their bilateral relationship. They have shared areas of influence and interests in Central America and have developed different policies toward the region that have often resulted in unwanted conflict. The triangular dynamic can be seen almost throughout the regional peace negotiations, dissipating after Esquipulas III, when Mexico distanced itself from the process.

The regional negotiations process has been analyzed within the context of this Mexico–Central America–United States triangle. We have omitted a discussion of the domestic situations of the three protagonists in this extended period, since they are beyond the scope of our objective, which is to study the negotiations process directly. Through successive approximations from the general to the specific this chapter attempts to explore the implications for Central America of the presence or absence of Mexico and the United States in the negotiations process for peace and development. This process and the peace alternatives for the region are analyzed from the advent of Contadora in 1983, with emphasis on the situation that emerged in 1987 with Esquipulas II— a key event for both Mexican and U.S. policy toward the region. At some junctures we will provide full descriptions of events that speak for themselves to confirm our theses, as we are well aware of the misinformation about some of them that exists in the mind of the North American public. Throughout the analysis we will see how Mexico and the United States relate to Central America and take on relevance in the process to the degree that they in fact become involved and participate.

It has been alleged in a number of forums—and here there is ample debate—that Presidents Salinas of Mexico and Bush of the United States are seeking to bilateralize their relations with the troubled region. Their point of departure is the concept that without eliminating the underlying problems between the perceptions of Mexico and the United States, it is still possible to cooperate on Central America. Is this really possible? The theory of conflict resolution says that "negotiation can resolve differences in two ways: either by moving the conflict from a situation of incompatibility to one of compatibility—that is, creating a structure in which, without resolving the basic differences, a dynamic of cooperation is created despite them; or by resolving or dissolving these differences."[7]

Thus, in the 1989 report of the Commission on the Future of Mexican-U.S. Relations and in the present debate, it has been noted that the bilateral relationship "has moved from historic conflict to diplomatic collaboration, and hence, to the problems of today." The document cites the development of "the special relationship" during the postwar period, the strengthening of diplomatic ties in the 1960s, and the modern characteristics of the problems between the two nations.[8]

The crisis and conflict in Central America have been met on the one hand by initiatives to resolve the conflict through dialogue and negotiation and on the other hand by efforts to impose political and military solutions. The first policy approach derives from the experiences of the Contadora mediation model, established in 1983 by Mexico, Panama, Colombia, and Venezuela, and its Support Group, founded in 1985, consisting of Peru, Brazil, Uruguay, and Argentina; these efforts have been taken up and continued by the Esquipulas II initiative which has served as a broader framework for negotiation. The second set of policies still under way in Central America relies heavily on military force to achieve foreign policy objectives. This was the strategy of the Reagan administration (1981–1989) and continues to be so for Reagan's successor, George Bush, through the so-called "two-track" policy and the more elaborate doctrine of "low-intensity conflict" (or high-intensity intervention, according to Central Americans). Low-intensity conflict in the context of the cold war and the East-West confrontation is a repeat of the concept of U.S. intervention in the form of covert operations, support for counterrevolution, threats, bribes, and political and economic pressure, combined for greater effect. Since 1989, the Bush administration has maintained its predecessor's priorities and objectives in Central America, using the same ideology to justify them, though its methods and style differ.

The U.S. presence in Central America, a product of its vision and its security interests (see Table 2.1), can be seen throughout the entire negotiations process, be it Contadora or Esquipulas, through regional travels by U.S. officials, telephone calls to the Central American presidents to pressure them during summits, the presentation of "alternative acts and plans" aimed at distracting attention from the regional emphasis on rapprochement and, of course, the military option. This took the form of the contra presence in Costa Rica during the administration of Luis A. Monge and for most of the 1980s in Honduras, which was

TABLE 2.1 Negotiation Models and Strategies of Contadora and the United States

	Contadora	United States	Differences
Diagnosis of the crisis	Economic backwardness and the struggles of societies to change structures of power and domination.	Foreign interference and conspiracy; Central America is a "test case."	As reflected in their approaches, the Contadora approach considered the struggle by opposition forces to be legitimate and worthy of inclusion in negotiations and a solution, whereas the Reagan-Bush approach considered them representatives of a foreign communist conspiracy that must be defeated.
Point of view	Central America's problems are internal and should not be treated as part of the East-West conflict. The principles of nonintervention and self-determination are fundamental.	The regional problem is an international matter, part of the East-West confrontation. Nicaragua is the first domino to fall in a program of Soviet expansionism; regional tensions are the result of internal conflict in Nicaragua and Nicaragua's threat to its neighbors, not Nicaragua's difficulties with the United States.	The United States ignored the violence and repression of military forces in Central America and saw a security threat as overriding any principle of nonintervention; by its intervention it almost regionalized the war.
Priority objectives	• Avoid the spread of armed conflict in Central America. • Build a climate of trust among the players.	• Restore hegemony. • Reverse and/or destroy the Sandinista revolution and other revolutionary movements in the area. • Displace Contadora in favor of more tractable forums for mediation. • Implement a neoliberal model in Central America through structural adjustment programs.	The United States created conditions for confrontation in Central America while Mexico sought dialogue and negotiation. Washington regarded Contadora as an obstacle.
Strategies	Political efforts to seek dialogue and negotiated political solutions involving all parties; an emphasis on self-determination, pluralism, demilitarization, and regional and international consensus.	A two-track policy with rhetorical support for Contadora and diplomatic activity; simultaneously arming pro-U.S. military governments and creating and arming the contras, installed in Costa Rica and Honduras.	The contra strategy became the principal source of regional tension, almost leading to war between Nicaragua and Costa Rica and Honduras. Contadora sought a regional accord, whereas Washington used the Tegucigalpa Bloc (El Salvador, Honduras, and Costa Rica) between 1981 and 1986 against Nicaragua and Contadora.

(continues)

Table 2.1 (continued)

	Contadora	United States	Differences
Actions, commitments, proposals	• The Mexican government insisted that the crisis in Central America not only derived from the countries in the area but also from U.S. hostility toward Nicaragua. • The solution to the regional conflict depends on each of the countries and the normalization of U.S.-Nicaraguan relations. • Contadora objectives document twenty points, among them principles of international law concerning human rights, national reconciliation, improvement of democratic systems, arms control, banning foreign military bases and advisers, and verification mechanisms. • The Contadora Peace Act, supported by the United Nations.	The Reagan administration insisted on these points: • Nicaragua's compliance with a commitment to democracy made to the OAS in June 1979. • An end to Nicaraguan aggression against its neighbors. • Withdrawal of foreign military advisers. • Restoration of Nicaragua's military parity with its neighbors. • Reagan insisted that support for the contras helped fulfill Contadora's objectives. • Contadora agreements and communiqués considered biased in favor of Nicaragua. • After Manzanilla, Reagan never again agreed to dialogue with the Sandinistas.	
Overall differences			The Peace Act of Contadora was viewed by the Reagan administration as inimical to U.S. interests, despite the fact that most of the points in the act offered significant guarantees for U.S. security. However, Washington first wanted to get rid of the Soviets, Cubans, and Sandinistas and then deal with other political issues.

Compiled by the author

used as a permanent base for assaults against Nicaragua; in addition, there was the entire military logistical apparatus in El Salvador and Guatemala that was used to support the counterrevolutionaries. We will also show how, throughout Contadora and seven of the presidential summits, the Reagan-Bush position permeated all regional events and U.S. agreements as well as differences with Mexico.[9]

Mexico, for its part, interacted with Central America both bilaterally (1978–1982) and multilaterally (1983–1986) under a broad plan for coexistence. Mexico oscillated between active pursuit of a principled policy (based on its traditional values of nonintervention, the self-determination of peoples, the peaceful resolution of controversies, the juridical equality of states, and cooperation for development) and yielding to external and internal pressures, related both to its interests in Central America and to its international context—all within the framework of Mexico's specific needs and its commitments in the area. This back-and-forth foreign policy derives from Mexico's national historical reading of certain situations and its own interests.

Thus we can see that Mexico's activism and conduct during the process that brought the Sandinista Front to power was later reinforced by Latin America, through a diplomatic juggling act via the Contadora initiative. Once Mexico had played its hand (and because of a certain "burnout" induced by its relations with the United States and some of the Central American countries, not to mention its domestic economic crisis) the country was left without any cards in the area. Bowing to national self-interest, Mexico turned inward after Esquipulas III and withdrew to some extent. The vacuum following Contadora and Mexico's active role was filled by the Esquipulas initiative and, within it, the participation of Oscar Arias, Vinicio Cerezo, and Daniel Ortega, in the main.

Throughout the mediation process—from Contadora to Esquipulas III—Mexico took action, made commitments, and assumed positions based on dialogue and political negotiation (see Table 2.1). Because of its principles and national interests, Mexico's activities in Central America almost always ran counter to the designs and strategies of the United States. In this regard, Luis Herrera Lazo states,

> The United States found every means possible to harass Nicaragua, and Mexico always upheld the principles of nonintervention and self-determination. The United States backed the government of El Salvador to put down domestic opposition militarily, and Mexico promoted the route of negotiation and dialogue between the parties. In response to the virtual military occupation of Honduras as a constant provocation to Nicaragua, Mexico sought to ease tensions between the countries. In

response to the economic and diplomatic pressures on democratic Costa
Rica to join in the harassment of Nicaragua, Mexico supported efforts to
avert conflicts and smooth over the differences between countries.[10]

More recently, the disagreement and confrontation between Mexico
and the United States over Central America have eased, because of
changes in the bilateral relationship and its international context. (In
this regard, see Chapter 4, by Gilberto Castañeda.)

This chapter, in brief, is a broad effort to interpret the march of this
"process of negotiation and war," an analysis of the diplomatic and
political realities of the region that takes into account the peculiarities
that the Mexican and U.S. presence stamps on the area and how this
presence has influenced the course of events. Indeed, readers of this
section will find the influence of this triangular perspective in the
discussion of the peace negotiation theories presented. This is an
academic and political appraisal of the entire negotiations process and
Latin American—and within them, Mexican—efforts toward pacification,
an easing of tensions, and a firm and lasting peace in Central America.

Mexico in Contadora and the United States in
the Tegucigalpa Bloc: Two Contradictory
Strategies in an Embattled Region

Some Background

In a merging of mutual interests and principles, Mexico (now an
intermediate power as a result of the oil boom that boosted its importance
for the United States), together with Venezuela, Panama, and Costa
Rica, played a strategic role in bringing about the Sandinista victory
in 1979. The consolidation of power by this revolutionary government
in Central America produced a major geopolitical change in the region.
Despite last-minute maneuvering to keep the Sandinistas from winning,
the Carter administration was prepared to let Somoza fall.[11]

Mexican President José López Portillo's active role in ensuring the
Sandinista victory reflected Mexico's view at that time that stability in
Central America was impossible without conditions conducive to sociopolitical change. For Mexico, this meant going beyond the Estrada
Doctrine of not interfering in other countries' internal affairs and
encouraging pluralistic change in the region. In aiding the consolidation
of the Sandinista revolution, Mexico's aim was to provide a third option
to hegemonies of East and West, as well as to avert radicalization and
foster pluralism in the region. This policy was pursued on the economic
front in August 1980 with the signing of the San José Pact, a "no-

strings" agreement to supply oil under preferential conditions, not just to Nicaragua but to all five countries of the area.

In 1980 and 1981, the intensification of the conflicts in El Salvador and Guatemala, the inauguration of Ronald Reagan as president of the United States (with his global East-West approach and his plan to transform the Central American question into a "test case"), the distancing of Costa Rica and Venezuela from Mexico's positions, and the deepening of the economic crisis all complicated Mexico's active policy in the area. On taking office, President Reagan began increasing the military component of U.S. policy toward Central America.[12]

In this context, under the administration of José López Portillo, Mexico switched from pro-change activism toward advocating stability through easing tensions. As part of this transition Mexico promoted a series of bilateral initiatives in the region, among them facilitating contacts between the Sandinista government and the United States in Manzanillo, and the French-Mexican declaration of August 1981, which asked the United Nations to recognize the Farabundo Martí Front for National Liberation (FMLN) as a major political force in El Salvador and include it in peace negotiations. As Mario Ojeda says,

> The French-Mexican declaration attempted to introduce an intermediate solution between the guerilla proposals and those of the civilian-military Junta, which meant the United States. In other words, it was trying to achieve the elections for a Salvadoran Constituent Assembly, called for March 1982, but with the participation of a broad alliance of sectors with ties to the guerilla groups.[13]

This declaration not only failed to win Latin American support—only Cuba and Nicaragua backed it—it accomplished just the opposite; Mexico paid dearly. On September 2, 1981, eight governments with distinctly different political regimes (Colombia, Chile, Argentina, Guatemala, Honduras, the Dominican Republic, Paraguay, and Venezuela) drew up a joint communiqué condemning the declaration. Given the nature and the polarizing effect of the conflicts in Central America, the difficulties and contradictions between U.S. and Mexican foreign policy in the area began to multiply. Nonetheless, the French-Mexican initiative received the support of the Non-Aligned Nations, the European Socialist International, and the majority of the Third World countries in the United Nations.

Costa Rica did not participate in the communiqué condemning the French-Mexican declaration, but it did promote the political riposte to it, the Central American Democratic Community (CDC) formed in January 1982. Strongly backed by the United States, it sought to legitimize the Salvadoran junta. Guatemala and Nicaragua were excluded from this effort on the grounds that the CDC would be composed only of legitimate governments elected by popular vote.

By September 1982, attacks on Nicaragua from U.S.-controlled contras based in Honduras and Costa Rica were sharpening the Central American crisis. Seeking to avert a direct confrontation with the Reagan administration, Mexico began to urge broader negotiations. Thus, Presidents José López Portillo of Mexico and Luis H. Campins of Venezuela sent a joint letter to Presidents Ronald Reagan, Daniel Ortega, and Roberto Suazo Córdova, exhorting them to find ways of arriving at a negotiated settlement between Honduras and Nicaragua and putting an end to border hostilities, as well as avoiding actions that would aggravate the situation. Mexico's cooperation with Venezuela in efforts to find new approaches, open up negotiating space, and defuse the conflict, which was on the verge of spreading regionwide, provoked a reaction from the United States. One month later (in October 1982), in an attempt to seize the initiative (especially from Mexico), the United States used the good offices of Costa Rica to convoke the Forum for Peace and Democracy. This forum, heir to the moribund CDC, was designed to forge a broad alliance between democratic governments and forces, according to its promoters.

Participating in the Forum for Peace and Democracy, also known as the Enders Forum, were El Salvador, Honduras, and Costa Rica, plus representatives from the governments of Belize, Panama, Jamaica, Colombia, and the Dominican Republic. The United States was represented by the assistant secretary of state for inter-American affairs, Thomas Enders. On the same day, newly elected president of Costa Rica, Luis A. Monge, in his inaugural address, exhorted U.S. allies in the region "not to trail behind the communist forces, for democracy must not be passive, on the defensive, but just the opposite." Thus, from the very outset, the Costa Rican president blamed the crisis on an alien conspiracy (read Nicaragua), situating it within the context of East-West confrontation.

The CDC and later the Enders Forum were clear indications that to implement its strategy, the United States was reconstructing a system of alliances in Central America among forces and governments that shared its objectives and approaches, heading off Mexican and other Latin American initiatives. Costa Rica, through Foreign Minister Fernando Volio, played a major role in protecting U.S. interests and curbing Mexican activity in the area. In fact, from 1982 to 1986, Costa Rica underwent a transformation from Mexico's ally in international forums to an open opponent of its policies.

For analytical purposes, we would like to pause for a moment. According to Volio, by refusing to attend the Enders Forum, Mexico was already manifesting hostility toward Costa Rica—hostility that would later be evident in the formation of the Contadora Group without Costa Rica. Volio charged,

> Not content with blocking Costa Rica, Mexico excluded it from the Contadora Group and the peace negotiations, simply because our country shared concerns and responsibilities with the United States. Likewise, because of its traditional flirtation with Marxist-Leninist totalitarians beyond its borders—yes sir!—and to score points in the sophisticated world of international politics and safeguard itself against communist expansionism, Mexico had an interest in consolidating and legitimizing the Nicaraguan regime of the Comandantes. This showed an irritating lack of consideration for Costa Rica, whose democracy, as the Mexican hierarchy well knew, would be in real jeopardy as long as the Sandinista system prevailed. That was when Mexico made a choice between Nicaragua and Costa Rica; between the survival of totalitarianism and democracy.[14]

Volio's position was essentially the position of the United States and the forum and reflected U.S. interests and concerns. Hence, in the forum, the crisis was framed and explained within the context of Cuban-Soviet expansionism via Nicaragua. Moreover, the foreign minister's understanding of democracy was limited to the Costa Rican–U.S. model, taking no note of the different pluralistic approach to democracy that was evolving in Nicaragua, but rather labelling it "totalitarian and expansionist." When Mexico proposed to move the Central American conflict out of the East-West focus it was, according to Volio, doing the Moscow-Havana-Managua axis a big favor.

Volio relates that when Contadora appeared on the scene in 1983, it fell to him to recommend the policy that Costa Rica should follow for its own ends and those of its allies:

> My Central American colleagues expressed their surprise, uncertainty, and discomfort at what they, too, considered an inopportune interference in the plans of the parties involved. To accept Contadora implied, certainly, that Costa Rica would lose its leadership role in the search for peace. I recommended giving the new Group a chance, warning them of the risks that we were running and alerting them, so that they could react in a timely manner if what they feared ever came to pass. . . . Some in our government and their intimate circles gladly embraced Contadora from the outset and recommended that Costa Rica join, abandoning its Forum allies (Honduras, El Salvador, and the United States) and thus distancing itself from them—including the United States, of course—in

an attitude very pleasing to the Socialist International, Mexico, and the Non-Aligned Nations.[15]

At a meeting in San José in late February 1983, the foreign ministers of Costa Rica, Honduras, and El Salvador made a last-ditch effort to revive the Enders Forum. However, their proposals met with no support among the Latin American countries, who were more in agreement with the Contadora Group and its proposals for a negotiated settlement; thus, the initiative found itself checkmated. Despite the economic crisis and the concern voiced in some conservative Mexican circles about the price of activism in Central America, Mexico, under the administration of Miguel de la Madrid, seized the initiative and formed the Contadora Group (Colombia, Mexico, Panama, and Venezuela), which would allow it to maintain an active, albeit multilateral, presence in the area.

After the birth of Contadora in 1983 and the incorporation of its Support Group (Argentina, Brazil, Peru, and Uruguay) in 1985, the initiative turned into a Latin American mediation effort that carried out joint activities with some Central American governments. Through it, Mexico pushed strategies for negotiation, dialogue, and peace, grounded in the principles of international law, the self-determination of peoples, and the defense of national sovereignty. Contadora was the negotiating tool that opened the door to alternative proposals in a permanent quest for peace; throughout its tenure it was instrumental in impeding the spread of the war in the area and preventing the direct invasion of Nicaragua by the United States.

To facilitate an understanding of the Contadora negotiating process and within it, Mexico's role as the group's leader, we have described (see Table 2.1) some of the features of the negotiation model, the war model, and the differences between the two; both models are broken down by analytical categories.[16] As usual in this type of theoretical construction, the table is a necessary reduction: The reality of the conflict and its political dynamic overflow in all directions. The intent of the model is merely to highlight differences between the negotiating approach and the Reagan approach.

As Jorge Castañeda and Robert Pastor write, the Contadora initiative

would eventually lead to a substantive change in Mexico's Central American policy from 1979 to 1982; however, during its initial years, it caused the country's influence in the region to expand, in harmony with its traditional sympathies and principles and its newly acquired responsibilities and ambitions. Contadora embodied one of the most important virtues of Mexico's new policy: the introduction of the problems of third countries into the bilateral relationship with the United States, making Mexico a valuable—though not always welcome—intermediary for Washington with regard to problems no longer strictly limited to bilateral relations.[17]

Through Contadora, Mexico sought to improve its relations with all the countries of the area. However, its close cooperation with the Sandinista government made its role as a neutral mediator suspect among the other governments. Despite the breadth and variety of Mexican diplomatic efforts—including cutbacks in Mexican aid to Nicaragua—this perception barely altered, for the region was already highly polarized around the conflict between Nicaragua and the United States. The so-called Tegucigalpa Bloc (Costa Rica, El Salvador, Honduras) had already openly taken sides with the Reagan administration.

From its inception, the broad Latin American alliance that found its expression in Contadora continuously ran up against the Reagan administration's strategy of domination, using military force. Mexico sought to pursue its policy in a multilateral Latin American context in order to avoid undesirable direct confrontations with the United States. Nonetheless, U.S. bilateral pressures were inevitable.

The strategic objective of U.S. interventionism in Central America—continued by George Bush after 1989—was and is to restore U.S. hegemony in the area. To achieve this, the United States managed to neutralize, wear down, or destroy any political, social, or military forces that opposed it. Employing a range of tactics, as exemplified in the "two-track" political/military policy and its subsequent amplification into "low-intensity conflict," the main U.S. priorities became the overthrow of the Sandinista government and the defeat of popular rebel forces in El Salvador. The doctrine of low-intensity conflict stems from U.S. analysis of its defeat in Vietnam and calls for limited direct use of U.S. forces and resources (a cheap war, in the words of the experts), in a coordinated military, economic, political, and psychological campaign. For the peoples that must endure it, though, the costs are terribly high.[18]

This almost permanent confrontation between strategies that has persisted up to this day (the one, to forge peace and encourage pluralistic coexistence; the other, to roll back revolutionary processes through war) are an academic/political reading of what has been characterized as the bloodiest war of all. The loss of human life and the economic costs in Nicaragua and El Salvador during the course of their armed conflicts have been proportionately greater than those suffered by the United States in World War II, the Korean War, or even the Vietnam War.[19]

The Reagan administration's diplomatic efforts in the region were pursued from 1982 to 1986 through the Tegucigalpa Bloc of Costa Rica,

Honduras, and El Salvador, an alliance against Nicaragua, and thus, against the nonexclusionary negotiations model favored by Contadora. During the Contadora process the Tegucigalpa Bloc became the main obstacle to the signing of the Peace Act and agreements to adopt political, diplomatic, and juridical measures over the years.

Beyond Washington's efforts to defeat identified enemies, the governments of the Tegucigalpa Bloc were also instrumental in U.S. efforts to reshape the economic structure and the political and juridical superstructure of Central America's societies. Hence, any foreign player who interfered in the implementation of this policy would be forced to pay a price.

As we have stated, Contadora was the foreign policy showpiece of Miguel de la Madrid's administration. His team was responsible for an unusual series of actions and initiatives designed to broaden the range of peace options. Without question, Mexico helped open up new vistas and alternatives concerning key negotiating areas and verification mechanisms to ensure compliance with the accords.

The critical juncture came in the fall of 1984. As Jorge Castañeda notes,

> the Contadora process drew to an end in September–October 1984, when the draft of a treaty on peace and cooperation in Central America was finally completed. It was initially accepted by the Tegucigalpa group and by Guatemala. Nicaragua temporized somewhat, because the proposed legal instrument included a series of domestic policy recommendations that, in the Sandinistas' view, violated the principle of non-intervention. However, Mexico finally convinced them—or they convinced themselves— and Managua announced its willingness to sign the agreement.
>
> The member countries of the Contadora Group began to circulate the document in the U.N. General Assembly. When U.S. officials realized that their allies in Central America had accepted an arrangement that left the Sandinistas in power and at the same time cut funding to the contras and withdrew U.S. advisors from the region, it began to work to nullify the accord. Their fury turned to apoplexy when they realized that things had gotten so out of hand because they had not paid any attention to Contadora. The draft treaty also included the withdrawal of Cuban military advisors from Nicaragua and the establishment of arms limitations in the region, but this was not enough for the Reagan administration. . . .
>
> Even when U.S. objections seemed reasonable or at least worthy of consideration, they were not the real reason behind U.S. opposition. At this point, it was evident that Ronald Reagan would never accept an agreement that left the Sandinistas in power. This was the real flaw, according to Washington: not the technical details, or a lack of preciseness.
> . . .

Later on, a number of similar opportunities presented themselves, but Mexico and its allies were never again so close to ratifying a treaty or ending their mediation effort with dignity: the group's inability to wring consent from Washington to a just and/or realistic agreement had been exposed, and this substantially reduced its influence with the Sandinistas. . . .[20]

In the transition from the Contadora–Esquipulas I negotiations model of May 1986 to the Esquipulas II model in August 1987, it is essential to point out the changes in some of the regional trends that had been under way since late 1986, since these contributed to a significant modification in negotiating strategies and movement toward the presidential summits of Esquipulas II. The most important among them are:

1. The erosion of the Reagan administration's Central America policy: This, among other things, was the product of the Iran-contra scandal, the reemergence of a Democratic majority in the Senate and the strengthening of that party (which altered the balance of domestic forces in the United States). All this rendered approval of military aid to the contras more difficult, as did the crisis within the contra camp (the resignation of the contras' top leadership, corruption, problems on the southern front, the impact of the public revelation of the contra-drug connection).

2. The stagnation of the Contadora initiative: The foreign ministers of Contadora and the Support Group themselves admitted to a certain impotence, due to a lack of willingness on the part of the Central American governments to search for peace, as well as U.S. pressure to distance themselves from Central America.

3. The Sandinista government's military, political, and diplomatic offensive: The clearest manifestations of this were the military defeats inflicted on the contras, on the one hand, and the complaint brought against Costa Rica and Honduras in the International Court in the Hague following its June 1986 ruling in Nicaragua's favor in an earlier suit against U.S. aggression.

4. The discrediting of the Luis A. Monge government in the wake of the Tower Report: The Tower Commission's report on the Iran-contra scandal exposed the involvement of Monge and officials of his administration in lending logistical support to the contras; later, U.S. pressure on newly elected president Oscar Arias to collaborate with its anti-Nicaragua campaign would be brought to light.

The Tegucigalpa Bloc was still together in May 1986 while Esquipulas I was under way. During the initial years of the Arias government, Costa Rica, later the promoter of the 1987 peace plan, persisted in its pro-U.S, anti-Sandinista policy, which included the same aspects of confrontation with Mexico that had characterized the previous administration's policy. "Nicaragua's regime is illegitimate," declared Oscar Arias, "The principal cause of the crisis in Central America, its overthrow would not be viewed amiss; Sandino would be the first to become a contra."[21]

This sudden change in attitude represented by Esquipulas II in so short a time altered the negotiating climate. At the same time Mexico's economic crisis deepened, contributing to the erosion of its role in Central America. Both its economic weaknesses and policy decisions taken as a result had consequences for Mexican policy. As Guadalupe González notes, Mexico's economic crisis caused it to make economic relations a priority. The governmental institutions responsible for financial relations valued close ties with Washington and tended to act outside the purview of institutions responsible for foreign relations. Secondly, efforts to open the Mexican economy, like rapid trade liberalization, greater openness to foreign investment, and the encouragement of the maquiladora industry, are believed to be part of a process of gradual integration with the U.S. economy, which will have serious consequences for national sovereignty, the independence of Mexico's goals, and the country's foreign policy principles. Indeed, these factors and processes will increasingly determine national goals.[22]

In sum, its economic crisis and the inward turning of its national goals notwithstanding, Mexico would be constantly confronted by the problem of maintaining a foreign policy toward Latin America—and Central America in particular—in line with its principles, traditions, history, and national security interests. At the same time, it would seek to avoid, or at least minimize, unnecessary conflicts and frictions with the United States, searching for commonalities that would allow it to put the accent on skillful and complementary management of negotiations on bilateral matters.

The Transition from Contadora to Esquipulas I

As we noted, from 1981 to 1986, Mexico clashed with the United States most of the time over its foreign policy toward Central America, both bilaterally and through the Contadora negotiating model (see Table 2.1). Bit by bit, due to changes in attitude, the presence of new players like Oscar Arias and Vinicio Cerezo, and the Contadora experience with dialogue, another negotiating model appeared that would take domestic matters directly into account "without intermediaries." This model can be seen in the tables presented for each of the summits (Tables 2.3 through 2.9).

The first meeting of Central American presidents in Esquipulas, Guatemala, on May 25, 1986, outside the Contadora process, reveals some interesting agreements:

1. To proceed with dialogues like Esquipulas I and acknowledge Contadora as the best political/diplomatic instrument.
2. To formalize these presidential meetings as a necessary and appropriate mechanism for analyzing the most urgent problems.
3. To have the Central American presidents sign the Contadora Act for Peace and Cooperation in Central America.
4. To design complementary mechanisms, such as the Central American Parliament.
5. To recognize that peace can only be the product of an authentic democratic, pluralistic, and participatory process.
6. To review and modernize the economic integration processes.

In the transitional period from Esquipulas I in 1986 to the presidential summit held in San José in February 1987, Oscar Arias began to draw up the initial version of the Arias Plan. Since it influenced the evolution of the regional negotiations process, we will stop here to look at the origins of this plan.

Guido Fernández, Costa Rica's ambassador to Washington during the Arias administration, indicated in January 1987 that Costa Rica sought to form an alliance of what it considered democratic countries, composed of nations from Europe and Central and South America, in order to pressure Nicaragua to enter into negotiations with the counterrevolutionaries.

On January 7, 1987, high-level U.S. officials (Elliot Abrams, Philip Habib, and William Walker) met in Miami with Costa Rica's Foreign Minister Rodrigo Madrigal Nieto to work on a diplomatic initiative for Central America.[23] Madrigal declared at the time that the intent of the proposal was to bring about the democratization of Nicaragua and that the details of the proposal were variations on this theme. It was also reported that the government of Costa Rica had discussed this proposal with a group of U.S. Senators from the Democratic party, led by Christopher Dodd, chairman of the Subcommittee on Hemispheric Affairs of the U.S. Senate's Foreign Affairs Committee, when they visited San José in December 1986. Former president of Costa Rica Daniel Oduber stated in the media that the new U.S. policy proposals coincided in many ways with the policy proposals of President Arias.

In Miami, U.S. officials backed the initial Arias Plan. It was timed to precede both the arrival of the foreign ministers of the Contadora and Support Group countries, who would be traveling to Central America in mid-January 1987, and the February 9–10 meeting of the Third Ministerial Conference in Guatemala, which would include the participation of the European Economic Community, the Central American countries, and the Contadora Group. This gathering witnessed the diplomatic unfurling of three peace proposals or negotiating models in their initial confrontation: the Reagan policy, the Contadora policy, and the Arias Plan, version one.

In the final declaration of the Guatemala meeting, Contadora was mentioned in twelve out of twenty-three points. Analysts expressed concern over the fact that, in point 10 of this document, the activities of Contadora and the Support Group were acknowledged as the only viable mechanism at that time for reaching a political settlement. The wording of the original version stated that they "continued to be the only viable mechanism. . . ." Costa Rica, El Salvador, and Honduras fought to give the Contadora initiative a temporary aspect, paving the way for a third option: the Arias Plan.

On February 13, 1987, two days prior to the meeting of Central American presidents in San José, the governments of El Salvador and Honduras publicly supported the Arias Plan. Elliot Abrams and Frank Carlucci (U.S. National Security Council advisor) also voiced their support. Nicaragua, on the other hand, attacked the Arias Plan, claiming that it was prejudicial to its interests and part of a unilateral U.S. scheme.

According to the versions leaked to the press, the original Arias Plan peremptorily demanded that the Sandinista government decide on it within fifteen days. The document made no reference whatsoever to the United States or to the aggression against Nicaragua. In any case, it represented a step backward in Contadora's progress—especially in view of the Latin American Declaration of Caraballeda in January 1986, in which the United States was already mentioned. This declaration had received strong international support as the basis for a realistic and effective agreement.

The first version of the Arias Plan attempted to supersede Contadora, offering a new negotiating platform that was considered less substantial because it referred almost exclusively to Nicaragua. Thus the "new" negotiating model not only failed to recognize issues already advanced by Contadora that were essential for a real peace, it legitimized and to some extent opened new spaces for the Reagan policy.

For reasons that are not entirely clear, that same February 13, 1987, in a bold about-face, President Arias sent Foreign Minister Madrigal Nieto on a tour through Central America to present a new version of the plan and discuss radical changes that he had made to bring it more into line with the positions suggested by the Democratic congressmen, with Christopher Dodd at their head—changes that clearly represented a more realistic model for dealing with the crisis in Central America.[24]

The points of agreement between Arias and Dodd, according to former president Oduber, had been there from the outset. Arias had always been inflexible about suspending military aid to the contras and putting an end to U.S. military maneuvers, but Sen. Dodd must have been very explicit with him about the recent changes in attitudes and perceptions reflected in U.S. domestic policy, especially in the aftermath of the Iran-contra scandal.

The reactions to this about-face were not unexpected: José Azcona, president of Honduras, declared at the next meeting (in San José) that he "could not sign a treaty of this nature, owing to prior commitments with the United States." In El Salvador, President José Napoleon Duarte held an emergency meeting with the Armed Forces High Command, demonstrating that he had no authority to make commitments that jeopardized the domestic progress of the war. Guatemalan president Vinicio Cerezo, who had been vacillating about attending the San José meeting because of the implications of the Arias Plan, version one, breathed a sigh of relief: The new plan did not compromise his policy of neutrality. The Arias Plan had been transformed from a variation of the Reagan plan to a variation of the final Revised Contadora Act for Peace that had been rejected by the Tegucigalpa Bloc in June 1986.[25]

The Presidential Meeting in Costa Rica, February 15, 1987

The meeting of presidents in Costa Rica on February 15, 1987—two days after the tour of Foreign Minister Madrigal Nieto, with the exclusion of Nicaragua and the continuing reluctance of Guatemala—marks an important step toward the realism needed to address the crisis in Central America. Despite its nature and objectives, this meeting was a preamble to greater flexibility and subsequent negotiations, though it also contained anti-Sandinista elements in the extreme and sought to distance the proposals from Contadora by offering a new platform for negotiations.

The meeting concluded with the signing of a document entitled, "An Hour for Peace in Central America," and a joint declaration was issued endorsing and supporting the peace plan proposed by Oscar Arias, though it was not signed. Each country made a commitment to study the plan contained in the document, *Procedure for Establishing a Firm and Lasting Peace in Central America,* and to put it up for discussion, approval, and signature at a meeting that would exclude none of the Central American presidents (read Daniel Ortega), to be held in Esquipulas, Guatemala, June 25–26, 1987. Nevertheless, it was clearly established that the new peace plan in its second version was not intended to replace Contadora, but to complement it; so said President Oscar Arias to Bernardo Sepulveda, Mexico's minister of foreign relations. Nicaragua, on the other hand, accepted the invitation to Esquipulas II, planning to complement the proposals (including some Contadora features) with domestic topics and bilateral issues.

These real changes in the dynamic and agenda of the negotiators are essential for an understanding of Mexico's withdrawal from the process, since what Contadora could not do out of respect for each of the countries' right to self-determination and sovereignty—the basis for Mexico's legitimacy as a mediator—was to point out and/or seek to influence opinions about the importance of domestic problems as a factor in regional pacification. However, as other proposals were eliminated, it skillfully obliged the players to confront the real issues. The very logic of the negotiations process led to a recognition that the Central American conflict could not have a lasting solution unless each country faced its own domestic difficulties. Furthermore, added Nicaragua, a halt to the U.S. aggression perpetrated by its contra surrogates was also essential for peace.

And so the scenarios for Esquipulas were constructed: Latin America (via Contadora) and the new Arias Plan opened up possibilities for a negotiating strategy from a perspective of coexistence, pluralism, and self-determination—interests and content highly at odds with the agenda of the Reagan administration.

With Oscar Arias as president, Costa Rica finally withdrew from the Tegucigalpa Bloc. The remaining bloc members, El Salvador and Honduras, together with the contras, placed obstacles in the path of the summit, which was postponed until August 1987 (see Table 2.2 for a chronology of the Esquipulas summits). The Reagan administration had a major interest in blocking dialogue among Central Americans within the framework of Contadora or Esquipulas. Consequently, it sought to prevent the development of a national and regional dynamic that could interfere with its strategy to topple the Nicaraguan government.

The easing of tensions had begun however, and despite numerous pressures and initiatives by the United States and the presentation of a last-minute "bipartisan" Reagan/Wright plan, the five months following the San José summit did not prevent Esquipulas II from being held. Circulating at Esquipulas II were four peace plans: the Contadora proposal, the Arias Plan, the Reagan Plan, and one by Honduras, which was very similar to the U.S. proposal.

What became overwhelmingly clear at this summit—what forced the Arias Plan to center stage, leaving the Reagan proposal in the wings— was that the Central American presidents would only be successful if they showed the determination to begin building the necessary trust among themselves, heeding their historical responsibility to make peace with their peoples and the international community.

On August 7, 1987, at the meeting called Esquipulas II, the presidents signed an agreement, *Procedures for the Establishment of a Firm and Lasting Peace in Central America,* demonstrating that notwithstanding their differences, they were capable of creating spaces for autonomy through negotiation and dialogue. Viewed in historical perspective, there were many limitations and problems with these agreements. But the Reagan policy suffered a setback that confirmed the U.S. president's inability to understand the changes that were taking place in Central America—in contrast to Mexico and Contadora. The efforts of Contadora and the Support Group, plus those of the United Nations and the OAS, were incorporated into the proposal.

Esquipulas II: A Historic Step Fraught with Obstacles—The "Central Americanization" of the Peace Process Begins

The document approved at this summit (see Table 2.3) stated in its introduction, "We have Central American paths toward peace and development," which translated in practice into a Central and Latin American responsibility and consensus. Esquipulas II was the product of a protracted, intense, and creative negotiations process that took the appropriate steps toward meeting Central America's most immediate strategic challenges: peace, development, and the enhancement of sovereignty and democracy. It should be recalled that these agreements were the result first, of the Contadora and Support Group initiative, with the participation of the European countries, and second, of the efforts of President Vinicio Cerezo of Guatemala and President Oscar Arias of Costa Rica. It was and is a great effort that they have participated in, responding to pressure from Central America's peoples to open the way for negotiations.

Thus the Esquipulas II accords were a step forward, chiefly in that they contributed to the peace process in Central America, expressed a Central American consensus, filled the ever-more dangerous negotiations vacuum in Central America, and eased the pressures (at least temporarily) of the low-intensity conflict that to this day burdens the vast majority of Central Americans.

Nevertheless, it cannot be ignored that for the Central American presidents (with the exception of Nicaragua's Daniel Ortega) and for the Democratic party in the United States, this process, even with its agreements (or precisely because of them), did not imply any real divergence from the Reagan administration's objectives. The basic goal of the U.S. model remained the same: to check and, if possible, defeat the movements for social change in Central America—chiefly the Nicaraguan Revolution, to keep it from serving as a role model for other peoples.

Esquipulas II: The Negotiating Model Unfolds; the Deadlines Pass

The conditions of the Esquipulas II agreement were not fulfilled, principally because the U.S. government and Central America's armies and ruling elites blocked compliance. Most directly, the virtually unconditional alignment of the Salvadoran and Honduran governments with Washington prevented implementation, particularly of provisions relating the contras, most of whom were hosted by Honduras. In addition to the disparities between the countries with regard to progress in meeting the domestic commitments they had assumed on August 7, there were differences on multilateral issues and, as ever, the question of U.S. interests, which presented the biggest problem. Areas of contention were the halting of aid to the contras, their presence in Honduras, security matters and the arms buildup in general, as well as the return of refugees and exiles. The United States, Honduras, and El Salvador supported proposals on these issues that were aimed at isolating Nicaragua.

The Reagan administration and conservative Republican sectors in the United States worked hard to block the agreements. The discussions held by the Reagan administration and these Republicans with the presidents of Honduras and El Salvador during the ninety-day grace period before the agreements were to go into effect centered on demanding compliance from Nicaragua alone. Even the president of Costa Rica, Oscar Arias, called for the Nicaraguan government to institute a dialogue with the Somocista counterrevolutionaries—though not directly, as President Reagan had urged—even though this was not stipulated in the Esquipulas II document. The document made a clear distinction between unarmed domestic opposition, with which governments were obliged to talk, and armed opposition.

The Reagan administration's strategy consisted of demanding a direct dialogue in Managua while maintaining congressional support for the so-called "freedom fighters," to keep the pressure on the Sandinistas to "democratize Nicaragua." Thus, Reagan sought to endow the contras with a political legitimacy that they did not possess.

These emphases took on importance after Esquipulas II as far as the Nicaraguan government was concerned, for they kept reiterating the need to "democratize Nicaragua" but not the other countries, as had been agreed. However, circumstances made it obvious that in the framework of Esquipulas II, the major thrust of the regional negotiations model was the plan shared by Presidents Vinicio Cerezo and Oscar Arias and important sectors of the Democratic party in the United States (though for different reasons and without an explicit agreement among them). Paradoxically, this model was also promoted by the Reagan administration, which sought to integrate it into its war-oriented strategy.

Viewed in perspective, the Reagan administration always wanted to make the contras take root within Nicaragua, so as to turn its counterrevolutionary war into an internal Nicaraguan struggle. It also attempted to exploit the weariness of the Nicaraguan people resulting from the war to topple Somoza and subsequent U.S. aggression through its contra surrogates, in order to generate a strong, broad-based opposition capable of reversing the revolutionary process or at least diluting it.

Esquipulas III: The Limits to Autonomy; the "De-Contadorization" of Esquipulas

For an understanding of the complexity of the interaction between the Contadora-Esquipulas models and the Reagan-sponsored plan and the difficulties involved, some basic elements that preceded the Esquipulas III summit must be analyzed.

One concerns the presummit travels of Gen. Colin Powell, National Security Council advisor, Elliot Abrams, undersecretary of state for hemispheric affairs, and special ambassador for Central America Morris Busby throughout the region—trips that were characterized by the *New York Times* as an unusual form of blackmail. Sen. Christopher Dodd even claimed in San José that the Reagan administration had intimidated the governments of Guatemala, El Salvador, Honduras, and Costa Rica.

Another is the presence of the Honduran, Salvadoran, and Guatemalan defense ministers at the summit, once again exposing the real power limits of the three presidents and heightening tensions at the summit. By their presence, these military men made it clear that their interests and points of view should and would be taken into account.

Another rather important but different element was the report by the International Commission on Verification and Follow-up (CIVS) (including representatives from Contadora and Support Group countries) that had been requested to verify compliance with the Esquipulas II accords as part of that agreement. The report revealed how thin the democratic veneer in Honduras, El Salvador, and Guatemala actually was. It left no doubt as to the key issues in the conflict and suggested that the negotiations process be broadened and understood as a series of actions, that verification of the accords take place *in situ,* and that mobile units under U.N. supervision commence operations. This CIVS document, over a hundred pages long, was taken to the presidential meeting on January 15, 1988.

At this third summit, the two viewpoints and strategies once again clashed:

1. The U.S. strategy: The U.S. government needed to close the negotiation openings created by the peace accords and demonstrate the Sandinistas' lack of compliance with the agreements. The little that Nicaragua had conceded, according to the Reagan administration, was basically the result of military pressure by the contras. The United States therefore exerted pressure on its allies in the region (Honduras and El Salvador) to condemn the Sandinistas.

2. The alternative strategy for peace: This strategy, which borrowed elements from Contadora and its Support Group, the Central American Parliament project, the Arias Plan, and the Democratic party, though with different nuances and alternative approaches, required that there be room to negotiate, that political and diplomatic options be kept open, and that the verification deadlines scheduled for after February 3–4, 1988, be observed (this was the date that the U.S. House of Representatives and Senate would vote on US$270 million in aid to the contras).

It was evident that the United States had learned the lessons of Esquipulas II. Once again, this was not surprising; hence, the presummit visits and pressures to remove this dialogue/obstacle to the Reagan administration's plans. Putting an end to this diplomatic scenario, with the help of José Azcona and Napoleon Duarte, was the U.S. intention. Duarte indicated that he was not going to cover for anyone and that Nicaragua's zero hour had arrived. Presidents Arias and Cerezo showed little optimism, in view of the minimal progress of the accords and low spirits deriving from U.S. pressure.

On January 15, the presidents had a document on the table that had been approved earlier by consensus: the CIVS report. President Arias opened the meeting with a call to "rectify instead of condemn and to ignore the prophecies of doom." Honduras, El Salvador, and Guatemala publicly criticized the CIVS report: There were specific complaints against Mexico and its alleged pro-Nicaragua bias, causing it to withdraw as a mediator.

Arias made use of a pragmatism born of urgency and indicated to Daniel Ortega that if Nicaragua would unilaterally take steps to open negotiations with the contras, the U.S. Congress would have no excuse to vote aid to the contras. If the United States were to approve aid, Arias felt that Esquipulas would have been for nothing. Ortega therefore made public his decision to enter into a dialogue with the contras and declare a cease-fire and an end to Nicaragua's state of emergency, thus rescuing the summit. Furthermore, he made it clear that the purpose of the dialogue was simply to agree on a cease-fire and that after turning in their arms, the contras would be reincorporated into civilian life through amnesty and other measures.

An understanding of what took place at the Costa Rican summit is crucial. Why Nicaragua's unilateral concessions? Why the termination of the CIVS, and hence the Mexican–Latin American verification effort? (See Table 2.4.)

At this summit, the main setback concerned self-determination and peace in the region, since U.S. pressure and threats to withdraw economic and other aid to the Central American countries had their effect on the presidents of the isthmus. While this was truer in some cases than others, all the presidents had a responsibility to see to it that the Reagan strategy was not as successful as it might have been.

Certainly, the most spectacular outcome of the summit was the direct dialogue with the contras agreed to by the delegation from Nicaragua, composed of Vice Minister Victor Tinoco and Chief of Military Intelligence of the Sandinista Popular Army (EPS) Ricardo Wheelock.

The Reagan administration's and contras' distorted interpretation of this agreement was that tripartite talks would be formalized between the domestic civilian opposition, the contras, and the Sandinistas—a dialogue that would not only include talks on a cease-fire but matters of domestic policy as well. By deliberately misinterpreting the agreement, the United States hoped to accomplish the following:

1. To lend an aura of legitimacy to the contras at a time (after Esquipulas II) when "irregular forces" had none, unless, as insurgent forces, they could count on real support within their countries.
2. To thereby gain a foothold in regional negotiations, in which they had not figured up to that point, since they were never accepted as real spokesmen for the Nicaraguan people.
3. To introduce the topic of domestic policy into the discussions with the Sandinista government. This implied power sharing, but

not an acceptance of the regime's offer of amnesty or a willingness to lay down arms. What Managua agreed to at the summit was simply a dialogue with the contras, and this subsequently took place.

Other setbacks, perhaps even the most serious, were connected with Contadora and the Support Group's disengagement from the tasks of monitoring and verification (through the CIVS), since the margin for autonomy that had opened up had largely been created by these countries in response to U.S. pressures. The U.S. objective of "de-Contadorizing" Esquipulas had been accomplished.

The CIVS was therefore replaced by the Executive Commission of the Agreements, composed simply of the Central American foreign ministers. Given the pressures those countries were under, it was not the most suitable body for verifying the dialogue, cease-fire, amnesty, and end to the state of emergency in Nicaragua. The "Central Americanization" of the negotiations was not (and is not) credible in the face of such successful pressure by the Reagan administration. Bruce Bagley, a researcher at the University of Miami, stated at the time, "The fact that Central Americans (since the Arias Plan and even more so after Esquipulas III) have taken the lead in what is going on, instead of Contadora, works to the advantage of U.S. interests. Oscar Arias with his Plan therefore has the upper hand, and thus the Central Americans are being favored by the United States."[26]

For Costa Rican Foreign Minister Rodrigo Madrigal Nieto,

the rejection of the CIVS report by some governments and the withdrawal of Contadora and its Support Group from the negotiations process occurred because the CIVS committed a procedural error; it had been assigned the task of verifying and following up events, not expressing opinions about political situations, which was not in its purview. The fact that the Central American countries wished to retain the right to verify [the agreements] and be the ones to decide how to turn verification and follow-up over to a specialized agency to avoid playing judge and jury, is highly significant. If there is an electoral problem, it will not be up to them to resolve it; instead, the task will be turned over to a specialized international agency of the OAS or the United Nations. If there is a refugee problem, it will be assigned to UNHCR, if there is a human rights problem, it will be assigned to the Human Rights Commission, with full guarantees by all that the Commission will be allowed to come and carry out an inspection.[27]

Madrigal reiterated,

the situation in Central America has been evolving such that all the presidents, without exception, believe that their relationship with their foreign ministers is the most viable, the most expeditious, and the most fruitful [way of getting things done]; thus, the greater part of the work can be accomplished by Central American hands. This does not mean that they are replacing Contadora as a mediating agency; however, given the fluid nature and the speed of events in ´ Central America, of the continuous possibilities for dialogue, for talking, for reaching agreements among the parties, *Contadora is a rather slow and cumbersome detour . . . a political agreement like Esquipulas is more viable than a legal mechanism like Contadora* [our emphasis].[28]

In contrast, Nicaragua fought to preserve the CIVS. Its concession to the other Central American presidents in this regard was in allowing the maximum room for negotiation. Moreover, after Esquipulas III, Nicaragua indicated its willingness to permit on-site verification of its compliance by the CIVS, something the other countries were unwilling to do.

In any case, at this point there were many factors that facilitated the possibility of maintaining this model for negotiation and dialogue. One of them, undoubtedly, was the Sandinistas' flexibility and desire for peace; another, the attitude of Oscar Arias and U.S. Democrats who favored coexistence with the Nicaraguan regime, despite its aggressive rhetoric. After the summit, Madrigal Nieto, laying on the pressure, declared that "the only thing left is to urge, but really urge Nicaragua to make basic changes. . . ."[29] However, how much more could Nicaragua concede? Why did Arias continue to be so indulgent of Azcona's and Duarte's failure to comply with the accords and so intransigent where Nicaragua was concerned? Contadora's elimination from this summit was taken as a virtual green light by some in the governments of Central America (and of course, the United States) to turn up the heat on Nicaragua. At that point, there was somehow a return to the plan of the CDC and the Enders Forum of 1982, since the promises to demobilize the contras had not been met.

Esquipulas IV: Between War and Intermittent Promises of Peace; Carlos Salinas de Gortari and George Bush Begin Their Administrations

After four postponements, the summit of Central American presidents was finally held. It was delayed by numerous disputes and some countries' insistence that it not be held until George Bush took office. President Bush was inaugurated, and there was no public mention of changes and/or new proposals for Central America.

Two elements would appear to be essential for an understanding of why the presidential meeting was finally held in February:

1. At the inauguration of Carlos Andres Pérez in Venezuela prior to the summit, President Daniel Ortega, understanding the unfavorable balance of forces in Central America, revealed a number of details and drafts of the proposal that he was taking to the summit. This proposal indicated a highly flexible attitude on the part of his government regarding both domestic and foreign (contra) issues. In addition, President Oscar Arias took this opportunity to exchange views with other Central American and Latin American heads of state (Fidel Castro among them) and other dignitaries, including U.S. Vice President Dan Quayle. Following these exchanges, President Arias insisted that they "were now in a better position to grasp the possible points of agreement, the differences that continued to persist among the governments of the region, and the international backing available for the area's peace process."[30]

2. The other element to bear in mind is the encounter between Presidents Vinicio Cerezo and Oscar Arias on February 7 in San José. The purpose of this meeting, according to Cerezo, was to "draw up a request to President Daniel Ortega, urging him to comply with the Esquipulas IV agreements reached in El Salvador. . . . This is not to pressure Nicaragua but a serious attempt to move toward democracy. . . . Nicaragua must commit itself to democracy, for if it does not, the international community will proceed to isolate it, with very stiff consequences in terms of international trade, economic development, and security."[31]

For reasons of national interest, explicit or not, Mexico had largely absented itself from Central America since Esquipulas III and turned inward, modifying and updating its foreign policy and distancing itself somewhat as a regional player. It returned to a bilateralist approach toward Central America, since at home—as we have already mentioned— a serious economic crisis was unfolding. The country was reformulating its economic strategy, searching for new options and undergoing an important rethinking of the role of the state in Mexican society, in the midst of the difficult external debt renegotiation. All this, plus the elimination of the CIVS during Esquipulas III, forced Mexico to alter its priorities. The country continued to maintain an interest in a self-determined Central America, but it had exhausted its role and its presence in the region. Besides, the presidential changeover in both Mexico and the United States permitted exploration of new terms in the bilateral relationship between the two countries, as well as those of each with Central America.

According to Oscar Arias, the new U.S. president, George Bush, would allow him "an opportunity for diplomacy at Esquipulas IV and would not seek a confrontation with the U.S. Congress over military aid for the contras in Nicaragua."[32] This view was based on the fact that Bush was just starting out his presidency, and among other things required a consensus in Congress if the domestic deficit was to be reduced; he did not need to open new battlefronts, much less concerning a topic as sensitive as contra aid.

The text of the Esquipulas IV presidential agreements made it clear that there was still some chance of revitalizing processes aimed at greater autonomy in Central America, despite U.S. interventionism. The commitments, agreements, and exhortations were rather biased in one direction, since the emphasis in the agenda was on Nicaragua.

In fact, if we examine the table of commitments, we can see that Daniel Ortega's willingness to begin a process of democratization and national reconciliation, expressed in concrete concessions, takes up about 75 percent of the space. Furthermore, other key issues were incorporated into the final document, such as the provision on the International Commission for Verification and Security and another connected with the need to revive the National Reconciliation Commissions (see Table 2.5).

One of the accords that attracted the most attention—and here we will stop a moment because of its implications—was the one in which Honduras and Nicaragua agreed to draw up a joint plan for the demobilization, repatriation, or voluntary resettlement of members of the Nicaraguan resistance and their families in Nicaragua and/or third countries. To accomplish this, the two countries would request technical assistance from the specialized agencies of the United Nations.

It should be recalled that the contras, as an armed force sponsored by the U.S. government, had frequently been responsible for the failures of peace initiatives during the period of Contadora and Support Group and Central America's Esquipulas meetings. Added to the actions of the permanent and/or roving U.S. ambassadors in each of the countries— and the parallel logistical structures created within the governments (of which the Iran-contra affair was a reflection)—the contras generated a series of pressures and obstacles that hampered the development of the Esquipulas negotiating model. This made it difficult to achieve any rapid progress toward peace or apply the basic principles of national sovereignty in the countries of the region.

The issues of who was to oversee the demobilization, who was to finance it, and where the contras would end up were a mystery—first, because of the contra leaders' unwillingness to accept disarmament

and demobilization, and second, because of U.S. sensitivity and opposition to this presidential resolution.

The summit maneuvers of the erstwhile Tegucigalpa Bloc (Costa
Rica, Honduras, and El Salvador, and now Guatemala) to oblige Nicaragua
to make "democratic" concessions to satisfy the Bush administration
cannot be ignored. Arias declared that he expected Nicaragua to abolish
press censorship, give the anti-Sandinista camp access to the television
station, and rewrite the new election law of 1988 to reduce the advantage
of the Sandinista party. These demands raised several questions: What
democratization, with what basic prerequisites and conditions, were
Ronald Reagan, Oscar Arias, Napoleon Duarte, José Azcona, and Vinicio
Cerezo talking about? What kind of democracy were they building in
their own countries? Would they finally agree to live alongside an
alternative regime like that of Nicaragua's Sandinistas or would they
look for gentler ways to strangle it and roll back the revolutionary
process?[33]

The Esquipulas IV agreements were termed "very soft" by the Bush
administration because they included no guarantees of compliance by
the Sandinistas. Bush therefore stated, "we have to put teeth into the
agreements, so they'll be respected. . . . It's all very well to make
commitments based on generalities, but we have to define procedures.
What does 'free elections' mean? I'd like to see some type of certification
of these elections."[34]

As was to be expected, the very day of the presidential communiqué,
some sectors of the contras rejected the plan for demobilization within
ninety days, because, among other things, March 31 was the date for
the last U.S. grant of humanitarian aid. According to James Baker, Bush
"would request new humanitarian aid, since he has the moral obligation
to seek new financing, even though there is a peace plan for Central
America that could lead to the dissolution of the Nicaraguan forces
backed by the United States."[35]

In any case, Bush had somewhat distanced himself from the contras,
perhaps in part because legal proceedings against Oliver North begun
January 31, 1989, could implicate him directly in the scandal.[36] Nor
did Bush, facing major budgetary and economic policy challenges, a
Democratic majority in Congress, and a political defeat in the rejection
of John Tower as secretary of defense, desire a partisan conflict over
the contra war.

Nevertheless the Bush administration had not assimilated the failure
of eight years of blunders by the Reagan administration and persisted
in its refusal to accept the Sandinista revolution. Noam Chomsky said
with good reason at this time that "the objective realities have not
changed for the United States; there is less hysterical rhetoric, but the

same policies have essentially been maintained." Chomsky was convinced that, tactically speaking, there were

> more efficient methods (than the contras) to strangle and destroy a small and weak country in a region of the world highly dependent on the United States—gentler methods, like economic and ideological pressures; the so-called "Chilean method," used against Salvador Allende, would be more effective. Bush thinks that with little investment he'll be able to keep on strangling Nicaragua. What they want there is what they call "democracy," and for them, that means rule by the business class. If you don't have this, you don't have democracy. I'm also sure that they'll attempt to build the parallel structures that the United States always tries to construct when it wants to undermine a country. In Nicaragua's case, they'll work with elements in the business community, opposition groups, etc.[37]

Thus, Vice President Dan Quayle was called upon to play the front man with respect to the contra situation. Quayle declared that "the Esquipulas IV agreement will not destroy the counterrevolution, and in case the Ortega government doesn't comply with its commitments, we will have to regroup the contras and decide on another strategy. The agreement is for elections, but what we need to see are actions."[38]

It is important to mention that at this time, Vinicio Cerezo spoke with George Bush and Dan Quayle in Washington and acknowledged that there existed differences between the United States and the Central American nations regarding the peace plan, which would encounter great difficulties without the backing, or at least the acceptance, of the U.S. government.

At a luncheon sponsored by the Carnegie Endowment for International Peace in Washington, Cerezo himself noted that he had "lacked the courage to propose specific measures concerning Nicaragua to his American colleague Bush, but he suggested that the five Central American presidents would perhaps do so in the future."[39]

After Esquipulas IV came the bipartisan agreement in the U.S. Congress to grant "humanitarian aid" to the contras—not to demobilize them as the presidents had agreed, but to sustain them until February 1990, just in case the democratization process and the elections in Nicaragua did not satisfy the United States and Nicaragua's neighbors. This resolution made it clear that Bush intended to keep the military option as a latent, deterrent element; even more serious was the fact that, with the sole exception of Daniel Ortega, the Central American presidents supported the plan, backtracking on the agreements that they themselves had adopted in Esquipulas IV.

Once again, the permanent tension between the principles, agreements, commitments, declarations, and degrees of autonomy of some Central American leaders and the hegemonic attitude of the United States was made manifest.

More and more, the agreements of Esquipulas II, III, and IV revealed what they really were: not a growing and simultaneous process of negotiation to defuse the various national conflicts and advance toward regional negotiations on substantive matters like peace, development, and self-determination, but rather, a process designed to focus regional negotiations on Nicaragua alone, hobbling the Sandinista regime and restricting it to movement only within the political and social canons and institutions of the rest of Central America.

The situation following Esquipulas IV brings us back to the first peace plan of Oscar Arias, where, just like today, the purpose of regional political action in concert with the United States was almost exclusively to put pressure on Nicaragua. At that time, the only thing that separated Arias from the Reagan administration insofar as Nicaragua was concerned was his desire to defeat the Sandinistas through ballots rather than bullets.

There is no doubt that a discussion of democratization in the context of the Central American crisis constitutes a high priority both theoretically and politically; the region's presidents were evading their responsibility under the accords to bolster their own democracies and demobilize the contras, under the pretext that there had been no democratization in Nicaragua. The real reason, however, was that, with the exception of Costa Rica (a representative democracy) and Nicaragua (a popular democracy), the rest of Central America had only known an occasional glimmer of democracy.

Why, then, was President Arias so interested in constructing the kind of democracy in Nicaragua that existed nowhere else in Central America? Arias kept referring to Honduras, El Salvador, and Guatemala as "developing democracies" ignoring the human rights violations, the death squads in El Salvador, the armies that put out any spark of democracy in the three countries, and the mercenaries in Honduras. The main argument of the Central American leaders, summarized by Arias, was to be found in the region's political and ideological position: a refusal to permit the consolidation of the Sandinista regime because of its pluralistic, popular democracy and its self-determination—in other words, sovereignty. This coincided with and complemented the U.S. position that compliance with the Esquipulas IV agreements, especially the demobilization of the contras, should be subordinated to the political evolution of democracy in Nicaragua and the holding of elections that were "truly free" in the eyes of the United States.

With the inauguration of Alfredo Cristiani of the ultraright National Republican Alliance (ARENA), the Salvadoran government hardened its position on the accords. Cristiani blocked the process that had begun, suggesting that the peace plan's proposal to demobilize the contras should also be applied to the Farabundo Martí National Liberation Front (FMLN). The comparison is specious for a number of reasons: The contras were an irregular force, financed and directed by the United States—not to mention that they operated out of Honduras and not Nicaragua, putting military pressure on the Sandinista regime; their conduct, in terms of negotiations and dialogue for peace and democracy with the government of Nicaragua, had been characterized as intransigent and unethical by many world leaders—among them, Javier Pérez de Cuellar and João Baena Suárez, secretaries general of the United Nations and the OAS, respectively. The FMLN, on the other hand, is an insurrectionist force that is part of the duality of power in El Salvador. Its tradition of dialogue and its search for negotiated settlements over the years has been evident in numerous proposals, many of them endorsed by Latin American governments, while the heart of the region's political and diplomatic dynamic was the plan to resolve the conflict by forcing the government of Nicaragua to make greater concessions to the opposition and the contras and to accommodate its domestic and foreign policy to the interests of the United States.

Esquipulas V: One More Effort Toward Peace

Like the previous presidential summits, this meeting was also postponed, this time for three months, owing to a number of uncertainties with regard to the agenda, in view of the many instances of noncompliance with Esquipulas II, III, and IV that had accumulated over the years.

As in the previous presidential encounters, a large mission of U.S. officials made the rounds throughout the region: Vice President Dan Quayle; Undersecretary of State for Inter-American Affairs Bernard Aronson, and his advisors Cresencio Arcos, John Glassman, Bill Cristol, Davis Baeckvith, and David Facelli, most of whom had been instrumental in implementing the Reagan strategy in the region (Arcos in particular was mentioned as "the real architect" behind the creation of the contras, when he served as a press attache in the U.S. Embassy in Tegucigalpa). The objectives and impact of the tour by Quayle, Aronson, and their advisors fit within the "pacification" model and the political style that the United States had been unfolding.

Concerning Nicaragua and its preparations for Esquipulas V, it must be mentioned that two days prior to the meeting, President Ortega met for twenty-three consecutive hours with representatives from twenty-one legal political parties in Nicaragua, and after fifty-three speeches and a long debate, they signed a series of agreements that had an unquestionable impact on the summit's outcome. They are, in brief:

1. The government of Nicaragua and the political parties called on the Central American presidents to approve the plan for the demobilization, relocation, or voluntary repatriation of the counterrevolutionary forces, as outlined in the Esquipulas II and Esquipulas IV agreements. The government of Nicaragua would declare an unconditional amnesty for former Somoza National Guards and contras, to go into effect as soon as the demobilization was complete.
2. The political parties called on governments with interests in Central America to abstain from covert activities during the Nicaraguan electoral process. All support to political parties would have to be in compliance with the laws of Nicaragua.
3. The president of the republic would make nine new commitments—among them, to suspend military recruitment until February 1990, to make the Supreme Electoral Council the final arbiter in matters within its jurisdiction during the electoral process, and to abrogate the law for maintaining order and public safety.
4. The political parties, with the backing of the president of the republic, proposed thirty new regulatory measures to the Supreme Electoral Council, designed to ensure the cleanest possible elections. Among them were voter registration lists, voting norms, the scrutiny of each of the ballot boxes, and the prohibition of ballot boxes on military installations.
5. The winners of the February 25, 1990, elections would take office on April 24 (the Assembly) and April 25 (the president and vice president).[40]

On attending his first summit, Alfredo Cristiani reiterated his demand that the demobilization of the contras take place simultaneously with a demobilization of the FMLN in El Salvador.

Hours before Esquipulas V, the four Central American presidents close to the Bush administration received a letter from the U.S. government containing the order "democratization before demobilization." Even worse, on August 2, four hours after the signing of the National Dialogue agreement in Nicaragua and two days prior to Esquipulas V, President Bush personally received Col. Bermúdez and other contra leaders to give them a single message: "We will continue to help you." A photograph of this meeting was circulated to area newspapers, with the clear intent of putting pressure on Central America's presidents.

Esquipulas V was finally held in Tela, Honduras. The degree of autonomy available to the presidents, though small, was somewhat of a relief, since they made some decisions on their own and did not entirely knuckle under to Bush expectations. The United States froze US$70 million in aid to Honduras, an action that was condemned by Sen. Christopher Dodd.

As seen in Table 2.6, the agreements reached in Esquipulas V targeted the factors responsible for the greatest tensions in the region and also helped consolidate the mechanisms for dialogue and agreement. Nevertheless, the United States continued to push through every possible means to prevent the *coup de grâce* from being delivered to the contras. "There was a telephone call from Baker to Arias at the summit that lasted more than an hour. Baker insisted that the contras not be demobilized, because the pressures on the Bush administration from the far right were very heavy."[41]

An essential feature of the summit was the out-of-court settlement between Honduras and Nicaragua, wherein Honduras promised to comply with the demobilization of the contras in exchange for Nicaragua's subsequent withdrawal of its suit against that country in the International Court of Justice at the Hague. Furthermore, President Cristiani remained isolated from the four other Central American presidents in his efforts to equate the contras with the FMLN. The final communiqué of the summit urged a constructive dialogue between the government and the FMLN to bring the war to a close. This represented a victory for the FMLN, which had made a variety of novel proposals for peace and dialogue, in contrast to Cristiani's and ARENA's project for an "all-out war."

In Nicaragua's case, the fact that the "democratization" issue was only partially discussed can be considered a major victory. With the signing of the agreements with the Nicaraguan opposition prior to the summit and the contras peremptorily ordered to disband under the supervision of international verification agencies, the strict timetable for demobilization represented a qualitative leap forward after the vagueness of Esquipulas IV. The U.N. International Commission for Supervision and Border Surveillance, made up of civilian and military contingents from West Germany, Spain, and Canada, would begin operations immediately, and together with the International Commission for Support and Verification (CIAV) composed of the secretaries general of the United Nations and the OAS, they would push for the demobilization of the contras by December 8, 1989, at the latest. This procedure would also involve a U.N. peace-keeping force.

The contras and the Bush administration continued to block these presidential agreements and persisted in their rejection of the demobilization, endeavoring to set conditions that had not been included in the accords. At this point, the *New York Times* reminded Bush that he "should not be obstinate about prolonging the life of the contras, since neither Nicaragua's domestic opposition nor even the U.S. Congress considers it of any use."[42] The majority of the contra leaders announced that they would return armed to Nicaragua as guarantors of their country's electoral process.

Nearly all of the U.S. political objectives for Nicaragua are present in the Tela agreements, and here, the contras were not a factor. Why, then, did the United States continue to block a practical diplomatic solution to its conflict with Nicaragua? The answer is that Bush would not accept the legitimacy of Nicaragua's elections if the Sandinistas won, and so, he kept the contras going.

Mexican Foreign Minister Fernando Solana stated that Esquipulas was "progressing very nicely, but many are concerned, as is the government of Mexico, of course, because at the moment, things appear to be at a standstill. We hope that the five presidents will make a new effort to get Esquipulas going, and we also hope that the multilateral organizations, specifically the United Nations and the OAS, manage to reactivate it so that it takes on a more definite and progressive orientation."

Esquipulas VI: Extraordinary Session

The background for this summit was the intensification of the war in El Salvador, owing to the failure of the meetings between the FMLN and the Cristiani government. Cristiani accused the Nicaraguan government, moreover, of collaborating militarily with El Salvador's armed rebel groups. In addition, there was the contras' failure to disband as agreed—an event that was to have taken place on December 7. The United States intended to keep on harassing Nicaragua until the elections in February 1990.

The summit agreements (see Table 2.7) indicate a clear support for President Cristiani and a rejection of the FMLN's activities. Signed by the presidents, even Daniel Ortega, they can be explained on two levels. In the latter case, the government of Nicaragua sought to facilitate the specific mechanisms for demobilizing the contras approved in Tela six months earlier. On the other hand, the signing by the other presidents can be explained by the existence of implicit pacts and conservative symmetries already discussed.

Nevertheless, the outcome of the sixth summit and the negotiations process was the continued presence of the contras. For Nicaragua, it meant the tactical sacrifice of a political friendship for a strategic arrangement, the subordination of solidarity with a guerilla movement to the needs of the state. What was clear at this point was that the demobilization of the contras and an acceleration of the peace process would depend more on Washington than on the area's presidents.

The Elections in Nicaragua, Current Situation, and Conclusions

Nicaragua's elections should be viewed as an important strategic moment in the process of democratizing the country, within the framework of the Esquipulas summits. The democratization process did not begin with the calling of elections nor can it be reduced to just that; it harks back to the revolutionary victory of 1979, the 1984 elections, and the establishment of democracy through an electoral process that restored the value of elections and the vote within a democratic state framework unheard of before 1990. An in-depth analysis of Nicaragua's electoral process would require another book, but let us point out some of its relevant features to permit an understanding of the turn of events just described.

Opting for the political alternative at this juncture (without discarding the military option embodied in the contras), the United States made opposition leader Violeta Chamorro's campaign its own. At a luncheon in New York for the heads of the British, French, and German diplomatic delegations, James Baker "suggested that the political parties of these countries finance the opposition in Nicaragua. . . . He made an identical request to the Japanese Minister of Foreign Relations and to Alois Mock, Austrian Minister of Foreign Relations and President of the European Democratic Union (UDE)."[43]

Furthermore, on October 17, 1989, after six weeks of effort by Bush, the U.S. Senate approved a $9 million package to finance Nicaragua's opposition coalition (National Opposition Union—the UNO). This vote granted $5 million to the U.S. National Endowment for Democracy (NED) to help develop the UNO party's organizational infrastructure, as well as some of its other electoral activities. The package included $400,000 to support electoral monitoring efforts by the "Council of Freely Elected Heads of Government," led by former U.S. president Jimmy Carter. It also allocated $4 million in direct support to the UNO, though half of this was designated for the Supreme Electoral Council. Presidential Press Secretary Marlin Fitzwater referred to Violeta Chamorro as "our candidate."[44]

Thus, the election scenario in Nicaragua in February 1990 (without the demobilization of the contras, which had been indirectly requested of the United States at each of the presidential summits) created an extremely tense climate at the time of the voting. It was (and is) obvious after the U.S. intervention in the Panamanian elections of 1989, that we were in the presence of a new kind of U.S. interventionism in Central America.

The key questions at this point were linked with the following problem: If the Sandinistas triumphed at the polls and this was confirmed by the U.N. electoral verification commission in Nicaragua, what would the attitude of the United States (along with the contras) and the other governments in the region be, and what would the scenario be if the Sandinistas lost?

The Sandinista Front lost the elections. The basic question is, Why did an electoral option publicly supported by the U.S. government obtain a majority? Indeed, more than half of Nicaragua's electorate chose to reject Sandinismo and back a formula clearly linked to the interventionist policy of the White House.

The Sandinista defeat has been attributed to a number of factors. One is the peace vote, resulting from exhaustion over the counterrevolutionary war and its impact, including wide-ranging destruction of Nicaragua's infrastructure, the involuntary displacement of many people, and compulsory military service. Hence the effectiveness of the UNO slogan, "while there is Sandinismo, there will be war." Another factor is opposition to the austerity measures undertaken by the Sandinista government that reversed social gains.[45]

The search for an explanation is part of the intellectual exercise necessary for making sense of this defeat. The framework for understanding why the Sandinista slogan "they shall not pass" was ultimately wrong is the U.S. aggression, the destruction of the economic and social infrastructure, the shortages of basic goods, and compulsory military service, among other things. This is what the people voted against. Despite the fact that the Sandinistas did not create this situation, it was their government that dealt with it.[46]

To conclude this brief analysis of the elections and view it from another angle, we share the view of another Mexican political commentator, who said:

> The defeat of the FSLN and its reorganization outside the government may in fact provide a strong impetus to the democratic left in Latin America, a left capable of criticizing neoliberalism with proposals, instead of rhetorical paradigms. . . . The FSLN now survives as a political force with impeccable democratic credentials. The electoral upset has paradoxically been transformed into a great moral and political good fortune. The voters have wrested from Sandinismo its statist rigidity, its messianic arrogance, its illusion of the infallibility of the masses. But they have

also disarmed the United States, deactivated the war, and transferred to the North Americans themselves and the international community the immediate responsibility of rebuilding the economy and compensating to some degree the great damage inflicted by this unjust and immoral war, this geopolitical game.[47]

At the time of the Esquipulas VII summit in April 1990, the reins of government in Nicaragua were being peacefully transferred by Daniel Ortega to President-elect Violeta Chamorro. The contras still had not disbanded, and discord within the newly elected coalition government was intensifying. Economic aid and backing from the United States and the international community had yet to arrive. The transition was uncertain. In this context, Esquipulas VII was held in Nicaragua to hasten and consolidate the demand for the disbanding and relocation of the contras (see Table 2.8).

This summit actually marks the close of a cycle, a period in the implementation of a negotiations model, and a sort of political birth. This would be the last summit attended by Oscar Arias and Daniel Ortega.

Ortega's electoral defeat, the institutionalization of the presidential summits in Central America as an instrument for conflict resolution, the regionwide election of governments with similar ideologies (conservative in their politics and neoliberal in their economics), and the gradual demobilization of the contras as a real possibility for discussion at Esquipulas VIII in Guatemala in June 1990 (see Table 2.9), plus the demand to demilitarize the region and find more equitable development alternatives within the framework of an end of the cold war, are elements that could make the war as we know it in Central America disappear in this decade of the 1990s.

In the balance, these ten years of negotiation in the context of the Mexico–Central America–United States triangle, Contadora, and the Esquipulas summits, where the war has been an expression of widespread social conflict, have left the peoples of the region as well as the institutions of the states much weakened. The political map of Central America has been altered for the 1990s, but the question of stability and the critical problems of the region remain, for not everything agreed to in the regional presidential summits and/or the national reconciliation efforts has come to pass. Likewise, the enhancement of democracy and development as strategic challenges are still pending, for the level of peace attained has not been sufficient to resolve the causes of the crisis.

The armed conflicts in El Salvador and Guatemala are still with us and the demobilization of the contras in Nicaragua, now a reality, has not been enough to set the stage for a national transition effort in Nicaragua. In these three countries, negotiations and dialogue among the parties are still sluggish, leaving the impression that the conflict may flare up again in the short or medium term.

Throughout this part we have seen how after Esquipulas III, Mexico had no cards left to play in the region, owing to the "burnout" induced by its triangular relationship with the United States in the Central American negotiations process, plus its domestic crisis and efforts to resolve it. Looking to its national interests, therefore, Mexico turned inward and lowered its profile in the region. We wonder if this trend will continue indefinitely.

Central American–Mexican relations are presently weak and are no longer as important as they were in the late 1970s and early 1980s. U.S. influence on both parties is greater, albeit different. The framework for all this is a multipolar world and the end of the cold war, which provides the United States with an excellent opportunity to "change course and promote nonintervention, respect for self-determination, collective self-defense, the peaceful settlement of disputes, respect for human rights, and support for democratic development."[48]

In economic terms, Mexico is rapidly progressing toward a free trade agreement with the United States. Such a pact and Mexico's current foreign policy imply risks and costs. According to Rosario Green:

> A close relationship with the United States could diminish Mexico's legitimacy in the diplomatic arena; it could provoke nationalist sentiments within the country and signify an excessive dependence on a rather unreliable partner. However, the existence of these possibilities should not favor policies of disengagement with respect to the United States, but rather, the clear perception of the risks Mexico is prepared to run and the price it is willing to pay. That is, while a good understanding between Mexico and the United States should be based on certain mutual concessions, they in no way should imply giving in. Sacrificing positions and openings is not the answer. Such is the case with regard to joint Latin American efforts, for example, or Mexico's participation in other areas and other integration efforts.[49]

Latin America and Central America are waiting to see what the nature of this relationship will be; they are also awaiting the outcome of Bush's "Enterprise for the Americas" initiative. However, why not accelerate the policy's timetable—that is, undertake a concerted effort toward democracy, development, and peace? The basic differences in Mexican and U.S. foreign policy are unlikely to disappear. It is possible that both will find structures for cooperation in foreign policy when the differences are not too serious. What is the range of options? The invasion of Panama destroyed this structure for cooperation, and, instead, the countries employed one that allowed for dissent—they agreed to disagree, as it were. What will Mexico's reaction be to this relative pacification? How will it respond to a new intensification of the conflict in the region? Why not establish a demilitarized zone in Central America under Latin American supervision, with the consent of the United States?

Within all these questions we add some final reflections. Will the Central American crisis of the 1990s be like that of the 1980s? Will the area's regimes continue to resort to authoritarianism? Will the topic of development be taken up in the forthcoming agendas? What sort of negotiations process will be able to address democratization in El Salvador and Guatemala under the new situations, since the old model is a failure? Will the 1990s witness the start of a dismantling of the armed forces of Central America, with 174,600 soldiers, 220 planes, 160 helicopters, and 100 naval vessels, and hundreds of armored vehicles? Will these resources and the more than 50 percent of the regional public expenditures designated for them be used to promote peace in the decade to come?

What will Mexico's role in Central America be during this new decade that has just begun? How will Mexico's closer ties with the United States affect Central America? Will Mexico's diversification of relations with Latin America fall behind as its ties to the United States are strengthened? Or can Mexico achieve a kind of equilibrium with the United States, perhaps by means of rapprochement with Europe, and continue to uphold the principles of self-determination and non-intervention in domestic affairs?

TABLE 2.2   Esquipulas Chronology: Summits of the Central American Presidents

Esquipulas I	Esquipulas, Guatemala	May 25, 1986
Esquipulas II	Guatemala City	August 5–6, 1987
Esquipulas III	Alajuela, Costa Rica	January 15–16, 1988
Esquipulas IV	Tesoro Beach, El Salvador	February 14, 1989
Esquipulas V	Tela, Honduras	August 6–7, 1989
Esquipulas VI	San Isidro, Costa Rica	December 10–12, 1989
Esquipulas VII	Montelimar, Nicaragua	April 3, 1990
Esquipulas VIII	Antigua, Guatemala	June 17, 1990

Source: The Esquipulas Process (Washington, D.C.: Center for International Policy, December 1990).

TABLE 2.3   Esquipulas II, August 1987

Reconciliation and Dialogue	Democracy	Foreign Intervention	Disarmament
• Creation of national reconciliation commissions. • Establishment of mechanisms for dialogue and cooperation. • Amnesty decrees for political prisoners. • Call for a cease-fire. • Attention to the flow of displaced persons.	• Necessity to lift states of siege and emergency powers and promote democratic processes that are pluralistic and participatory, with press freedom. • Election of representatives to a Central American Parliament.	• Halt to extraregional aid to irregular forces or insurrectionist movements. • National territory is not to be used to attack other countries. • The search for regional negotiation mechanisms for security, verification, and monitoring.	No agreements.

Verification of Accords	Integration and Development	Human Rights	
• Establishment of the International Commission on Verification and Follow-up, with the secretaries of the OAS and UN, the Contadora Group and its Support Group, and the Central American foreign ministers. • Timetable for compliance.	Necessity to accelerate regional development and create more egalitarian societies free of misery.	No agreements.	

Source: Emma Molina, "Los ejercitos siguen en la agenda regional," Boletín ACAFADE, June/July 1990, pp. 9–13.

TABLE 2.4 Esquipulas III, January 1988

Reconciliation and Dialogue	Democracy	Foreign Intervention	Disarmament
• Total compliance with the accords on dialogue, cease-fire, and amnesty decrees.	• Total compliance with accords on states of siege and emergency powers and promotion of democracy, press freedom, and pluralism. • An end to operation of special tribunals. • Real freedom in electoral processes. • Election of representatives to Central American Parliament.	Absolute need to promote specific verification of the halt of aid to irregular forces and nonuse of national territory for attacking other states.	Arms regulation; agreements on security and disarmament.

Verification of Accords	Integration and Development	Human Rights	
The Commission on Verification is thanked and its mission deemed concluded.	• The international community is thanked for supporting development in the region. • Social and economic conditions are considered the cause of the Central American conflict.	No agreements.	

Source: Emma Molina, "Los ejercitos siguen en la agenda regional," Boletín ACAFADE, June/July 1990, pp. 9–13.

TABLE 2.5 Esquipulas IV, February 1989

Reconciliation and Dialogue	Democracy	Foreign Intervention	Disarmament
• Nicaraguan commitment to promote reconciliation. • The FMLN in El Salvador is called on to cease hostilities.	• Nicaraguan commitment to promote democratization through reform of the Electoral Law, guarantees of press freedom, elections February 25, 1990, a balanced Supreme Electoral Tribunal, and the presence of UN and OAS electoral observers.	• President of Honduras requests the presence of a UN peacekeeping force to prevent its territory from being used by irregular forces. • Nicaragua agrees to withdraw its suit against Honduras in the International Court of Justice.	• Agreement on a joint plan to demobilize, repatriate, or relocate the Nicaraguan Resistance.

Verification of Accords	Integration and Development	Human Rights
No agreements.	No agreements.	No agreements.

Source: Emma Molina, "Los ejercitos siguen en la agenda regional," *Boletín ACAFADE,* June/July 1990, pp. 9–13.

TABLE 2.6 Esquipulas V, August 1989

Reconciliation and Dialogue	Democracy	Foreign Intervention	Disarmament
• Call on the FMLN to cease fire immediately. • Recognition of efforts of the government of Guatemala to promote reconciliation through a permanent dialogue.	No agreements.	• Encourage an out-of-court settlement of Nicaragua's suit against Honduras in the International Court of Justice.	• Approval of a joint plan for demobilization, repatriation, or relocation of the Nicaraguan Resistance.

Verification of Accords	Integration and Development	Human Rights
• Request to UN to verify security between Honduras and Nicaragua.	• The Central American Commission on Environment and Development is convoked.	No agreements.

Source: Emma Molina, "Los ejercitos siguen en la agenda regional," *Boletín ACAFADE,* June/July 1990, pp. 9–13.

TABLE 2.7 Esquipulas VI, December 1989

Reconciliation and Dialogue	Democracy	Foreign Intervention	Disarmament
• Condemnation of terrorist activities and support for President Alfredo Cristiani of El Salvador. • Call for the FMLN to cease hostilities.	No agreements.	• Request to the UN that the United States involve itself more directly in peace efforts. • El Salvador and Nicaragua exhorted to put an end to the distancing between their governments. • Insistence upon an out-of-court settlement between Honduras and Nicaragua.	• Request that funds for the Nicaraguan Resistance be channelled to the International Commission for Support and Verification. • Nicaraguan Resistance called upon to cease all actions against Nicaraguan electoral processes and civilian population. • Demobilization of Nicaraguan Resistance and FMLN considered fundamental. • Request for full deployment of UN peacekeeping force and an acceleration of efforts to prevent arms supplies to FMLN or Nicaraguan Resistance.

Verification of Accords	Integration and Development	Human Rights	
No agreements.	• International cooperation considered a parallel and indispensable element to regional peace efforts. • Gratitude expressed for progress of the Special Plan for Cooperation of the EEC and United Nations Development Program.	• Ratification of commitment to fully respect human rights.	

Source: Emma Molina, "Los ejercitos siguen en la agenda regional," *Boletín ACAFADE*, June/July 1990, pp. 9–13.

TABLE 2.8 Esquipulas VII, April 1990

Reconciliation and Dialogue	Democracy	Foreign Intervention	Disarmament
• Satisfaction over the upcoming dialogue among Salvadorans and the agreements among Guatemalans.	• Consolidation of democracy through clean electoral processes is pointed out (Honduras, Costa Rica, and Nicaragua). • Mention of Nicaragua's free and honest elections. • Recognition of Daniel Ortega's role in promoting and strengthening representative democracy. • Expression of satisfaction over the ratification of the Central American Parliament's constitution.	• Call for the U.S. government to support and contribute to the demobilization of the contras.	• Need for immediate demobilization of the Nicaraguan Resistance.

Verification of Accords	Integration and Development	Human Rights	Drugs
• Agreement to set a timetable for pending negotiations on security and disarmament.	• Agreement on points to discuss at the next summit: (1) economic integration, (2) integration of production, (3) foreign debt, (4) better distribution of social costs of economic adjustment. • Call to the international community to reinforce, consolidate, and broaden economic support. • Gratitude for offers by Canada and Japan to help overcome political and social obstacles and promote development. • Satisfaction expressed over progress of the Special Plan for Cooperation. • Call for financing commitments in the next meetings sponsored by the UNDP. • Acceptance of proposals by Colombia, Mexico, and Venezuela to provide aid for education, health, agriculture, and energy in Central America. • Satisfaction expressed over work of the Commission on the Environment and Development. • Reminder to Ministers of Health to develop new health initiatives for Central America.	• Ratification of commitment to respect human rights. • Support for the implementation of development programs for the displaced, repatriated, and refugee population. • Request to the international community to maintain and broaden its support for displaced persons.	• Agreement to eradicate drug trafficking.

Source: Emma Molina, "Los ejercitos siguen en la agenda regional," *Boletin ACAFADE,* June/July 1990, pp. 9–13.

TABLE 2.9 Esquipulas VIII, June 1990

Reconciliation and Dialogue	Democracy	Foreign Intervention	Disarmament
• Support for Guatemalan dialogue. • Progress noted in Salvadoran dialogue and FMLN again called upon to end violence.	• Central American Parliament constitutive treaty goes into effect.	• Insistence that Honduras and Nicaragua seek an out-of-court settlement.	• Call to proceed urgently with negotiations on security, verification, and arms control and limitation.

Verification of Accords	Integration and Development	Human Rights	Drugs
No agreements.	• Panama (present as an observer) invited to integrate with Central America. • Military powers exhorted to channel resources toward development in the region. • Gratitude expressed for international community's (especially Europe's) backing for regional integration. • Recognition of the need to strengthen the Central American Group to participate in international agencies and events. • Joint strategy outlined for participation in world trade. • Call for economic reactivation to end poverty in the framework of economic democracy. • Call for restructuring, bolstering, and reactivation of Central American integration to establish an economic community in the region. • Request for international help to renegotiate the foreign debt.	• In the first agreement of the meeting, the commitment to respect human rights is ratified.	• A meeting of antidrug authorities is planned.

(continues)

Table 2.9 (continued)

Verification of Accords	Integration and Development	Human Rights	Drugs
	• Call for strengthening activities of Inter-American Development Bank and Central American Bank for economic integration in area.		
	• Need expressed to reconstruct and transform productive systems so that social welfare is improved.		
	• Call to establish regional mechanisms to protect ecosystems.		
	• Call for promotion of programs of food security and self-sufficiency in basic grains.		
	• Support for education and for scientific and technical research.		
	• Call to study mechanisms for cooperation (especially the proposals of the Sanford Commission).		
	• Need recognized for improvements in health and protection of children and in education.		
	• Approval of the Special Plan for Cooperation and the creation of the Economic and Financial Commission as the coordinating agency.		

Source: Emma Molina, "Los ejercitos siguen en la agenda regional," Boletín ACAFADE, June/July 1990, pp. 9–13.

Notes

1. See Chapter 3 by Pedro Vuskovic, which includes an in-depth analysis of the main features of the Central American crisis, as well as the different approaches and development strategies that are being promoted.

2. The various alternatives for development and growth in Central America are also dealt with in Chapter 3.

3. This comparison between the two historical eras has been made by other authors. Guillermo Castro Herrera, "De ayer y mañana en la crisis de hoy," "El Gallo Ilustrado," *El Día,* 1 October 1989, p. 8.

4. Oscar Arias has stated, "The United States is frequently wrongheaded in its relationship with Latin America. The United States should learn that we Latin Americans agree with it about the ends, but not necessarily the means . . . one would expect more respect from the United States as to the Latin American way of achieving these ends. The United States has always thought in terms of war, generating great tension in the region's relationship with it, since Reagan believed that the contras were necessary to force Daniel Ortega to negotiate; he also tried to involve Costa Rica in the Central American war. Reagan wanted us to make our territory available—as he had in other countries—so that he could open a new southern front. I would not accept this. Then came the pressure." Interview by Miguel Reyes, *Excélsior,* 24 June 1990.

5. The first chapter, by Jesús Hernández, discusses the triangular events between Mexico, Central America, and the United States.

6. Fernando Solana, Ministry of Foreign Relations of Mexico, *El Día.* To expand on this, see Rodrigo Jauberth Rojas, *Costa Rica–México 1978–1986: de la concertación a la confrontación* (Mexico: PECA-CIDE, 1987), pp. 92ff.

7. Gabriel Aguilera, "Centroamérica: concertación y conflicto, una exploración," *Revista Nueva Sociedad* (July–August 1989), p. 35.

8. Report of the Binational Mexican-U.S. Commission, *El Día,* 11 March 1989, International Section.

9. Colin Danby suggests that during the 1980s, the amount of U.S. aid allocated to Central America was determined by two objectives: to defeat the left and to pressure the governments of the region to reform their economies along "structural adjustment" lines. Danby states that security objectives have determined where the greatest amounts of money have been allocated and that this foreign aid has been the main tool of U.S foreign policy; the level of U.S. aid to Central America will diminish to the degree that its security concerns in the area wane. Colin Danby, "Perspectivas sobre la ayuda de Estados Unidos a Centroamérica en la década de los 90" in *Cooperación externa y desarrollo en Centroamérica* (San José: Concertación Centroamericana de Organismos de Desarrollo, 1990).

10. Luis Herrera Lazo, "Geopolítica de la región: el sureste, el istmo, el Caribe," Seminar on the Southern Border, November 1984, mimeo.

11. This U.S. commitment to bring down Somoza can be seen in this interview with General Omar Torrijos: "When someone collaborates in a plan with the White House, things have to go well. [But] we had some difficult

moments. Rodrigo Carazo, President of Costa Rica, called me and said, 'Omar, the battle is lost. The number of dead returning from the southern front is impressive. The criminality of the National Guard is impressive. But equally impressive is the valor of this generation of unarmed Sandinistas, ill-equipped, and badly trained. . . . We knew that if we lost, the consequences could be disastrous for Costa Rica or Panama.' It was only when Carlos A. Pérez stationed planes from the Venezuelan Air Force in Costa Rica and Panama that we felt secure." Interview with Omar Torrijos, *Cuadernos do Terceiro Mundo* 29 (Brazil), (November–December 1980).

12. Richard Fagen, *Forging Peace: The Challenge of Central America* (New York: Basil Blackwell, 1987), p. 10. Furthermore, he points out, "in 1981, Washington launched a campaign of threats against Cuba, initiated a covert war against Nicaragua, and substantially increased military aid to El Salvador. In 1982, U.S. aid to the Salvadoran military doubled; in 1983, the United States constructed four military bases in Honduras and began maneuvers that brought thousands of U.S. troops to Central America. In 1984, military aid to El Salvador doubled again (and this time included AC-47 gunships), and the CIA mined the harbors of Nicaragua. In 1985, Green Beret advisors were sent to lightly armed—and formally neutral—Costa Rica. In 1986, military aid grants to Guatemala were renewed." In addition, see Christopher Dickey, "Central America: From Quagmire to Cauldron," *Foreign Affairs* 62 (January 1984), pp. 659–694.

13. Mario Ojeda, *Mexico: el surgimiento de una política exterior activa, Foro 2000* (Mexico: Secretaría de Educación Pública), pp. 144–145.

14. Fernando Volio Jiménez, *El militarismo en Costa Rica y otros ensayos* (San José, Costa Rica: Editorial Libro Libre, 1985), pp. 181–183. ·

15. Ibid., p. 199.

16. The contents of the model are a synthesis of the bibliography and documents consulted, chief among them, Claude Heller, "México, Estados Unidos, Centroamérica," in *La política exterior y la agenda México–Estados Unidos,* ed. Rosario Green and Peter Smith (Mexico: Fondo de Cultura Económica, 1989). See also, *Boletines de Coyuntura Centroamericana PECA-CIDE.*

17. Jorge G. Castañeda and Robert A. Pastor, *Límites en la amistad: México y Estados Unidos* (Mexico: Editorial Joaquín Mortiz-Planeta, 1989), p. 228.

18. To expand on this theme, see: David Brooks and William Hartung, "Presencia estratégica de EUA en América Latina," (Centro Latinoamericano de Estudios Estratégicos [CLEE], 1986, mimeo); José Rodolfo Castro, *La GBI y sus costos para C.A.* (Managua, Nicaragua: CRIES, 1987); Sara Miles, "The Real War: Low Intensity Conflict in Central America," in *NACLA Report on the Americas* 20 (April–May 1986), pp. 17–48; and Tom Barry, *Low Intensity Conflict: The New Battlefield in Central America* (Albuquerque: The Resource Center, 1986).

19. See Pedro Vuskovic Céspedes, *Fisionomía de una región* (Colección de libros Relaciones México-Centroamérica, PECA-CIDE), pp. 15–17.

20. Castañeda and Pastor, *Límites en la amistad,* pp. 230–233.

21. Declarations of President Oscar Arias Sánchez during his four-year administration, see information bulletins 1986–1990, PECA.

22. "What is clear," concludes Guadalupe González, "is that in Mexico we are dealing with a process of economic opening that is irreversible, given its depth and scope; nevertheless, how it will adapt and the influence it will exert on Mexico's foreign policy, understood in the broadest sense, are still unclear. This reflection is relevant despite the fact that it comes in the aftermath of these events, for it shows why Mexico since the end of the de la Madrid administration began to turn inward and re-evaluate its role in Central America and its position with respect to the United States." Guadalupe González, "Tradiciones y premisas de la política exterior de México," in Green and Smith, *La política exterior,* p. 52.

23. At this meeting, it is rumored, the principles and draft of the first plan were drawn up. The origins of the first and second version of the Arias Plan are controversial. There is talk about the participation of Democratic Senator Christopher Dodd, of President Arias' personal advisor, John Biehl, and others.

24. The unbridled demands of Nicaragua and the criticisms of the plan by Contadora, the Support Group, and the secretaries general of the United Nations and the OAS, plus Vinicio Cerezo's reluctance to sign an agreement that compromised Guatemala's neutrality and the change in attitudes mentioned in this chapter, may have combined to produce this beneficial metamorphosis.

25. See "Continue el forcejeo," *Envío* (Instituto Histórico Centroamericano, March 1987); Rodrigo Jauberth Rojas, *El Plan de Paz de Oscar Arias: ¿Intervencionismo de nuevo tipo o negociación regional?* (Mexico: CIDE, 1987). Furthermore, it should be noted that the distance that separated Cerezo and Arias at that time concerned Guatemala's differences with respect to an eventual regionalization of the armed conflict and not any real disagreement about U.S. objectives. The transformation of the Arias Plan from the first to the second version can only be ascribed to these elements.

26. "Oscar Arias' Peace Plan," *Miami Herald.* See also *Boletín Hemerográfico Informativo,* 1986–1989 (Mexico: Edit. CODELIDE [Coordinadora por la Defensa de las Libertades Democráticas en Costa Rica]).

27. El Rechazo del Informe CIUS. See also information in *Boletín Hemerográfico Informativo,* 1986–1989 (Mexico: Edit. CODELIDE).

28. Ibid. These arguments by Madrigal and the presidents of the area aroused a great international polemic, because this meant that they questioned the objectivity of the CIVS report and at the same time made it clear that there were other alternatives for democratization and self-determination.

29. Ibid.

30. "Centroamérica: punto clave en Caracas," *Universidad* (Costa Rica), 10 February 1989, p. 26.

31. Frida Modak, "Hasta que se hizo la cumbre," *El Día,* 14 February 1989.

32. President Arias has always declared himself "with Bush on 99 percent of the issues." The Arias-Cerezo margin for autonomy has become more and more oriented toward the Bush-Baker duo than exploring alternative policies; see Carlos Sarti, "La nueva política exterior norteamericana," *Revista FLACSO* 7 (April–May 1989), p. 1.

33. As to coexistence with Nicaragua, Gabriel Aguilera, "Centroamérica: concertación y conflicto," has some ideas, stating "the triumph of the Nicaraguan

insurgents situated the region's problems within a political crisis that had several manifestations. . . . The new order in Nicaragua meant a partial denial of the common elements that had served as the foundation for consensus in Central America, offering socialism instead of liberal democracy, a planned economy instead of a market economy, etc.," p. 9.

34. Modak, "Hasta que se hizo la cumbre," p. 15.

35. "Estados Unidos, pongale dientes al plan de paz de Centroamérica," *Excélsior,* 16 February 1989; *El Día,* 20 February 1989.

36. See "Bajo el gobierno de las sombras," published by the Christic Institute, cited by Carlos Morales in the newspaper "Universidad de Costa Rica," January 20–26, 1989. Also, the Costa Rican weekly *Adelante,* 20–26 January and 3–9 February 1989. Other sources: *La Otra Guatemala* and *Proceso,* 642 (1989).

37. "¿Persiguirá Bush métodos más suaves de estrangulamiento para Nicaragua?" Exclusive interview with Noam Chomsky by I. William Robinson, *El Día,* 15 February 1989. *Boletín Hemerográfico Informativo* (Mexico: Edit. CODELIDE).

38. Modak, "Hasta que se hizo la cumbre," p. 16.

39. "Cerezo no se atrevío a proponer medidas sobre Nicaragua," *El Día,* 4 March 1989.

40. *Envío* 96 (August 1989), p. 9.

41. *Envío* 96. In addition, see *Boletín Hemerográfico Informativo* and *Boletín Entre Líneas* (Programa de Análisis de la Realidad Centroamericana, ALFORJA, Costa Rica).

42. *New York Times* and *El Día* (IPS), 10 October 1989.

43. *El Día,* 28 September 1989, p. 17.

44. *Excélsior* and *El Día,* 18 October 1989, international sections. We will not comment on the implications of a foreign government publicly and "generously" financing a candidate's electoral campaign.

45. See Carlos Vilas, "Especulaciones sobre una sorpresa: las elecciones en Nicaragua," (preliminary version) and Rodrigo Jauberth, "Commentaries" (on the above). Papers presented in the cycle, "América Latina a la hora de las elecciones," March 1990, Instituto Mora, Mexico.

46. Vilas, "Especulaciones."

47. Adolfo Aguilar Zinser, "Los votantes nicaraguenses dieron a la democracia electoral un sentido concreto," *Excélsior,* 2 March 1990, Front Section, p. 26.

48. PACCA, *Changing Course* (Washington, D.C.: IPS, 1984). See also Morris J. Blachman, Douglas C. Bennett, William M. LeoGrande, and Kenneth Sharpe, "The Failure of the Hegemonic Strategic Vision" and "Security Through Diplomacy: A Policy of Principled Realism" in *Confronting Revolution,* ed. Blachman, LeoGrande, and Sharpe (New York: Pantheon, 1986), pp. 329–350 and 351–368.

49. Green and Smith, *La política exterior,* p. 28.

CHAPTER 3

Central America: Regional Crisis and Alternatives for Peace and Development

PEDRO VUSKOVIC

THIS CHAPTER DEALS WITH THE TRIANGULAR relationship between Mexico, Central America, and the United States, viewed from the Central American perspective.[1] Aspects of the regional agenda will therefore be emphasized, despite the fact that the Central American crisis itself is not the object of our study. Since Mexico's relations with the United States dominate the entire triangular relationship, other essays in this volume discuss them.

Mexican–Central American relations are also important for an understanding of this triangle.[2] However, they have been strongly influenced by Mexican-U.S. relations as well as by historical dynamics within Mexico; hence, they are explored in other parts of the book. The bonds between the United States and the Central American region are also essential to the relationship and are examined by Rodrigo Jauberth in Chapter 2.

A variety of new elements provide content to the relationship. U.S. efforts to consolidate a geoeconomic zone that will allow it to meet the global challenge of this decade are the general framework for inter-American relations. The rush to seal the recent trade agreements between Mexico and the United States is extremely important for the region, since these accords mean that we will be sharing a border with the United States in the very near future and facing grave political challenges and serious economic dilemmas. Central America will not be the same, nor will it be able to integrate itself into this process or a similar foreign relations framework. Furthermore, the kind of peace process that Central America has pursued has generated the political conditions for recent homogeneity in economic strategy at the same time that it has retained the structural elements that are at the root of the regional crisis.

The object of these notes is to visualize possible scenarios for the triangular relationship. To do this, it will be necessary to review the immediate background of the 1970s and 1980s, for it is here that the elements of the current agenda were born; finally, the chapter will conclude with an overview of possible future relations between the parties to the triangle.

Recent Background

The general background of the triangular relationship has been examined in the previous chapters. The object of this section is to accent some elements that will help explain the current relationship and provide clues to the future.

The 1970s

Toward the late 1970s, the triangular relationship could be characterized by three basic elements: first, U.S. influence over the region within its eroding hegemony; second, an active Mexican presence; and third, the simultaneous but separate impact of the convulsions in El Salvador, Guatemala, and Nicaragua.[3]

The United States maintained its hegemony over the region. By contrast, Mexico, whose aspirations of becoming an intermediate power had grown, favored change and increased its political presence in Central America to bolster its international position—particularly with respect to the United States. The possibilities that oil seemed to offer and the danger to its national security led Mexico to break its characteristic restraint with regard to its Central American foreign policy; hence, its interest in encouraging social movements and preventing foreign intervention.

In Central America, there was already (and still is) an economic, social, and political crisis, though the degree and nature varied from country to country. The crisis sprang from structural causes within the region itself, but its origins, evolution, and outlook were framed in the larger context of the international system and how the region fit into it—specifically where relations with the United States, and to a lesser extent Mexico, were concerned.

Between 1950 and 1980 Central America's gross domestic product (GDP) more than quadrupled; per capita GDP doubled. But this strong growth hid some enduring problems and worsened others. Income distribution remained sharply skewed: By the late 1970s, the wealthiest 20 percent in most Central American countries received around 60 percent of national income.

Central American economies became more open and vulnerable— while exports grew even faster than total GDP between 1950 and 1980, they were outpaced by imports, which stood by 1980 at roughly six-and-one-half times their level in 1950. Growth was accompanied by significant urbanization, an expansion in public services, and a broadening of the infrastructure network, without structural changes like agrarian reform.

As a result, the social structure became more complex and diversified. However, the varied and dynamic sectors that were emerging found their social demands for participation blocked by political systems allied with the interests of the oligarchies. The political regime associated with this pattern of dependent and concentrated growth was an authoritarian system with the military at its core. The extreme poverty and social inequality, plus the constant exclusion of large segments of the population from political participation, and the consistent refusal to legalize opposition parties generated broad-based insurgent movements.

By the late 1970s, the balance of relations was altered along three axes: the crisis in the relative international position of the United States, a greater activism on the part of Mexico, and unrest in each of the Central American countries.

The 1980s

The panorama of the 1980s was defined by U.S. efforts to restore its hegemony on a worldwide scale (particularly in Central America), the deepening economic crisis in the United States and Mexico, and U.S. constraints on Central America.[4]

During that decade, within a strategy aimed at rolling back social processes all over the world, Central America was the object of a messianic vision of U.S. destiny and its security interests, which presupposed the exercise of U.S hegemony as an indisputable right. Direct political aid was supported by three pillars: the "Caribbean Basin Initiative," official aid for development, and the doctrine of "low-intensity conflict," consisting of force, destabilization, and, more recently, "low-intensity democracy"—a term that we have coined to refer to the intervention in and exploitation of electoral processes as part of this strategy.[5] Thus, as a result of the U.S. "democratization" policy, there were virtually no direct coups by the armed forces in Central America during this time—which is not to say that the political processes that unfolded count as legitimately democratic. Nonetheless, the United States regionalized the Central American conflict with this policy, and, although without intending to, legitimized a presence in the region of foreign players like European and Latin American nations.

In the early 1970s Mexico's development strategy, based on industrialization through import substitution, underwent a crisis. However, it was not perceived for two reasons: the surge in oil prices and the ease with which Mexico could borrow abroad. These two factors permitted a decade-long postponement of the outbreak of the crisis, but at the price of an erosion of the resource supply (oil) and a debt of $86.1 billion by 1982. The debt burden was already unsustainable by 1982; it would either be repudiated or Mexico would have to find a mechanism to handle it. The latter option was possible through an infusion of fresh resources, which made the debt grow all the more rapidly and encouraged imports, leading to a negative balance of trade. This in turn required restricting imports and expanding exports, which generated a trade surplus, but at the same time unleashed a recession.

This is how trade policy became the fulcrum for economic policy. It implied the nullification of the domestic, or import substitution, strategy—there was no alternative but to open the economy under the new approach. The new Mexican strategy provided for three sources of growth: the maquiladora industry, the attraction of foreign investment, and export production.

In the meantime, Canada worked to expand its commercial integration with the United States through the Free Trade Agreement, signed in October 1987.[6] This drove Mexico to bolster its ties with the United States: In 1985, the two countries established a bilateral agreement on subsidies and compensatory taxes; in November 1987, a basic trade agreement was signed; in October 1989, Mexico's president signed six bilateral accords; finally, in June 1990, there was an agreement to open talks on eliminating all tariff barriers to bilateral trade (estimates are that it could take from one to three years to conclude the pact).

In the 1980s the economic, social, and political crisis in Central America sharpened. Economic growth stagnated, and per capita income in the region as a whole dropped from $1,126 in 1980 to $950 in 1989 (at 1980 prices), falling back to levels of the late 1960s.

Despite the Caribbean Basin Initiative, Central American exports fell roughly 40 percent during the 1980s, and the region's trade deficit grew more than 70 percent. The unit values of export products generally fell by an average of 25 percent; thus, the losses deriving from the deterioration in the terms of trade amounted to roughly $6 billion between 1980 and 1989.

While public spending for social programs was cut, real wages eroded, even where GDP had risen. All this is indicative of an ongoing process of income concentration.[7] Moreover, this increasing concentration of wealth did not generate increasing investment and demand within the region.[8]

Income from external resources, though positive by and large, was not used for development but to subsidize the war in the region.[9] The conflict in El Salvador entailed resource costs as high, relatively speaking, as those incurred by the United States in the Korean and the Vietnam Wars combined. The cost of the aggression in Nicaragua was double that. By middecade, "extra" military expenditures (over and above the "normal" levels of 1975) would be responsible for half the size of the fiscal deficits in Central America.[10]

The number of poor rose in both proportional and absolute terms. The reduction in health expenditures, among other things, during those years has meant that half the population has no access to basic services, that one in every ten children dies before the age of five, and that two-thirds of those who do survive suffer from malnutrition.[11] The halt in spending for education has led to an increase in the number of illiterates and a decline in the quality of education. The abandonment of infrastructure and basic services projects, together with the cumulative debt, keep 10 million people without potable water.

All this explains the persistence of the conflict throughout the 1980s. One measure of the intensification of the war is the rising toll in human lives. More Salvadorans and Nicaraguans have died in the "low-intensity conflict" than U.S. citizens in the Korean or Vietnam Wars. In terms of per capita losses, not even World War II had an impact on the United States similar to that of the civil war in El Salvador by 1989 or the aggression in Nicaragua.[12]

Another social expression of the conflict and the crisis that has had a significant impact on the agenda of the triangular relationship are population movements, which have touched some 15 percent of Central America's inhabitants.[13] The refugees are in the millions; of them, some 160,000 can be found within the region itself, about 300,000 are located in Mexico, and there is talk of a million Salvadorans in the United States. The number of people displaced within their countries is of a similar order of magnitude.

Another response to economic marginalization has been the growth of the "informal sector." Around 1982, 29 percent of the economically active metropolitan population of the region constituted the urban informal sector; in Nicaragua alone it has now burgeoned to 60 percent and has a tremendous impact in some service sectors, in macroeconomic terms.[14]

No less important is the rise in crime, insecurity, and civil violence in the region that has even led to the segregation of urban spaces, with wealthy and often foreign enclaves existing like islands in a sea of misery and territories controlled by gangs and organized crime.[15]

In the political sphere, the most significant change is the incorporation of new social groups into political life. Ethnic groups, base communities, women's associations, religious groups, people's organizations, human rights defense groups, union organizations for wage earners and guild societies for the self-employed, and other nongovernmental associations (like ecologists) began to build a social network that opened up spaces in Central America's political systems that cannot be shut without the risk of causing polarization and conflict. These associations were encouraged, moreover, by support from numerous U.S. nongovernmental organizations (NGOs) not connected with the policy of the Reagan and Bush administrations: Over 100 international NGOs contribute from $200 to $300 million annually; these funds are channeled through some 600 local organizations, which in turn connect up with 5 million Central Americans.[16]

In brief, during the 1980s there was a major change in the nature of the triangular relationship. The United States attempted to bolster its world presence, basically in military terms, and turned the region (most especially Nicaragua) into the privileged object of its foreign policy. In so doing, however, it facilitated the participation of a number of international players. The crisis in Mexico and Central America, moreover, made the task easier. Using the debt as a lever, the United States managed to co-opt Mexican activism and introduce the formation of a North American trade bloc as a medium-term goal. In Central America, however, far from being resolved, the problems worsened: If poverty and income concentration ignited the conflict during the 1970s, they fanned the flames in the 1980s.

Key Elements in the Current Relationship

This section explores the key elements in the triangular relationship—elements that spring in part from the immediate past and from the new environment as well. The instability of the international situation (and U.S. policy in this context), the formation of a North American trading bloc, the presence of foreign players, and the persistence of the structural underpinnings of the crisis in Central America constitute the ingredients of this triangle.

The International System

Around the world, national economies are becoming integrated into large regional economic and political blocs. The European Common Market is set for closer integration in 1992, and an Asian bloc appears to be emerging under Japan's leadership. The Free Trade Agreement between Canada and the United States has been in effect since 1987. The strengthening of these tendencies and, in particular, the incorporation of Mexico into this trade bloc will affect Central America's international position.

The links between the United States and Japan have yet to be defined. Will a "Pacific Bloc" emerge that includes the United States, or will there be competition between Asia and North America? According to one interpretation, the 1989 invasion of Panama can be viewed as the use of force to "contain" a powerful competitor, Japan.[17]

The consolidation of a strong Europe (the economic bloc with the largest GDP and trade in the world) could induce that region to alter the nature of its presence in Central America.

Another factor that is not entirely clear is the path that the worldwide economic reconversion will take. Are we in the presence of a new and protracted expansionary cycle or is there a possibility of stagnation in the world economy (especially the U.S. economy), with its consequent side effects in Mexico and Central America?[18]

Certainly, the world has not yet defined the conditions necessary for the insertion of dependent countries into the international economy. When such conditions are determined, though, the difficulties that lead to a definitive readjustment will "change the rules of the game" for the triangular relationship.

All this is relevant in terms of the role that other powers can play in Central America. When it raised what were essentially local conflicts to a regional level, the United States created the conditions conducive to the involvement of various international forces, such as European and Latin American governments; thus as a side effect, it provoked by other means exactly what it wished to eradicate: the foreign presence in the region. Ten years later, there would be a whole field of players, and Central American policy would be less polar; other forces, with other objectives and methods that sometimes converged, sometimes diverged, and sometimes clashed, would be an obstacle to the implementation of U.S. policy, significantly reducing its room to maneuver.

In the late 1970s other players in the region were almost nonexistent. By the end of the 1980s the United States was still the main source of development aid to Central America, accounting for 36 percent of such assistance to the region. Latin America, however (with the exception of Cuba), accounted for 22 percent and Europe 14 percent. During the 1980s European aid to Central America quadrupled, reaching 8.3 percent of its worldwide total.[19]

Right now, the United States continues to exert a substantial but no longer exclusive influence. As the international geoeconomic context determines, this is potentially important in the development of new scenarios. In the meantime, the United States will be obliged to share the decision about who receives economic aid and under what conditions with other parties.

In summary, the international alignment of forces may alter the framework for Central America's insertion into the world market, especially if a geoeconomic confrontation between the different blocs ensues. While the trend is for the region to gravitate toward integration into a North American common market, the presence of other players and the appearance of other, divergent interests in the region are elements that may alter it.

The United States

In principle, the Bush administration is continuing its policy of regrouping U.S. hegemony by means of the three instruments mentioned above. The events in Panama from 1988 to late 1989, as well as in Nicaragua in early 1990, are also manifestations of the policy of low-intensity conflict. However, in the future, the economic mechanisms are likely to be given priority, with the external debt the main instrument; Central America's debt amounted to nearly $20 billion in 1989 and implies a $14.3 billion debt service payment between 1989 and 1997. While the debt is not the cause of the crisis, it remains an important determinant of Central America's future.[20]

The changes in the international system and the new global challenges require modifications in strategy. Bush's June 1990 "Enterprise for the Americas" initiative and his efforts to get Japan and Europe to supplement dwindling U.S. aid to Central America are manifestations of this. Central America figured heavily in the June 1990 initiative, even though the scope of the project is rather limited.[21] It coincides with the privatization strategy already in vogue in the region. The problems for Central America will be not so much the direction of change as the pace—especially where lowering trade barriers is concerned—first, because of U.S. protectionism and second, because the Central American economies are unprepared for competition.

At almost the same time the Bush initiative was announced, James Baker proposed that (additional) foreign aid be coordinated among the

United States, Japan, Canada, the European Economic Community (EEC), the Inter-American Development Bank (IDB), and the World Bank, in addition to Venezuela and Mexico. With this proposal, the United States plans to share the economic burden with its allies, reducing the flow of U.S. resources toward the region. It is also attempting to exploit its position of dominance to recover hegemony over the foreign presence and decrease the relative autonomy created for Central America by Esquipulas in the wake of the difficulties in the developed world.[22] In so doing it would make it possible for the United States to bring Central America's development strategy into line. Furthermore, the adoption of the criterion that funding will be conditioned on the Central American countries' maintenance of "a firm respect for human rights and the rule of law" suggests that Washington determines what constitutes human rights and law and decides when they are violated.

Thus, while U.S. policy toward the region continues to pursue hegemony, the content of the policy and the methods for ensuring that it is carried out are turning toward the geoeconomic sphere.

North American Integration and Its Repercussions for Central America

One expression of the renewed efforts to broaden the U.S. perimeter of relations is the construction of a North American common market.

At present, over one-quarter of U.S. exports are destined for its immediate neighbors, and one-fifth of its imports derive from them. Mexico and Canada send 64 and 77 percent of their respective exports to the U.S. market, which generates 64 and 68 percent of their imports, respectively.[23] Direct foreign trade between Canada and Mexico accounts for less than 1 percent of the total volume moved within North America. However, the figure is far higher for indirect trade through the United States. *Thus, there is already a de facto trade bloc in North America, even though it has not yet been formalized.* Two separate agreements do exist, however: one between the United States and Canada, and the other between the United States and Mexico. In addition, in March 1990, Canada and Mexico agreed to open up a "new era of trade."

We are witnessing unprecedented changes in the economic policy of the countries of North America, but these changes are not necessarily moving in the same direction; while Canada and Mexico are progressing toward greater openness, the United States is undergoing its greatest protectionist phase since the 1930s. This instability has caused great uncertainty and makes it difficult to make any predictions. In any case, events in the coming years will change Central America's trade policy and its international economic relations, with effects extending well into the next century.

Nearly two-thirds of Mexico's exports are channeled to the United States, but in terms of income the U.S. market actually represents closer to 80 percent.[24] Moreover, two-thirds of direct foreign investment in Mexico is of U.S. origin. It can therefore be said that the Mexican-U.S. common market is already fully operative in terms of merchandise, a good percentage of services, and capital flows.

Mexico has virtually no substitute for the U.S. market, especially when it comes to manufacturing exports, while for the United States, Mexico ranks as its number three trading partner. Although the United States does have other options, they are limited, as recent experience would indicate. Mexico's $8.6 billion cutback in imports from the United States from 1981 to 1983 had a major impact on the U.S. trade deficit, since the United States could not find alternative markets.

Mexico is already a major market for the United States. Furthermore, it is a highly significant potential market. Given its income distribution, Mexico can add 8 million consumers with an average income of over $10,000 annually. In addition, for a variety of reasons (among them Mexico's protracted economic recession, inflation, population growth, and migration) Mexico's situation and U.S.-Mexican relations occupy an important place in the U.S. international agenda, especially for the Bush administration. All this indicates a trend toward closer economic ties that will ultimately lead to an unequal interdependence.

Based on experience, we can predict that economic synchronization will result in foreign policy synchronization, manifested largely through foreign aid grants and trade concessions.[25] The emerging association of foreign policy with unequal interdependence in North America is establishing a different framework for Central America's insertion into the international system and changing the familiar parameters of its relationships. The future holds new scenarios with new room to maneuver and new constraints that must be analyzed.

Central America is not an important market for the components of this North American trade bloc. The Central American market does not account for even 1 percent of the exports or imports of Canada or the United States. It accounts for between 1 and 2 percent of Mexico's exports, mostly petroleum, but far less than 1 percent of Mexico's imports. Nevertheless, in view of its level and distribution of income, Central America represents a potential market of 2.5 million consumers with an annual per capita income of over $10,000.

For Central America, the problem is different. In 1989 North American (Canadian, U.S., and Mexican) markets were the destination of 45 percent of its exports and the origin of 40 percent of its imports. The

United States accounted for most of this trade, 31 percent of Central American imports and 43 percent of the region's exports. In 1981 the United States received only 31 percent of Central American exports, so its role as Central America's largest trading partner has increased.[26] Mexico, Central America's neighbor to the north, does not have substantial economic ties to the region, except as an oil supplier. Canada's relevance as a Central American trading partner is negligible.

In terms of trade and economic relations in general, without offering any value judgments, the establishment of a North American common market is likely to have no immediate direct impact on Central America, in contrast to that of the Free Trade Agreement on Mexico. However, it may have an indirect impact in the sense that Mexico's comparative advantages are similar to those of Central America (cheap labor and tropical natural resources). Moreover, the growth of the maquiladora industry will tend to concentrate in Mexico and, obviously, direct foreign investment will find additional incentives to gravitate toward that country instead of Central America. It may be that in the medium term, there will be greater trade opportunities with Mexico, from which imports could be purchased that are now bought from the United States.

From the Central American standpoint, the options for meeting the challenge of northern integration are limited, for the region really has no influence. Its room to maneuver is narrow, since it lacks the infrastructure necessary to produce competitive manufactured goods up to the standards of the North American or even the current Mexican market. At the same time, a drastic fall off in demand for Central American goods can be anticipated. This has already begun to be felt with the region's main export products, and Central America has no alternative goods to export in their stead.[27] In addition, there has been an erosion in the comparative advantage that cheap labor represents, because of technological changes that displace it in the manufacturing process, sensitivities that could develop in the United States in response to the flood of Asian goods assembled in Mexico and Central America, and Mexico's perception that it can negotiate the exploitation of its own labor resources from a position of privilege, to the disadvantage of its neighbors to the south.

Furthermore, there is a possibility that the U.S. market will be closed to some countries for political reasons. This is highly improbable where Mexico is concerned, for trade between the two countries is largely carried out between enterprises (which is not what occurs in the region to the south). However, in the case of Central America, it is much more of a possibility. The use of the market as a political tool is highly probable, feasible, and has already occurred: It was used against Nicaragua from 1985 to 1990 and against Panama from 1988 to 1989.

In brief, the development of a North American common market will create new dilemmas for Central America that will alter both the framework for its insertion into the external market and its relationship with the United States and Mexico.

The Central American Agenda

Another key element in the content of the triangular relationship springs from the internal dynamic of the region. The situation in Central America is dominated by a negotiations process aimed at resolving the region's conflicts and, likewise, efforts to devise alternative development strategies in one or another direction. The winding down of the regional conflict, the weariness of the contenders, and international arbitration of the disputes—in sum, the "pacification" of Central America—do not imply a resolution of the causes of the crisis, nor attention to the origins of the confrontation.

Actually, for ten years the international community kept up a positive net flow of resources to the region, financing an economic "breather" in the troubled area, after which the crisis and the conflict took up where they had left off a decade earlier. Thus, Central America bears the heavy burden of the leftover problems of the 1970s, and the new challenges of the times, since both the region and the world have changed. In point of fact, the basic problems of sovereignty, democracy, and development of the 1970s remain the same.

Even with the region pacified, its military expenditures reduced, and its external debt forgiven, the crisis is unlikely to be resolved. In economic terms, the future is not promising, for there has been an erosion of productive resources: human resources, capital, the environment—expressed in migration and the "brain drain," the deterioration and obsolescence of infrastructure and equipment, and environmental degradation and the exhaustion of natural resources.[28]

Thirty-seven million people will inhabit Central America by the year 2000. The challenge is immense. In terms of economic growth, just to maintain the per capita income level (which, given the distribution of income, has led to continuing political explosions) would require GDP to grow at 3 percent annually. To provide jobs for just the new people who will join the work force (not to resolve current problems), ten times the number of full-time jobs currently available will have to be created.[29] The situation is no different for food, health care services, education, and housing.

At the political level, new players must be acknowledged who have not yet been incorporated into the system—in particular, popular social forces that have traditionally been excluded. There is a profound instability within the alliances that sustained the old social order and a relative lack of clear goals, or at least a set pace for them, among society's dominant groups. This can be attributed to changes that have taken place in the local ruling sectors and has been manifested in the following: Private enterprise has tended to transfer its vigor and leadership from traditional sectors toward new forces that have found their expression in institutions like the Salvadoran Development Foundation (FUSADES) in El Salvador or the Coalition for Development Initiatives (CINDE) in Costa Rica; such groups have been encouraged by direct funding from the U.S. Agency for International Development (AID). In addition, the terms of the political negotiation do not in themselves guarantee the mediation instruments to prevent the conflict from reverting to violence. In this context, a number of strategies have struggled to impose their solution to the crisis.

Foreign and multinational interests, as well as the "modern" and "competitive" sectors of the local ruling classes, support a strategy of subordinating the Central American countries to the world market. This will result in an atomized regional relationship between the individual countries of the isthmus and the rest of the world, relegating possibilities for integration to a secondary plane.

In the macroeconomic dynamic, the acquisition of foreign exchange has chiefly been what has guided the productive apparatus, setting the pace and determining the level of the reactivation. This productive orientation is grounded in the growth of the nontraditional export sectors, the assembly of manufactured and agro-industrial goods (supported in the Caribbean Basin Initiative) as the key to growth, direct foreign investment linked to the reexport (or maquiladora) industries and, eventually, the exploitation of Central America's geographical position.

From this standpoint, structural changes like the privatization of public enterprises, reductions in social spending, and economic deregulation based on a broad criticism of the outsized growth of social expenditures have been considered the main causes of the financial disequilibria. In addition, such changes are seen as productive reconversion, with a view toward enhancing international competitiveness by creating new comparative advantages in the export sectors (incorporating advanced technologies where necessary), especially through cost reductions facilitated by a contraction in wages.

In contrast, diverse nongovernmental international forces from the United States, Canada, and Europe, plus a broad range of local social sectors—modern factions of the ruling strata on a national level, middle-class groups, and not a few sectors of the traditional working class (salaried employees, laborers, and campesinos long linked to the formal sectors)—have promoted a strategy aimed at creating a "greater room to maneuver" with regard to external sector constraints and eradicating extreme poverty. Within this framework, the point of regional integration would be to permit the Central American economies to deal with the international markets as a group from a regional platform.

This orientation seeks the elimination of the economic, social, and political structures deriving from the preservation of precapitalist colonial patterns (fundamentally, through agrarian reform) and the political problems that they imply, a greater capacity for state action through the socialization of strategic sectors (such as banks and foreign trade) and a more audacious management of economic policy, with social expenditures geared toward "complementary" activities designed to eradicate critical poverty.

Moreover, the combination of revolutionary forces and the demands by many emerging forces—sectors of the population by tradition forcibly excluded from participating—may give rise to a different strategy based on autonomy, the satisfaction of basic needs, and a restructuring of production to reduce the heterogeneity of the domestic productive apparatus and promote integration as the basis for economic growth.

Two Scenarios

The potential scenarios for relations obviously derive from a combination of the elements and values examined in the previous section. The object of this section is to explore possible variations with a look to the future.

The Trend Projection Scenario

A projection of the current trend, the contradictions of the situation notwithstanding, indicates a strong North American bloc (led by the United States and including Canada and Mexico) with close ties to Latin America and the Pacific, with the participation of Japan. In the context of a major restoration of trade between Latin America and the United States, we can visualize fluid relations between the North America bloc and the countries of Latin America, as well as special relationships with certain Central American countries, Costa Rica, for example.

The United States, for its part, may rectify its economic imbalances with a slightly expansive but stable period. This would allow it to maintain a policy toward Central America that pairs two great objectives: to preserve its hegemony and to add on Central America as an extension of the recently incorporated Mexican market. This would be possible through the mechanisms previously described. Without contributing any more to the financial flows already committed, the United States would endeavor to optimize aid resources by employing them regionally and mobilizing new resources—financial organizations and other world powers. This is the meaning of the aforementioned Baker proposal.

Other players in the area would be increasingly constrained. The withdrawal of the USSR and Eastern European presence would alter the global challenge and the anatomy of resource flows toward the region. As for the official aid for development, there is rising unanimity that it should be channeled more toward promoting growth than fostering structural changes or attending to social needs, both of which favor U.S. policy objectives.

Europe remains an unknown quantity, but it is most likely to lower its profile. First, Germany, the dominant country in the bloc, is an EEC member with little interest in Central America; second, Europe must meet the challenge of absorbing the Eastern European countries or turning them into its geoeconomic zone. In any case, even if Europe could maintain a presence with a certain degree of independence from the United States, the latter could still find means other than economic to restrict its movements.

Finally, the orientation of the Central Americans themselves would make this a viable scenario. In recent years, the conditionality of financial flows toward Central America has steered stabilization and adjustment policies toward greater openness and privatization, with an emphasis on the promotion of nontraditional exports and the maquiladora industry. Up to now, these efforts have not constituted a "pure" application of the orthodox neoliberal paradigm, but they are generally oriented around its basic premises. Once the main policy elements entailed in its application are defined, a new phase of tight constraints and homogenization will fully begin in Central America—and the external debt is most likely to be the key instrument.

Because of its content and format, the meeting of Central American presidents in Antigua, Guatemala, on June 17, 1990, seems to have been a prologue to a strategy of development under U.S. hegemony. This meeting is relevant, for a set of long-term measures began to emerge here. According to the presidents, these steps are aimed at promoting the sustained development of Central America through an outward-oriented strategy and establishing mechanisms for consultation and coordination to boost the participation of the Central American economies in international trade. The ultimate goal of this strategy is the efficient, vigorous reinsertion of the region into the world market, with the specific hope of allowing the Central American nations to take advantage of Mexico's incorporation into the North American common market. The strategy's orientation would facilitate a rapid opening of the economies and their integration into the world of the

North. Briefly then, for all intents and purposes, the U.S. border would lie south of Darién, Panama.

In line with this, integration itself is undergoing real changes. From a process that tended to augment economic potential, forging links between national productive structures, it has turned into "an integration oriented toward third countries, in line with the international markets, to deal with the world economy as an organized bloc in a much more competitive fashion"—an association for trade and negotiations, it would seem.

The above paragraphs describe what we visualize as the trend projection. This would appear to be the most viable scenario, the one with the most possibilities. However, there are elements that can alter these tendencies. Thus, it is not enough to study only the most viable scenarios; we must construct alternatives, based on an "objective image" (i.e., what we would like to have) and the room to maneuver that reality ultimately allows.

The Greater Autonomy Scenario

The goal of greater autonomy is not merely an exercise in optimism, but derives from the obligation to acknowledge room for players who can alter the trend through their own policy.

Many events and efforts could lead to a different scenario. Through cooperation with other powers, the geoeconomic struggle could help the region forge its ties to North America in a much more integrated manner, with relative autonomy created by the counterweight of its economic and political relations with other blocs (a topic discussed by Gilberto Castañeda in Chapter 4).

The development of the international system may lead to the creation of powerful European and Asian blocs that have major differences with the United States. In that context, there would be no Pacific Rim bloc, at least, not one based on a substantive relationship between the United States and Japan. This would provoke the presence of external powers with their own agenda in Central America. These powers might or might not coincide with U.S. policies, allowing the Central Americans a certain latitude. For example, the reaction to the Baker plan to consolidate foreign aid under a U.S. design has met with resistance. The argument for a parallel arrangement with the so-called Group of 24 (in which the United States currently participates under the aegis of the EEC to channel aid to Eastern Europe) is not accepted by the Europeans for Central America.

This scenario, moreover, would probably unfold in a situation where the United States has to deal with the challenges of its economic imbalances (the fiscal and trade deficits). In this environment, Latin America's own position could be different, with more subregional variations and a greater degree of autonomy from the United States and its policies.

The consequences of all this would be manifold. For example, with external support, regional integration could swing toward a strengthening of the productive sector to meet the requirements of the domestic market. In this regard, the contributions of the EEC to boost trade, plus the reactivation of the Central American Common Market could encourage production for the home market.

In that context, a greater Mexican voice in the North American common market would mean some constraints on its relations with other blocs. Right now, Mexico is not only moving rapidly toward integration with the United States, it is also forging ties with Europe and Japan. Naturally, the precise significance of this phenomenon will depend not only on Mexico's plans, but on the international climate.

However, greater autonomy will also depend on Central American determination. Until now, increased autonomy was linked to the design of development strategies aimed at bending fully to the winds from the North. Now though, there are a number of factors that can alter this trend.

On the one hand, the imposition of the "new" policy in Central America is occurring at a time when the limitations of the most extreme neoliberal experiments of the Southern Cone have been exposed. Moreover, their rather limited successes have tended to broaden the margin for dissent by important sectors of the local ruling class with the pattern of development promoted by the international financial agencies and the United States. This is evident, for example, in the more open attitude toward the reactivation of the Central American Common Market now found in some sectors that only a few years ago had declared it moribund and useless. Finally, the local ruling classes have begun to perceive that the social costs of adjustment at any price can render their plans to open the economy politically inviable.

Naturally, the content, nuances, and sociopolitical forces behind any efforts to construct a more autonomous scenario are varied and cover a wide range of possibilities that it is not within our purview to analyze.

Conclusions

This chapter has described the elements that we consider crucial to the relationship between Mexico, Central America, and the United States. Our examination concludes that:

1. Four simultaneous dynamics make up the triangular relationship: the evolution of the international system; the U.S. situation and that country's resulting policies; what is happening with and within Mexico; and the evolution of the Central American crisis and the region's plans. The parties to the triangle have been linked chiefly by: external debt and trade policy in the case of Mexican-U.S. relations; low-intensity conflict and U.S. economic policy (Caribbean Basin Initiative and official aid for development) in the case of Central American–U.S. relations; and diplomatic policy and Mexico's energetic assistance in the case of Mexican–Central American relations.

2. The formation of a North American common market, the persistence of the underlying structural factors in the Central American crisis, and the use of the external debt as a political and economic tool have been the main features of the current situation and have been instrumental in determining the trend.

3. The evolution of the international climate has been a key factor in the situation of the triangular relationship and its outlook. Central America, a region with scant potential, situated on the immediate perimeter of the United States, has been subject to the tendencies, instabilities, and troubles of the international system. Nevertheless, this system offers not only limitations and tight constraints, but creates opportunities as well.

4. The U.S. presence and its activities have been and continue to be a determinant of the region's future. The country's military presence, political and ideological influence, and strong economic commitment make it the main extraregional player in Central America. However, partly due to its own policies, the United States no longer enjoys an exclusive presence in the region.

5. Despite the vulnerability of the region, Central American determination and skill can create room for autonomy to meet its challenges with plans developed by and for Central Americans. Judging the events of the past decade apart, the Central Americans reveal the potential for maintaining significant margins of autonomy, although under extremely adverse conditions.

Notes

1. In what follows, Central America will be considered five countries (excluding Panama and Belize), except where otherwise indicated.

2. In this regard, see the collection *Relaciones Centroamérica-México* by various authors (México: PECA-CIDE, 1986).

3. Actually, the relative position of the United States as the number one power in the world has been eroding since the postwar era. By the 1970s, a

series of circumstances gave a more balanced character to the triangularity. The Reagan administration—which we do not presume to judge in this work—attempted to restore the leadership position of the United States through an emphasis on military aspects; however, this did not imply a resolution of the basic disequilibria in U.S. power. Thus, while the structural underpinnings of U.S. leadership continued to erode, its interventionist policy in Central America was reinforced.

4. Thus, in another way, we reiterate the subordination of Mexican–Central American relations to Mexican-U.S. relations. These latter were almost entirely exclusive, since from the time of its independence, Mexico had constraints imposed on its relations with Central America. This topic is covered by Jesús Hernández in Chapter 1.

5. Naturally, neither trade measures, official aid for development, economic destabilization, nor the exploitation of democratic processes are new tools for promoting the more or less coherent objectives of the various U.S. agencies that execute the country's foreign policy; however, during this period, such activities were carried out under the aegis of low-intensity conflict, which directed the other components of U.S. policy.

6. The Free Trade Agreement provides for the total elimination of tariffs and administrative obstacles in the space of ten years. See Gerardo Bueno, "El tratado de Libre Comercio entre Estados Unidos y Canadá," *Comercio Exterior* 37, 11 (Mexico, November 1987); Paul Wonnacott, "The United States and Canada: The Quest for Free Trade," *Policy Analyses in International Economics* 16 (March 1987); Pedro F. Castro Martínez, "El Acuerdo de Libre Comercio entre Estados Unidos y Canadá," *Comercio Exterior* 39 (April 1989); Eduardo Morales Pérez and Antonio Galicia Escoto, "Acuerdo de Libre Comercio entre Estados Unidos y Canadá," Banco de México Office of International Organizations and Agreements (Document Series, 25, January 1988). Canada's trade volume is estimated to increase to $5 billion per year, creating 350,000 new jobs in Canada by 1995.

7. CEPAL, *Centroamérica: situación actual y perspectivas de la economía y la integración* (Mexico: 1989).

8. This is evident in capital flight: In 1986 there were $2.5 billion deposited in U.S. bank accounts under the name of Central Americans. See International Commission for the Recovery and Development of Central America, *The Report of the International Commission for Central American Recovery and Development* (Durham and London: Duke University Press, 1989), p. 23. For every export dollar earned in Honduras, 58 cents leave the country; in Costa Rica the figure is 60 cents, according to René L. Cáceres and S. Seninger, "Redes regionales, estructuras jerárques y fuga de la riquieza en Centroamérica: un análisis de la cadena de Markov," *El Trimestre Económico* 49, 3 (July–September 1982), as cited by René L. Cáceres and George Irving, "The Reconstruction of the CACM and European Cooperation in Central America," in *Central America: The Future of Economic Integration,* ed. George Irvin and Stuart Holland (Boulder: Westview Press, 1989).

9. Pedro Vuskovic Céspedes, *Centroamérica: posibilidades estratégicas de los distintos espácios de desarrollo* (Working document) (Mexico: PECA-CIDE, 1988).

10. Pedro Vuskovic Céspedes, *Centroamérica: fisionomía de una región* (Mexico: CIDE, 1986).

11. Spending under the health system declined from roughly $15–20 per capita at the start of the decade to $8–10 in 1987, except for Costa Rica, where it fell from $30 to $16. A. I. García and E. Gomariz, "Las mujeres definan el futuro," in *América Central hacia el 2000,* ed. Edelberto Torres-Rivas (coordinator) (Venezuela: Nueva Sociedad, 1989), p. 145; International Commission for the Recovery and Development of Central America, *The Report of the International Commission* (Durham, N.C.: Duke University, 1989).

12. Vuskovic Céspedes, *Centroamérica: fisionomía de una región.*

13. International Commission for the Recovery and Development of Central America, *Report.*

14. Pedro Vuskovic Céspedes and René Escoto, "Algunos problemas y alternativas de los pequeños países periféricos de América Latina: el caso de Centroamérica y el Caribe" (Nicaragua: CRIES, 1989), mimeo.

15. René Poitevin, *Guatemala: un futuro democrático incierto en América Central hacia el 2000* (Venezuela: Nueva Sociedad, 1989).

16. International Commission for the Recovery and Development of Central America, *Report.*

17. Xabier Gorostiaga, *After the Panama Invasion, What Next?* (Nicaragua: CRIES, 1990).

18. Orlando Caputo, "Algunas características fundamentales del capitalismo en los años 70 y 80," (Preliminary research) (Mexico: PEDEI-UAP, March 1987).

19. Pedro Vuskovic Céspedes, *Centroamérica: disyuntivas del desarrollo* (Preliminary research) (Managua: CRIES, October 1990).

20. CEPAL, *Notas económicas de América Latina y El Caribe* (Mexico: 1990); World Bank, *World Debt Tables 1989* and *Annual Report* (Washington, D.C.: various years); Bulmer-Thomas et al., "Políticas de ajuste en Centroamérica," *Cuadernos de Ciencias Sociales* 9 (Costa Rica: FLACSO, 1987).

21. Pedro Vuskovic Céspedes, "Iniciativa para las Américas: ¿nueva versión de la Doctrina Monroe?" *Pensamiento Propio* 73 (Nicaragua, August 1990).

22. Indeed, during the last five years, despite the differences among the countries of the region and U.S. policy to undo initiatives with a relatively autonomous regional perspective (however limited, incoherent, and contradictory) this was only possible because of the dissension among the Northern countries.

23. United Nations, "Proyecto regional para la superación de la pobreza. Bases para una Estrategia y un Programa de acción regional," RLA/86/004, July 1988; *Comercio Exterior,* Anexo Estadística, 39, 5, (May 1989).

24. Sidney Weintraub, *México frente al acuerdo de libre comercio Canadá–Estados Unidos* (Mexico: Ed. Diana, 1989).

25. David Lewis and Al Gariazzo, *Europa Comunitaria y Centroamérica: de la solidaridad a los negocios* (Preliminary research) (Managua: CRIES, 1989).

26. *Series Estadísticas Seleccionadas de Centroamérica,* SIECA 22 (Guatemala, April 1989).

27. The prospects for "traditional" export goods, in terms of a substantial and stable growth of the market and prices, are poor. The possibilities for "nontraditional" goods are limited, for a number of reasons. Nevertheless, the opening of Central America's economies demands an effort to expand this potential, in view of the region's external gap.

28. An extensive bibliography on this subject is cited in this text. International Commission for the Recovery and Development of Central America, *Report*; Jeffrey H. Leonard, *Natural Resources and Economic Development in Central America* (Washington, D.C.: IIED, 1987).

29. Vuskovic Céspedes and Escoto, "Algunos problemas y alternativas."

CHAPTER 4

Central American–
Mexican–U.S. Relations:
Present and Future

GILBERTO CASTAÑEDA

"He awoke and the dinosaur was still there."
—Augusto Monterroso

IN THE RECENT PAST, CLOSE TIES BETWEEN Central America and Mexico have favored social change in the region, counteracting and in some cases even reducing U.S. influence in the region. These ties were especially important in the late 1970s with the rise of revolutionary movements in Central America.

The change in the triangular relationship has been characterized by a strengthening of relations between Mexico and the United States, chiefly at the economic level but with important political repercussions; at the same time, there has been a weakening of relations between Central America and Mexico on the political and diplomatic levels. This is especially visible in Mexico's diminished participation in the search for solutions to the social confrontations in Nicaragua, El Salvador, and Guatemala and has been accompanied by a reinforcement of U.S. hegemony in the region.

These trends undercut a long-standing historical relationship that has benefitted movements for social change in Central America and helped Mexico uphold its principles as a sovereign nation despite U.S. harassment.[1] A key question is whether Mexico will accelerate its current political and diplomatic retreat from the area and how much more it will tend to base its regional role on economic relations.

To establish whether such extremes are likely, we must determine how much the historical terms of the Central America–Mexico–United States triangle have been modified. U.S. interference in the region has grown in recent years, especially in economic and ideological terms, and has entailed new military aspects. Particularly in evidence is an interventionism grounded in the war on drugs and a larger direct military presence, of which the 1989 invasion of Panama is no more than one facet. The Central American countries are also becoming increasingly dependent on the United States, despite the fact that they are receiving less U.S. economic aid.

The need for social change in Central America remains pressing, especially in Guatemala and El Salvador. International pressure has fostered peace negotiations under the assumption that they will lead to political stability and open up opportunities for development. But so far, negotiations have not proven sufficient to effect the changes that countries like Nicaragua, El Salvador, and Guatemala so urgently need or to produce stability.

The cause of instability and backwardness in Central America continues to be a highly exclusive and concentrated socioeconomic structure subordinated to foreign interests, chiefly those of the United States. There is immediate prospect for change, especially given the current world context. The current modifications in Central American–Mexican–U.S. relations portend an even greater subordination of the region's countries to their powerful neighbor to the north. This subordination will increase as the world situation pressures the weaker countries and limits their possibilities for self-determination and development.

It would appear that Central America has no choice in the medium term but, as in times past, to suffer "malign neglect" by the United States. The region will regain importance for the United States only when some danger—a new victory for the forces of revolution, for example—jeopardizes U.S. interests and goals, as defined by the administration of the moment. Only then will the needs and viewpoint of the region be considered in any way.

The implications of the changes in the triangular dynamic for Central America go beyond foreign policy issues, despite their importance (see Chapter 2). They also touch on the prospects for the development of the region and each of its countries (see Chapter 3) and include a consideration of migratory flows toward Mexico and through it to the United States, the problems of drug trafficking, and payment of the external debt—aspects that are analyzed here.

This chapter addresses:

1. The context of Central American–Mexican–U.S. relations, including the effects of current global changes on Latin America in general and Central America in particular. The analysis seeks to contribute

to the considerations about Central American–Mexican–U.S. relations that appear in Chapter 3.

2. Mexican-U.S. relations: their main parameters, current changes,
   and possible evolution.

3. Mexican–Central American relations in the context of Mexican-
   U.S. relations, stressing the most relevant implications of Mexican-
   U.S. relations for the area, particularly with regard to the foreign
   debt, regional migration, and the war on drugs.

The Context of Central American–Mexican–U.S. Relations

Global Overview

A series of changes in the world economy has had considerable impact
on Latin America in general and Central America in particular. Among
them are the greater interdependence of production processes around
the world and the increasing internationalization of capital. These trends
have generated strong pressures to open national economies, although
countries like the United States reserve protectionist practices for
themselves that they reject for other nations. These processes, moreover,
have given rise to increasing economic integration through global
agreements like those sanctioning the unification of the countries of
the European Economic Community in 1992, or bilateral accords like
the Free Trade Agreement between the United States and Canada.
Significant de facto integration already exists between Mexico and the
United States, and a formal agreement is in the offing that will have
a significant impact on Central American–Mexican–U.S. relations, as we
will see below.

At the same time, there is an emerging trend toward the transfer of
the hub of the world economy from the Atlantic Rim to the Pacific
Rim, with the United States (chiefly the West Coast) as the fulcrum.
This process is not over and may yet be modified by changes in the
dynamic of European unification wrought by the transformation of
Eastern Europe. This trend may portend a closer alliance between the
United States, Japan, and the rest of the newly industrialized countries
(NICs) of the Pacific. There is also the possibility of a greater rapprochement between the United States and the People's Republic of
China, at least at the economic level; the Bush administration's in-
dulgence of China's leadership following the Tiananmen Square massacre
is significant. In the midst of all this, Central America appears as a
bridge between the Atlantic and the Pacific, and there are a variety of
interests that would expect to profit from the situation, the Japanese

among others. However, for the moment, U.S. hegemony in the region is unchallenged.

Nonetheless, the United States is clearly on the decline as a world power, chiefly in terms of the economy, but also politically and militarily. Of course, this does not mean that the United States—and especially U.S. capital—has lost its dominion over large areas of the globe, particularly in Latin America and, above all, Central America.[2]

At the same time peripheral economies are being buffeted by advances in fields like biotechnology, materials sciences, and the engineering of products, which are tending to reduce demand for the mineral and agricultural resources of peripheral countries, eroding traditional areas of comparative advantage. The situation most affects raw materials exporters like the countries of Central America, whose elites are now interested in a competitive insertion in the new world market on the basis of even lower wages, lower taxes and social services, and tighter control over the populace. These comparative advantages may be sustainable to some degree for certain areas of economic activity or products, chiefly in the maquiladora industry.[3]

Added to this is the international financial crisis, which has taken a heavy toll on Latin American countries at the same time that they are being pushed by the International Monetary Fund (IMF) and World Bank to open their economies and incorporate them more fully into the world market. According to these institutions, the economic adjustment that they impose will "allow" the countries to pay the debt, emerge from the crisis, and insert themselves competitively into the market. This may be possible in cases like that of Mexico and Brazil, but it implies greater social inequalities and growing difficulties for democracy, owing to the damage caused by adjustment to the mass of the population in these countries and the limits imposed on the exercise of national independence. For countries that do not manage to adjust, the costs will be higher, since on top of the inequalities inherent in the process are the effects of the economic and social imbalances that such policies generate and, in many instances, the privations and problems that have built up over time.

Furthermore, we are witnessing the internationalization of communications, notably satellite transmissions received into the home via the family television over circuits largely controlled by U.S. firms. This means that information is derived from a few sources, which transmit ideologies that affect our ability to know and understand reality. There is a high degree of selectivity in the broadcast material, which translates into information and broadcasting control, with information filtered through the great multinational communications networks. For example, entire countries—even major countries like the People's Republic of

China after Tiananmen—disappear from the news, while others become the focus of attention (e.g., Cuba, which is the object of harassment right now) through the whim of these companies.[4]

We have experienced an internationalization of politics that, while not entirely new (at least in Latin America), has become accentuated and consolidated within the hegemony of neoconservative thought. This ideology profits from the current influence of neoliberal thought at the economic level—which it complements—and from the existence of groups and movements like international liberalism, the Christian Democratic Party, and the Socialist International. Politics has not only lost its former local flavor, it responds increasingly to international conditions and directives instead of the needs and interests of the respective countries. The market is now increasingly viewed (at least in the various power circles) as the great articulator of human activity and, thus, as a parameter that determines and influences not only economic but political decisions as well.[5]

To this complex dynamic must be added the changes in the countries of Eastern Europe and the possible incorporation of all or some of them into a united Europe. This incorporation could pave the way for a European Free Trade Treaty to be signed with the nonmembers of the EEC. Such a treaty could lead to a major reshuffling of economic and political alliances worldwide, with unpredictable results for both Latin and Central America.

For the moment, it is clear that multipolarity and an easing of political tensions will not necessarily lead to an easing of international economic tensions. Rather, North-South economic relations may become polarized and jeopardized by a growing marginalization of the natural resources and the labor markets of the Third World. While relations among the countries at the center of the economic dynamic are becoming ever more important, their relations with peripheral nations are generally losing their former importance. The paradox lies in that, by the same token, the attraction of the central countries over the periphery is growing, leading to a trend toward an ever-greater disintegration of the less-developed countries. Of course, this is not occurring without some resistance and does so within a framework of struggle and contradictions. The Persian Gulf War is an example of the kind of tensions that can be generated, connected in this case with the control of energy resources and their prices.

Associated with all this is the rise of neoconservatism and the U.S. tendency to exploit the economies of peripheral countries to reassert its hegemony and domination in Latin America. This is an outcome of the policy instituted by the Reagan administration in 1981. From then on, the United States became the spearhead for the neoconservative offensive, chiefly against the countries of the Third World: No more New International Economic Order or New World Information Order (except for those deriving from the laws of capitalism); no more OPEC-type producers' associations, much less concerted action to address the external debt issue; no more multilateral agencies with a growing international influence (the U.N. in general, but also the United Nations Educational, Scientific, and Cultural Organization [UNESCO]). Right now, narrowly defined efficiency is the key, and there appears to be no room for equity, sovereignty, or democracy as understood by the peoples who struggle for their social and national emancipation.

In all this, the growing interest of the United States in promoting the so-called "democratization processes" in Latin America (and especially Central America) plays a major role. The experiment with military dictatorships a failure, it has become clear to the United States that to guarantee its national security, more effective and extensive controls over civil society are needed—controls capable of growing and spreading along with the growth and organization of society. The United States has instruments at its disposal like the National Endowment for Democracy, which has already demonstrated its effectiveness in Central America with its support for what turned out to be the winning candidates in the recent elections in Costa Rica, Honduras, and Nicaragua.

The new interventionism requires new methods even at the economic level. This is the motive behind the "Enterprise for the Americas" initiative unveiled by President Bush to the Latin American and Caribbean diplomatic community in Washington June 26, 1991. Based on trade, investment, and debt reduction, this initiative seeks to foster regional pacts that would dampen efforts toward Latin American integration independent of the United States. To carry out this plan, the United States will work with the Inter-American Development Bank (IDB) and contribute $100 million annually, hoping that Japan and Europe will provide matching funds to the tune of $300 million a year. The scope of the initiative and its great limitations are evident when we consider that the resources designated for investment are insignificant even for Central America, where "Nicaragua alone needs double that amount to sustain its 'normal' operations, not to mention productive reconversion."[6]

While Bush's proposal has generated some expectations in certain Latin American quarters, the lessons of history have tempered enthusiasm for it. Not a few people remember that similar promises have been made before when the world or continental situation threatened the United States—for example, the "Good Neighbor Policy" of Franklin Delano Roosevelt and the Alliance for Progress of John. F. Kennedy.

Roosevelt's policy was abandoned once the war was over; Kennedy's was replaced by other measures, such as support for dictatorships, in the wake of the difficulties encountered by the alliance and pressures from hardliners in Washington. We must also recall the Kissinger Report's proposal for economic aid to Central America—a proposal that was swiftly forgotten as progress was made in achieving a bipartisan consensus on the Reagan administration's policy in the region.

Latin American Overview

Latin America runs the risk of remaining on the sidelines of the present world economic dynamic. More and more, it is losing its sovereignty, while U.S. influence in the region expands. The self-determination and Latin American solidarity enshrined in the Torrijos-Carter Treaties and the support for the Nicaraguan Revolution have faded. Now, not only are the immediate prospects for new initiatives of this type dim, even the "democratization processes" under way face great obstacles and limitations.

In the 1970s, while a number of Latin American countries were dominated by military dictatorships, their macroeconomic situation was not critical. The situation is now reversed: The military is no longer in government, but the economies are in deep crisis; the civilian presence in government merely constitutes a relative "breather," while the national sovereignty of the countries is under siege. The imposition of structural adjustment policies by the IMF and the World Bank is an indication of this.

Latin America is now a sinking archipelago, and Latin Americans have shown neither the concern nor the capacity necessary to restore the joint vision that existed up to the 1970s. On the contrary, dominated by neoconservative ideology, Latin Americans are proving incapable of formulating their own responses to the violent changes that have overtaken them.[7]

Furthermore, the obstacles to the regional integration processes are growing. For Central America, in addition to the difficulties inherent in the process of reactivating the Common Market there are the counterpressures generated by policies like those of the IMF, which favor an individualistic, competitive insertion of the countries into the emerging world market.

The current situation is overshadowed by the effects of the tendencies imposed by an extremely hostile and unstable external environment characterized by a persistent decline in the terms of trade (17 percent between 1980 and 1987, according to figures from the United Nations Economic Commission for Latin America and the Caribbean—ECLAC).

Most of all, Latin America is faced with an external debt equal to 80 percent of its regional product. Despite the fact that it is unpayable, as the creditors themselves have acknowledged, the region's governments have failed to present a united front in this regard and consider themselves obliged to pay, transferring capital to the industrialized nations and, hence, subsidizing the capitalist reconversion that then turns against their own countries.

The IMF's formulas and goals are hurting Latin America's economies, forcing the great mass of the people into the position of beggars or criminals. The burgeoning of the so-called "informal sector," hailed as a panacea for the crisis by the elite theorists of neoliberalism, is therefore no accident; neither is the social stratum—consciously produced or not—that nourishes the narcotics trade, which flourishes because large segments of the population directly or indirectly benefit from the illegal cultivation and marketing of drugs and from the capital invested by drug traffickers for money laundering.[8]

There is a general consensus that economic problems are at the bottom of drug production. Despite this, the United States does little. Despite efforts to substitute other crops for coca, Washington refuses to provide price guarantees or open its markets to the new products, as in the case of the achiote producers of Peru.[9]

The war on drugs thus represents one more burden for the countries of Latin America. Not only does it oblige governments to fight peasant poppy and marijuana producers and deal with their demands for new sources of employment under conditions that do not allow for competition with the prices paid by drug lords, it requires the commitment of economic and human resources to the pursuit, capture, trial, and incarceration of those implicated in this highly profitable enterprise. Finally, the war on drugs has become a new pretext for domination and abuse by the United States.[10]

In this context of crisis and difficulties, the trend of increased Latin American migration toward the more industrialized countries is not surprising; in the case of Central America, this chiefly means the United States, with Mexican territory as the principal means of access. The importance of these migrations is obvious. In El Salvador, for example, remittances from family members outside the country now constitute that nation's main source of foreign exchange.

Neither is it odd in this context that, since the mid-1980s, the armed forces have withdrawn from government in Latin America, even though this phenomenon does not necessarily imply the building or rebuilding of democracy. On the contrary, the new incumbents take up their burden as a lesser evil: "if we do not govern, the military will," they say, and they demand patience and cooperation from their peoples. No dredging up the past, much less demanding justice for the crimes of then and now; no complaints or mobilization against the growing deterioration in the already precarious standard of living, either—in other words, a limited democracy, with even electoral activity constrained.

But reality is stubborn. Hunger and desperation are more powerful than excuses and threats, and rioting and looting, as recent events in Venezuela and Argentina indicate, are impossible to prevent, repression notwithstanding. For the moment, the democratic impulse reduced to electoral rites is what can be anticipated, with the United States as the final arbiter of the process. The outlook is discouraging, although the neoconservative euphoria would appear to be premature and we have still not reached "the end of history."

Central America

The prospects for solving the problems that beset the peoples of Central America are very dim. The likely outlook is a rather long period of difficulties.

The past decade opened in Central America with the sounds of the Sandinista victory in Nicaragua. Once again, as with Cuba in 1959, a small country within the U.S. sphere of influence was asserting independence. The 1990s began with the electoral reversal of the Sandinistas, providing new evidence of the enormous difficulties and challenges faced by any revolutionary struggle in the region. The impasse in El Salvador and the prolongation of the social conflict in Guatemala confirm this.

At least for now, U.S. might has clearly managed to roll back the popular revolutionary surge that Central America witnessed in the early 1980s. It has been assisted by the prevailing international and regional climate, which the United States itself helped to create. According to the Report of the Sanford Commission, progress in easing world tensions will tend to distance the region from the East-West focus and may permit more room for autonomy. However, it may also lead to a situation where the basic problems that burden the region are forgotten by the international community. Furthermore, European unification in 1992 and the trend toward a greater integration with Eastern Europe may underscore this tendency and decrease flows of economic resources toward the region.[11]

Current Mexican-U.S. Relations

Relations between Mexico and the United States have a long, complex, and conflictual history. While the United States was seeking to expand its dominion and hegemony, Mexico desired independence and sovereignty. All the while, Central America served as a point of conflict. Thus, it is a history that has generated confrontation and "intense and sometimes bitter" feelings between the peoples of both countries and their governments.[12]

The recent improvement in bilateral relations by Presidents Carlos Salinas de Gortari and George Bush is therefore very important, especially after the highly aggressive tenure of the Reagan administration. One example of this change in attitude was the official visit of President Salinas to Washington in October 1989. Analysts all spoke of a new chapter in relations between the two countries. Mexico is now important for the United States, while U.S. importance for Mexico has significantly increased.[13]

Nonetheless, the recent discussion of a "new relationship" should not obscure the long-term, structural inequities in U.S.-Mexican relations. Nor is there unanimity on this question in Mexico. Some counsel acceptance of the new realities.[14] Others warn Mexicans not to forget their history or ignore the exploitive nature of U.S. capital.[15] Still others, recognizing the force of the economic dynamic between the two countries, call for a new relationship which ends U.S. bullying of Mexico.[16]

The Structure of Bilateral Relations

Circumstances aside, the essential difficulty with the "new relationship" lies in the fact that "Mexico will never be as continuously important to the United States as the United States is to Mexico." Moreover, the global impact of the United States "as an economy and as a culture on Mexico will be many times greater than that of Mexico on the United States."[17]

The relationship has at least three basic components: territorial contiguity; asymmetry of power; and Mexico's economic and technological dependence on the United States.

Territorial contiguity "means that Mexico constitutes a key zone in what the great power considers its first line of national defense." Moreover, the concentration of economic, and hence, political ties determines that relations between the two countries "go significantly beyond the framework of government-to-government diplomatic relations and traditional trade. Thus, relations between the countries exhibit a high degree of complexity, and the policies that they establish to regulate these relations tend to affect them only partially."[18]

The asymmetry of power, in turn, derives from the huge disparities between the two countries. Since the mid-nineteenth century, the United States has had three times the population of Mexico, fifteen times its gross domestic product, and an immense military superiority. Approximately two-thirds of Mexico's trade is carried out with the United States, while conversely, trade with Mexico accounts for just 3 to 6 percent of U.S. international transactions. "Under such conditions, negotiations tend to be unequal, and thus, disparities pervade the entire relationship."[19]

To this must be added the fact that the United States has eight times the income per capita and, in absolute terms, twenty-five times the economic output of Mexico. And as if this were not enough, despite its current problems, on a worldwide scale, the United States ranks first in military and economic terms, fourth in land area, and fourth in population.

These conditions are relative, however. Asymmetry of power, for example, does not necessarily imply a one-sided relationship in practice, as in the case of Mexico's activist foreign policy toward Central America. Moreover, there is the question of whether the stability of Mexico is a concern of the United States.[20]

In an attempt to decrease the importance of the United States in its economy, Mexico has made an ongoing effort to diversify its international relations, up to now with little success. It has also worked for greater Latin American integration, again with little result.[21]

Relations between Mexico and the United States are thus full of contradictions. While their relationship is dominated by conflict, both countries are moving toward closer economic ties because of physical proximity and changes in the international economy. It is not merely a question of improving interstate relations but of improving intersocietal relations as well, especially along the border. In the long run, such relations may turn out to be stronger determinants of the integration process between the two countries. This implies huge political and ideological challenges for Mexicans and the defense of their sovereignty, as well as for those in the United States who do not share the idea for their own gain.

Growing Mutual Importance

Mexican-U.S. ties are growing in importance, but the negative side to the relationship between the two countries has not disappeared. This is illustrated by the thrashing that Mexico received at the hands of the Reagan administration, a situation that reached its height in 1986 with the anti-Mexican hearings instituted by Sen. Jesse Helms.

These bilateral relations have a broad agenda. Topics like drug trafficking, Central American and Mexican migration to the United States, political stability in Mexico, and Mexican oil sales for the U.S. strategic reserve, among other things, are key issues in various quarters in the United States. The importance of these questions bolsters the interventionist tendencies of the major power sectors of that country.

The new cycle of U.S. interest in Mexico began with the Mexican oil boom in the late 1970s, when the relationship between the two countries was becoming more complex. This new interest was a consequence not only of more intense bilateral relations but also of a more active Mexican foreign policy, chiefly where Central America was concerned. Thus, if we do not take the changes of the last few years into account, pronouncements like those of Secretary of State James Baker at the opening of the VII Binational Meeting between Mexico and the United States on August 7, 1989, might appear to be inconsistent. On that occasion, he said that the United States "has no relations more important than those it maintains with its neighbor and friend, the Republic of Mexico. These are not just words, but the solemn commitment of the United States." These are pronouncements dictated by a world context that has generated new needs, especially in terms of long-term bilateral relations, given the prospect of establishing a North American common market together with Canada.

Progress toward a common market aside, the reality is that closer economic ties between Mexico and the United States are inevitable. In the early 1980s, analysts like Richard Fagen maintained that even during that decade there would be an "increase in the alliances between the Mexican state and foreign private capital . . . [and] the alliances between foreign private and Mexican private capital. In many cases the Mexican state would intervene as an intermediary in such alliances. In others, the state would be one of the main participants."[22]

In this context, a growing number of voices—even in the United States—are calling for a "new relationship." To this end, they propose broad cooperation with Mexico, saying, "Assuring this cooperation should be a major [U.S.] foreign policy objective."[23]

Such is the context of the change in attitude by the Mexican government toward its U.S. counterpart. It takes place within the framework of Mexico's decisions on how to handle the economic crisis. It is essential to build relations with the United States. It is a step that must be taken despite the ever-present reservations, the mistrust and differences, and the belatedly positive U.S. attitude, which only materialized with the Bush administration.

The Context of the Change

The change on the part of the Mexican government occurred during the administration of President Miguel de la Madrid Hurtado (1982–1988). Mexico's worsening economic problems—with their consequent political impact—and the importance of the United States to the country's prospects for solving them (especially where the renegotiation of the external debt and Mexico's economic reconversion process were concerned), played a significant role. Thus, the Mexican government made a tangible effort to seek an improvement in bilateral relations with its U.S. counterpart, at first, chiefly at the international policy level. This was a time when, on the one hand, the Mexican government was somewhat isolated in Latin America as a result of the French-Mexican Declaration, which recognized the FMLN as a belligerent force in El Salvador. On the other, the Reagan administration escalated its activities against Nicaragua and turned up pressure on Mexico to alter its policy toward that country.[24]

The obstacles that would lead to an ebbing of the revolution in Guatemala and an impasse in the war in El Salvador were already beginning to make themselves felt. The Reagan administration's anti-Mexican offensive intensified, largely due to Mexico's role in Central America. At the same time, Europe withdrew its support for the region, at least in terms of its earlier encouragement of social change, which had been promoted by several parties and governments affiliated with the Socialist International.

This combination of circumstances led to a modification in the Mexican government's position toward the region. It even had negative repercussions on the future of the new Nicaraguan state, since it was in this context that Mexico's conflict with Nicaragua over the oil debt arose. Mexico cut crude oil supplies in 1985, demanding the payment overdue. The situation was later resolved under the San José Agreement.

In the process, the Mexican government shifted from direct action aimed at social change in Central America to support for multilateral Latin American participation through the Contadora Group. This group was devoted chiefly to seeking a negotiated political settlement to the interstate conflicts, particularly the one between Nicaragua and its neighbors, Honduras and Costa Rica. Contadora sought primarily to prevent military conflict in the region and thus achieve a certain stability that would permit the most urgent changes demanded by the people. However, this would not be possible.

Along with peace negotiations Contadora promoted economic reactivation. Among these mechanisms was the Commission to Support the Economic and Social Development of Central America (CADESCA). Contadora managed to center efforts by other Latin American countries and the European Economic Community around this organization. However, after the Esquipulas III meeting in January 1988, the Central American presidents distanced themselves from the group insofar as peace efforts were concerned, seeking to "Central Americanize" the negotiations.

The Mexican government began devoting more attention to domestic and economic problems and made payment of its foreign debt a priority. In foreign policy, it sought to avoid unnecessary confrontations with the United States, though with little success, owing to the Reagan administration's anti-Mexicanism. With the election of President Carlos Salinas de Gortari, ties between Central America and Mexico have weakened further. Meanwhile, the region must face greater challenges emanating from the invasion of Panama and the Sandinista reversal at the polls.

The Present

An essential feature of current Mexican-U.S. relations is a broadening of the bilateral agenda and the trend toward a "new relationship." Mexico's recent initiative to establish a Free Trade Agreement with the United States, its support for the war on drugs and the curbing of illegal immigration to the North are examples of this. Nevertheless, these steps have created new problems inside both Mexico and the United States and have a different tempo and purpose in each country.[25]

The current Mexican-U.S. agenda covers four main areas: trade, migration, drug trafficking, and the environment. It has led to the creation of an Office for Border Affairs in both the Mexican Ministry of Foreign Relations and the U.S. Department of State and the formation of a subgroup to deal with the rise in illegal migration. These, of course, are not issues likely to be resolved in the short run, due to their inherent complexity.

Within this agenda, Central America is notable for its absence. In spite of this, the region is not a topic beyond the scope of the bilateral relationship, as the speeches of Presidents Salinas and Bush revealed during the official visit of the Mexican president to the United States in October 1990.[26] Nor are the government and the people of Mexico likely to forget the history of their relations with the United States and the nature of their bilateral relationship.

Mexican–Central American Relations in the Context of Mexican-U.S. Relations

Will Mexico weaken its historic ties with Central America and its support for social change and move toward links based almost exclusively on economic interest—primarily links between states and economic power sectors governed by international capital interests?

Whether this happens or not depends on the international situation, the course of Central American–Mexican relations, and the current bolstering of Mexican-U.S. ties. Of particular importance is Central America's growing dependence on the United States and, in general, the traditional U.S. clout within the triangular relationship.

Until about 1979, there was little political hierarchy in Central American–Mexican relations and scant economic significance. Central American affairs seemed to be important for the Mexican state and Mexican society because of "their significance for Mexico's difficult relationship with the United States." Nevertheless, since the late 1970s, Central America has been transformed into a place of risks and decisive opportunities for Mexico, which has led to confrontation with the United States.[27]

Historically, overcoming the problems derived from its proximity to the United States has been a constant concern for Mexico. This concern is shared by the forces of social change in Central America and some of its power circles, creating a sense of unity with Mexico, though often only temporarily.

U.S. intervention in Central America has been a permanent focus of attention for Mexico and an occasion for new tensions with the United States, which fears Mexican hegemony in the isthmus. Mexican governments have tended to support and contribute to the search for political solutions to conflicts in the area. In this, they have had the backing and even the urging of the people; at the same time, the social movements in the region have identified with Mexico and sympathized with it. This still holds true, transcending the traditional anti-Mexicanism of Central America's ruling class.

For Mexico, removing temptations to U.S. intervention in the area has been a fundamental goal. In so doing, it has sought to prevent a "double U.S. border" (that is, at both ends of its territory) sustained in the south by Central American regimes closely allied to the United States. For the movements for social change and, on occasion, for certain area power sectors, Mexico's presence has served as an important counterweight to U.S. pressure.[28]

Such is the historical triangularity of relations between Central America, Mexico, and the United States, grounded in closer ties between Central America and Mexico (see Chapter 1). The main objective of this rapprochement has been to reduce or mitigate U.S. influence in the region and thus lessen the danger that this country poses to Mexico's national sovereignty. Despite this, the changes in Mexican-U.S. relations, combined with the current weakening of Central American–Mexican

ties and the growing influence of the United States are having a profound
affect that may permanently alter the relationship.

Current Central American–Mexican Relations

Mexico's political and diplomatic activism in Central America began
with the government's support for the Torrijos-Carter Treaties, signed
in September 1977, and above all, its backing for the Nicaraguan
Revolution.[29] Mexico likewise supported the revolutionary movement
in El Salvador, though to a lesser degree.[30] It also participated to a
limited extent in Guatemala.[31] By this means it contributed to a political
and diplomatic flowering of new social forces in Central America that
could no longer be ignored. There were moments when U.S. hegemony
in the region appeared to be on the wane.[32]

Despite this, from late 1982 on, Mexico began to alter its position,
attempting to foster a multilateral participation that, instead of resolving
domestic social conflicts, would seek a certain regional stability to put
the social crisis on hold. This would serve as a point of departure, it
was thought, for a new attempt to resolve the crisis through changes
in the economic base. As everyone knows, this strategy has made little
headway, and Mexico's chief concern would now appear to be the
economic reactivation of the region and the creation of palliatives for
the crisis.

This change in Mexico's Central American policy grew visible with
the formation of the Contadora Group in 1983. It was accentuated with
the presidential accords of Esquipulas II in 1987 and became virtually
absolute after Esquipulas III in early 1988. Mexico's domestic problems
and its rapprochement with the United States, the rising U.S. interventionism in the region under the Reagan administration, and the
obstacles to new revolutionary gains (including the advancement of
the Sandinista project) were contributing factors.

Despite this, the historical basis of Mexico's commitment to social
change in the area has not altered. While the traditional accumulation
model sustained by agro-exports and authoritarianism in Central America
is now unviable, the new one that is to replace it has not yet materialized.[33] Thus, the causes of social conflict in Central America remain,
with all their negative implications for the peoples of Central America
as well as Mexico.

In our view, social change continues to be important for Mexico. It
is vital that the new order struggling to establish itself in the region
be grounded in changes that will permit stable, independent, and
democratic states to emerge with which closer ties can be forged.
Mexico can count on the same interest and mobilization of effort on

the part of Central American and U.S. sectors who share this objective. Clearly, the foreign policy differences that divide Mexico and the United States are not going to go away, at least in the short run. These differences are profound and constitute the underpinnings for the Central America–Mexico–United States triangle.[34]

In spite of this, Central American–Mexican relations run the risk of deteriorating. This could occur if the current trend toward closer Mexican-U.S. ties continues under its present terms and if the obstacles to Central America's movements for social change continue to grow. The resurgent U.S. influence within the triangular relationship will not be easy to overcome; it can be seen at the economic level in general and in the payment of the external debt in particular, and touches on sensitive issues like illegal migration and the war on drugs.

The Economic Issue

The economic aspect of Central American–Mexican–U.S. relations is dominated by one theme of strategic importance: the possibility of a North American common market composed of Mexico, the United States, and Canada. This possibility and the integration dynamic between Mexico and the United States has a number of implications for the triangular relationship and for each of the countries involved, since the United States is the dominant component.

The basis for U.S. hegemony is not only its traditional political and military power in the region, but also its economic clout. This inequality is even greater now with the recent rise in U.S. protectionism and Washington's tactic of closing the U.S. market as leverage (e.g., the trade blockade of Nicaragua).

The nature of the triangular relationship is illustrated by the traditional weakness of economic ties between Central America and Mexico. While Mexico initially showed an interest in fostering the structural changes needed in the area, its ability to influence and lend support was limited. The rigidities of the systems of domination and accumulation and the very power groups within the Central American countries themselves, combined with U.S. counterpressures, were stronger.

In addition to these structural barriers were other paradoxes. In 1977, when the oil boom hit, Mexico—as a producer—greatly benefitted, while Central America and the Caribbean—as consumers—did not. In light of this, Mexico and Venezuela sought to offset the situation with the San José Pact, signed in 1980. The current Persian Gulf crisis has recreated the problem, however, but Mexico and Venezuela are no longer in a position to counteract it.

Furthermore, without meaning to, Mexico is presenting new obstacles to Central American efforts aimed at a "competitive" insertion in the new world market. Some of Mexico's comparative advantages in today's competition for foreign investment are similar to Central America's, like cheap labor and natural resources. In addition, however, the country can boast of oil, economic and political stability, and a more educated work force. Mexico is therefore more attractive to foreign investors. The situation is even more serious when we consider that such difficulties will reinforce the regressive economic policies applied by the governments of Central America. Unable to introduce the structural reforms dictated by this competitiveness, they will revert to a greater contraction of wages and social services and, hence, an increase in authoritarian and repressive forms of control that will exacerbate social conflicts.[35]

The Debt Problem

Financial problems add to the obstacles to Central America's economic reactivation and its "competitive" reinsertion into the world market. These problems include debt and the enormous capital flight provoked by armed domestic conflict and U.S. intervention; they are compounded by the government corruption and squandering of public finances that are prevalent in Central America. Here again, Mexico's recent history has unintentionally hurt Central Americans and its own interests in the region.

Since the administration of Miguel de la Madrid (1982–1988), the Mexican government has made a priority of seeking less onerous debt payment conditions through bilateral negotiations with its creditors. In this, it has had the backing of the U.S. government. Mexico has managed to renegotiate its debt, achieving a reduction of the balance owed, lower interest rates, and fresh funds on a multinational basis—albeit after severe restrictions on public expenditures and major modifications in the state apparatus that have had both political and social repercussions.

Whether or not Mexico finally achieves its economic objectives, any progress that it makes will in part be prejudicial for the Central American countries. This is evident when we consider that such progress is the outcome of bilateral negotiations that respond to the situation of each individual case and that the region's situation is not comparable to Mexico's. In Central America, the adjustment falls on a populace severely battered by a crisis superimposed on generations of injustice, on peoples suspicious and discontented with their leaders and confronted with very high levels of per capita debt.[36]

In practice, the Mexican precedent translates into the idea that the debt can and should be paid within the framework of an economic Darwinism that puts the smaller, weaker nations at a serious disadvantage. The government of Costa Rica, for example, has already undertaken talks with its creditors to establish the possibility of reaching a Mexican-type agreement with them. However, what is being discussed is whether the weak economies of the small, poor Central American countries will obtain a result at least similar to Mexico's—on what terms can they pay their debt? But more importantly, *should* the debt be paid?

In this regard, we must bear in mind that the IMF's adjustment policies are recessive, contrary to the interests of the people, and, in the case of Central America, entail measures that hinder efforts at regional integration. Integration, in the view of many experts, is one viable alternative for the economic recovery of the area at a time when protectionism and the formation of trade blocs among the industrialized nations is the dominant trend.

Despite this, because of the Bush "Enterprise for the Americas" initiative, some Latin American circles are beginning to regard integration in a peculiar light; they see it chiefly as a means of linking themselves to a future North American or hemispheric common market. In so doing, they run the risk of frustrating the essential goal of Central American integration, which is to open up the possibility of achieving and enhancing democratization and the exercise of sovereignty.

Under these circumstances, a rapid and easy recovery of the Central American economies is unlikely. On the contrary, the picture points to a worsening of Central America's historical calamities. The prognosis is the persistence of the structural causes at the heart of the discontent and popular rebellion.[37]

Because of this, the regional scenario suggests an increase in migration (chiefly toward Mexico and the United States), a rise in crime and drug trafficking, persistent and even more serious political instability, and a creeping social disintegration, which in countries like Guatemala and El Salvador is clearly evident after so many years of crisis. For Mexico and many other countries with ties to Central America, this is an undesirable situation, but there are serious obstacles to any effort to modify it.

The Migration Issue

In view of these circumstances, a rise in Central American–Mexican–U.S. tensions is probable. The growth of Central American migration to Mexico (and from there to the United States), the dramatic population displacement provoked by the armed conflicts in the region, and the absence of political and economic solutions to the crisis make such a possibility likely. Of course, the situation varies, according to the country involved.[38]

Given its grasp of the situation and the interests at stake, as far as the U.S. government is concerned, there is no question that Mexico must guarantee a containment of migration—both its own and foreign—toward U.S. territory. For Mexico, given its interests with respect to both the United States and Central America, either option means conflict with one of the parties. The outcome is linked to the recent reforms in Mexico's General Population Law and its application and also to the actions of the subgroup established during the VII Binational Meeting between Mexico and the United States held in August 1989 to deal with the mounting illegal migration to the United States. For Central America, in turn, encountering a hardline Mexico that punishes its efforts to survive would surely contradict its conception of a friendly Mexico concerned about supporting independence and democracy for the peoples of the region.[39]

This consequently heightens the need for Mexico to help find a speedy solution to the regional crisis. It will not be easy, of course, since other basic problems that must be addressed are the failure of the agro-export model and the abuses of authoritarian regimes in Central America. Only then will it be possible to think about a durable reactivation of the region's economy, political stability for the countries, and the prevention of confrontation between these regimes and their peoples—all of these factors that spur migration but which are difficult for Mexico and Central America to address on their own.

The War on Drugs

The war on drugs began in 1986 with the decision by the Reagan administration to put a halt to illicit narcotics traffic. It thus became a burning issue for the national sovereignty and security of the Latin American countries.[40] At the same time, it profoundly affected civil safety and exacerbated racist and xenophobic attitudes in the United States.[41]

Pursued in countries like Mexico and Colombia, drug traffickers find a favorable climate for drug cultivation and marketing in countries as diverse as Guatemala and Costa Rica. In Guatemala, the narcotics trade is chiefly the result of the armed domestic conflict, government corruption, and a military command and business sectors who have no qualms about drug trafficking.[42] In Costa Rica, the main cause is corruption.[43]

At the same time, the United States is using the war on drugs to increase its military aid to the countries of the region or to install troops where they are not already stationed. In the same way, when trying to involve Costa Rica in the U.S. strategy to topple the Nicaraguan Revolution, Washington took steps to form a military alliance between the two countries, even though Costa Rica had abolished its army in 1948.[44] Under the pretext of the war on drugs, military aid is channelled to regimes like Guatemala's, known as persistent and systematic violators of human rights that otherwise would encounter difficulties in obtaining such assistance. Likewise, coining terms like "narco-guerrilla" and "narco-terror," antidrug propaganda is being used to discredit revolutionary movements.

Local armies carry out antiguerrilla campaigns under the guise of action against the drug lords and their plantations, even using defoliants in important areas of the jungles in El Petén in Guatemala. This has caused major ecological damage.[45]

Furthermore, the war on drugs has led to an open violation of the laws of several countries, with the consent of some local authorities. This is true for Honduras, in the case of the 1988 capture and deportation of accused drug trafficker Ramón Matta Ballesteros to the United States for trial and sentencing. These actions provoked a strong popular reaction that ended in the destruction of the U.S. Consulate in Tegucigalpa.[46]

Thus, the conditions that lead the United States to pursue its interventionist activities are multiplying. Far from being resolved, the domestic conflicts in Central America are becoming ever more complex.

A Likely Prospect

If the situation persists, Central America faces grave consequences, which affect Mexico as well. However, there is a possibility that this situation can be reversed, by taking advantage of certain favorable conditions. Some issues can already be identified that could lead to closer bilateral relations between Central America and Mexico and the elimination of possible tensions with the United States (e.g., tensions that could arise if Central American migration to Mexico and through it to the United States persists or even increases). A strengthening of Mexican–Central American bilateral ties should permit an increase in the relative importance of each to the United States, restoring the aspects taken on by the triangular relationship in the late 1970s and early 1980s. Mexican-Venezuelan and Mexican-Brazilian relations, plus support from the rest of Latin America, could play a significant role in strengthening these actions.[47]

Migration and Central American instability are sensitive issues for Mexico, and resolving them is tremendously important for the peoples of the region. Nevertheless, any solution must take into account the economic aspect at the heart of these problems.

No one doubts the enormous economic difficulties confronting Central America, nor does anyone believe that the simple reactivation of production and trade flows is sufficient. However, they may serve as an important point of departure. Mexico and Central America could advance toward reactivation, for instance, by devising joint activities linked with the promotion of new formulas for handling the debt—particularly Central America's debt with Mexico, which is basically derived from oil purchases. Other actions could be an updating and effective application of the "Partial Scope" trade agreements signed by Mexico and the Central American countries, and above all, the resolute support of Latin America for the reactivation of the Central America Common Market through governmental and nongovernmental agencies. In this respect, both Mexico and Latin America in general can play a singular role in international forums and in relations with the United States by discouraging and, where possible, blocking actions promoted by the IMF and the World Bank that interfere with regional integration. An updating and broadening of the San José Pact could also be promoted, particularly insofar as the use of its resources by Central America is concerned.[48]

It is also important for Mexico to use its influence (especially in light of the significance of its own political stability for the United States) to make Washington understand that instability in Central America is harmful to Mexico and that achieving political stability requires ending the armed domestic conflict in El Salvador and Guatemala, restoring democracy. For Nicaragua, it is important not to stifle the political efforts of the populace and its representative organizations.

As for the war on drugs, Mexico and Central America must reach their own agreements without U.S. pressure. This is especially important where pressures that compromise their sovereignty and national interests are concerned. Nicaragua's proposal to the Contadora Group in this regard could serve as a starting point.

Thus, Mexico and Central America could profit from the multiple ties that bind them at various levels (particularly cultural and political ties) through regional players with a constructive position toward bilateral relations between the parties. In all this, we repeat, a renewal of the Latin American spirit and the support of other extraregional countries is both urgent and indispensable.

General Conclusions

We can conclude that Central American–Mexican relations, which have historically favored social change in the region, have been weakened. Nevertheless, we have not reached a point where the underlying criteria for these relations have vanished, nor have the social groups that support them disappeared. However, if the current trend persists, Mexican–Central American relations may become so weak that Mexico ceases to be a counterweight to U.S. policy in the region, and Central America loses the advantages of the triangular relationship.

Modifications in the triangular relationship are a result not only of the domestic changes in Mexico and in its international relations (chiefly with the United States), but also of the greater complexity of the Central American situation, on the one hand, and its international context, on the other. There has been a notable growth of U.S. hegemony and the obstacles to social change in the region, as well as a distancing of the Central American governments from Mexico since Esquipulas III.

The implications of this situation for the region cover a broad spectrum of topics that go beyond foreign policy. They touch upon the economic prospects for the region and each of its countries, the external debt, Central American migration, and drug trafficking. In all this, the United States plays a significant role and has concrete interests that do not generally coincide with those of Central America.

If the current trend intensifies, the outlook will be a Central American–Mexican–U.S. relationship without its traditional triangularity, perhaps collapsing into linearity. Central American–U.S. relations may be mediated by Mexican-U.S. relations, mainly in the economic sphere. In fact, Mexico's commitment to social change in Central America appears to have been replaced by closer economic ties—including economic cooperation and technical assistance to the region. However, these are grounded in rather weak economic relations between Central America and Mexico that are taking some time to develop.[49]

In consequence, we can state that the United States will retain its hegemony over Central America for the foreseeable future. The basis for this affirmation is the growing economic dependence of the Central American countries on the U.S. economy and greater U.S. government interference in the region's internal affairs. This is already occurring through the adjustment policies of the IMF and the World Bank, the war on drugs, and the curbing of Central American migration to the United States. This increased interference can also be seen in the promotion of the "democratization processes" now in vogue. In addition, all this is occurring at a time when neither the European Economic Community, the new capitalist countries of Asia (chiefly Japan), nor the countries of Eastern Europe are able or trying to dispute the U.S. hegemony.

The outlook for a modification in the current trend in the triangular relationship will be determined largely by a series of uncertain prospects, chief among them the development potential of the Latin American integration processes within the context of South-South relations. The same holds true for the prospects of encouraging the processes of social change in the region for the moment, through a bolstering of the political power of the Nicaraguan people and the advance of the real democratization processes in El Salvador and Guatemala. The course of the triangular relationship will depend on these things and the ability of the countries to forge regional and international alliances to strengthen these possibilities.

In this regard, we should not underestimate the role that the forces of social change in the region can play in profiting from the favorable conditions created by Central American–Mexican relations. Through Mexico, for example, Central America could more effectively seek out the Latin American and international support it requires to address the crisis, and both Central America and Mexico could obtain the help they need to reverse the current anticipated trend in the triangular relationship. In all this, the importance of Mexico to the United States, particularly in recent years, cannot be ignored—an importance that is likely only to increase.

In the meantime, if the current orientation of U.S policy toward Central America and the weakening of the traditional triangular relationship persists, social conflicts in the region will simply be prolonged and the complexity and costs involved in resolving them will increase on every level. If these conflicts persist, the prospects for social coexistence in countries like El Salvador and Guatemala, already severely chastised by their domestic conflicts, will worsen further, with repercussions not only on the region and its immediate neighbors but on the United States as well, through increased Central American migration, a rise in drug trafficking, and a general worsening of the social instability of the area.

We believe, therefore, that for the peoples of Latin America and the North American people as well, encouragement and support for foreign policy measures more in line with the reality of Central America is crucial. This means policies that acknowledge the historic roots of the social conflicts in Central America and the need for profound social change to resolve them. For the present, what is needed is a political solution for the armed domestic conflict in Guatemala and El Salvador, and respect for the will of the people. We are talking about contributing to the self-determination of the peoples of Central America and the real exercise of their right to peace, democracy, and development.

An understanding of these needs by U.S. citizens and their support for the processes of social change in Central America is urgent. The influence that the Mexican, Chicano, and Hispanic communities in the United States can bring to bear in this respect is significant. The activities of organized groups in U.S. society must be translated into concrete U.S. foreign policy orientations. The key issue at hand is to reduce the burdens of the increased U.S. hegemony and domination in the area on the prospects for the peoples of Central America. Clearly, progress in this direction would also represent an important step in the achievement of similar objectives by other Latin Americans and for the prospects of freedom of important sectors of the U.S. people.

Notes

1. Suffice it to recall the U.S. offensive against the government of Zelaya in Nicaragua in 1909, U.S. intervention in Guatemala in 1954, and the Carter administration's opposition to the assumption of power by the Nicaraguan Revolution in 1979. On each of these occasions, Mexico and the United States found themselves diametrically opposed (see Chapter 1).

2. "From a domestic standpoint, the problems that [the United States] faces are linked chiefly to the economy: an unprecedented federal deficit, a rising debt that is turning it into the world's greatest debtor, a large trade deficit (despite the fall of the dollar and a relative dependence on foreign capital), a growing loss of competitiveness, and a decline in the economy in global terms. In addition, a technological lag, albeit relative, that puts it in second place with respect to Japan and the Federal Republic of Germany . . . in the distribution of the world's Gross National Product, the United States had 40 percent in 1965; 29 percent in 1975. Today, the figure is around 25 percent according to 1986 IMF figures . . ." Isabel Jaramillo, "Estados Unidos: la política exterior, la perspectiva global y el Tercer Mundo," in *Cuadernos de Nuestra América*, 6, 13 (July–December 1989) (Havana: Centro de Estudios sobre América).

3. Pedro Vuskovic Céspedes, *Centroamérica: disyuntivas del desarrollo* (Mexico: PECA-CIDE, forthcoming).

4. Augustín Cueva during a cycle of conferences organized in March 1990 by the students of Master's Degree Program in Economics and International Policy (MEPI) of the Center for Economic Research and Teaching (CIDE).

5. Augustín Cueva, Inaugural speech at the VIII Central American Sociological Congress, Guatemala, November 1987.

6. Pedro Vuskovic Céspedes, "Iniciativa para las Américas: ¿nueva versión de la doctrina Monroe?" in *Pensamiento Propio* VIII, 73 (Managua: August 1990), pp. 5–8.

7. Cueva, MEPI-CIDE conference.

8. According to estimates by Carlos Caballeros, president of the Bankers Association, drugs in Colombia generate some $4.6 billion annually—that is, 87.8 percent of the country's exports of goods and services. The same source points out that some $1.5 billion are repatriated and "laundered" through the simulation of productive activities included under various monetary categories within the Colombian balance of payments. The figures may be higher. There are estimates that report gross annual sales of $35–80 billion to the United States and Europe. The importance of this activity to the Colombian economy is illustrated by the fact that, since 1976, there has been a monetary category denominated "remittances of dollars by Colombians abroad," a crucial instrument for the stability of the country's international reserves. Rafael Vergara, "Colombia en lucha por la esperanza," in *Otra Guatemala* 11 (México, D.F.) (May 1980), p. 31.

9. IPS, "Abandona EUA a productores que sustituyeron cultivos de coca," *Excélsior,* 4 July 1990.

10. Suffice it to recall the invasion of Panama and the naval blockade of Colombia in late 1989, as well as the Reagan—and now the Bush—administration's insistence on carrying out joint military operations against drug traffickers through a multinational force headed by the Pentagon. In the meantime, the Drug Enforcement Agency (DEA) has been carrying out "covert" and illegal activities in countries like Mexico—with whom the Bush administration claims to be seeking a "new relationship"—and, together with the Special Operations Forces of the Pentagon, undertaking joint activities with armies like that of Bolivia (since 1986) and, more recently, Peru.

11. David Lewis and Alicia Gariazzo, "Europa Comunitaria y Centroamérica: de la solidaridad a los negocios" (Managua: CRIES, 1989), mimeo.

12. "For many Mexicans, the United States is still the country that stole half their national territory in the middle of the last century, that invaded and conspired against it during the Revolution, that opposed the reforms of Cárdenas and the nationalization of the oil industry in the 1930s, and that continues to covet, invade, and despoil the Republic. . . ." For many North Americans, "while their historical memory is much shorter and probably less accurate, there is a series of equally rich images: Mexico as a corrupt, barbarian country, overpopulated and impoverished, opulent but not modern and now, arrogant and aggressive." Richard R. Fagen, "La política de las relaciones Mexico-norteamericanas," in *Las relaciones México–Estados Unidos,* ed. C. Tello and C. Reynolds (Mexico: Fondo de Cultura Económica, 1981), pp. 378 and 379.

13. Mexico needs capital, technology, and access to large export markets, but it also has a surplus of unskilled labor, energy, and other natural resources. The United States lacks oil, some raw materials, and unskilled labor, but has capital and technology and is the largest market in the world. Abraham Lowenthal, "Estados Unidos y México," in *México EEUU 1986,* ed. Gerardo M. Bueno (Mexico: El Colegio de México, 1986), p. 55.

14. "If Mexico were torn by revolution, the United States would be unable to escape its consequences. At present, with the exception of the U.S.S.R. for

strategic reasons and Japan for financial ones, probably no country can affect the United States as much as Mexico." Robert A. Pastor, "Introduction" to Jorge G. Castañeda and Robert A. Pastor, *Límites en la amistad: México y Estados Unidos* (Mexico: Joaquín Mortriz/Planeta, 1989).

15. "Viewed from the present, when Mexico has the United States as its principal market, the resolution of national differences is occurring substantially through the strategic inevitability of compromise and rationality of negotiations between sovereign peoples urgently in need of a real agreement, not just words." Juan María Alponte, *La Jornada,* 10 August 1989.

16. "Never to forget our history nor what it has cost us to be fated to live alongside our powerful neighbor. . . . For the United States, Mexico has been nothing but a land for conquest and a source of wealth (natural or man-made) that the Americans can expropriate whenever they please. . . . The aim is to integrate us into the U.S. economy and obtain free access to our raw materials, our labor force, and of course the pocketbook of every Mexican." Arnold Córdova, *UnomásUno,* 11 August 1989.

17. "I believe that it is perfectly possible to think about economic integration with the United States as a reality, but at the same time, it should be negotiated, administered, in some cases curbed and others promoted. It is not something that should be rejected out of hand. . . ." Leonardo Kourchenko, Interview with Jorge G. Castañeda, *La Jornada,* 11 March 1989.

18. Richard R. Fagen, "La política," p. 379. "It is precisely the structure of the relationship that is the key factor in keeping Mexico from negotiating its problems with the United States on an equal basis. On the other hand, it is also what has obliged Mexico on numerous occasions to bow to unilateral decisions by Washington, with no alternative but resignation." Mario Ojeda, "El futuro de las relaciones entre México y los Estados Unidos," in *Las relaciones,* ed. Tello and Reynolds, p. 384.

19. Ojeda, "El Futuro," pp. 384–386.

20. Comisión sobre el Futuro de las Relaciones México–Estados Unidos, *El desafío de la interdependencia: México y Estados Unidos* (Mexico: Fondo de Cultura Económica, 1988), p. 26.

21. "Despite the fact that the widespread economic crisis in Latin America has eroded the integration process, Mexico has not flagged in its efforts to strengthen it. It has broadened its partial scope agreements with many countries and signed others with Central American and Caribbean nations, in addition to negotiating several trade agreements that benefit a variety of industrial areas." Jorge Alberto Lozoya, "Política exterior: apertura a nuevas ideas," *Excélsior,* 7 December 1989.

22. Fagen, "La política," p. 365.

23. Lowenthal, "Estados Unidos y México," p. 69.

24. "The differences between the international policies of Mexico and Washington led to crisis in the second half of the 1980s, owing to the convergence of several factors. Our country's new policy toward Central America—both as an activist and leader and as a moderate and mediator—had become an obstacle to U.S. objectives in the region. The Reagan administration defined U.S.

aspirations in the area more precisely and broadly than ever before, and this turned simple disagreements into real confrontations." Castañeda and Pastor, *Límites,* p. 235.

25. In his address to the U.S. Congress during his visit to Washington in October 1990, President Salinas pointed out the need for "broader and more certain access" to the U.S. market, recalling that "to ensure that Mexico remains one of the most open economies on an international level, we need greater reciprocity." Concerning undocumented workers, he called for an end to the myths: "Mexican workers do not displace anyone; they toil efficiently and with dignity for wages often below market rates, filling positions that American workers do not occupy." Because of this, he demanded legal protection for these workers and an end to discrimination against them, as well as a real solution through "a far-reaching political understanding." As to the war on drugs, he stated "the responsibility for the war on our territory is exclusively Mexican and thus, there will be no joint military operations on our soil"; he accepted coordination and cooperation as effective measures in the areas of information and evaluation, as well as joint application of the law and the attack on money laundering. *La Jornada,* 5 October 1990.

26. In his speech welcoming President Salinas, President Bush stated: "we must discuss how democracy can be restored in Panama and how free and just elections can be held in Nicaragua." In turn, in his address to Congress, President Salinas said, "Mexico desires the restoration of peace in Central America, the consolidation of democracy and a new beginning for development" and he added, "growth and job creation are needed to curb migrations to the south of Mexico or their transit to the United States." *La Jornada,* 5 October 1990.

27. Adolfo Aguilar Zinser and Rodrigo Jauberth Rojas, Presentation of the collection *Relaciones Centroamérica-México* (Mexico: PECA-CIDE, 1987), p. 10. This was largely the outcome of a foreign policy that had been evolving toward a growing activism since the administration of President Luis Echeverría Alvarez (1970–1976). It involved an active diplomacy chiefly oriented toward the search for joint action with the other countries of the Third World. Nevertheless, it was an activism that addressed questions of a global nature that did not always imply a direct confrontation with U.S. interests. With the administration of José López Portillo (1976–1982) this situation intensified considerably. This was partly because of Mexico's greater autonomy during these years, fostered by the oil boom, and above all because of the intensification of the revolutionary struggles in Central America, a favorable international climate, and a United States weakened by the changes that had begun to take place on a world scale, the defeat in Vietnam, and the discredit to the government brought about by the Watergate scandal.

28. The Mexican government's backing for the Nicaraguan Revolution occurred in the context of its alliance with the government of Costa Rican president Rodrigo Carazo, when he opted to help the anti-Somoza forces. See Rodrigo Jauberth Rojas, *Costa Rica–México 1978–1986: de la concertación a la confrontación* (Mexico: PECA-CIDE, 1987). At the same time, Mexico was a valuable

help to the de facto military government of General Humberto Mejía Víctores, when in 1985 he chose to promote an "active neutrality" in the U.S.-Nicaraguan confrontation through his support for the Contadora peace efforts. It is significant that this occurred after a history of continuous confrontation between Guatemala and Mexico, accentuated after the assault by Guatemalan troops on the El Chupadero refugee camp in the Mexican state of Chiapas on April 30, 1984. Gilberto Castañeda S., *Guatemala: crisis social política exterior y relaciones con México 1978–1986* (Mexico: PECA-CIDE, 1987).

29. Mexico, for example, led the opposition in the OAS to the Carter administration's initiative to send an inter-American force to Nicaragua to "supervise" the government transition after Somoza's defeat, and it provided important political, diplomatic, and economic backing for the new regime, although this was later reduced.

30. The French-Mexican declaration recognizing the FMLN as a representative political force is perhaps what is most significant. Viewed with hindsight, it is the start of what are now the FMLN's negotiations with the Salvadoran government.

31. Mexico backed the resolutions against the persistent human rights violations in Guatemala until the advent of the civilian government in 1986 and has maintained a constructive position with regard to the refugee question. Its position is notable for its insistence that the repatriation of refugees be on a voluntary basis and that there must be a commitment by the Guatemalan government to guarantee and respect their rights, which include a return of their lands, the majority of which have been confiscated by the military and the leaders of the civil patrols.

32. See Nora Hamilton and Manuel Pastor, Jr., eds., *Crisis in Central America* (Boulder: Westview Press, 1988), "Introduction," pp. 1–11.

33. In 1988, for example, the enormous weight of agro-exports in the economies of the region could be seen in foreign exchange earnings. In the case of Guatemala and El Salvador, the importance of coffee is evident: 34.8 percent and 58.2 percent, respectively, followed by sugar in Guatemala (6.6 percent), and shrimp in El Salvador (3.3 percent). For Honduras, Nicaragua, and Costa Rica the weight is distributed between two main products, respectively: bananas (40.8 percent) and coffee (21.3 percent); coffee (39.9 percent) and cotton (24.9 percent); and coffee (27.7 percent) and bananas (20.2 percent). CEPAL, *Estudio económico de América Latina y el Caribe 1988* (Mexico: August and September 1989).

34. The strongest grounds for these differences are provided by Mexican history itself, which is linked to the costly, bloody, and almost constant struggle to become an independent nation. Suffice it to recall the struggles for independence in 1810, the Reform of 1857 and the fight against the French invasion, the Mexican Revolution and U.S. intervention against its consolidation.

35. The promotion of new export sectors in Central America would have to be massive "to begin to modify the current inequalities. To achieve this, there must be at least substantial improvements in access by the population to the land, to domestic credit, to the basic means of production—all, processes

that are generally moving away from the present course of the region." Gerardo Timossi Dolinsky, *Centroamérica: deuda externa y ajuste estructural* (San José: DEI-CRIES, 1989), pp. 105–106.

36. "In 1987 Central America's debt surpassed $18.1 billion. One year before it had already represented nearly 84 percent of regional GDP, and its service consumed practically 40 percent of the total exports of the area—that is, three and a half times what it did at the beginning of the decade." However, the results obtained by the countries of the Isthmus in the negotiating rounds with their creditors "have always proven to be well below those obtained by other Latin American debtors, though there has been a trend toward making the terms of the renegotiation—initially very onerous—more flexible." Timossi Dolinsky, *Centroamérica,* pp. 30–31.

37. "The progressive recurrence to devaluation as an economic policy instrument, combined with fiscal exemption of export activities, resistance to serious tax reform, and conservative wage and social policies, inevitably leads to a more exclusive and polarized society. The attempt to promote the maquiladora industry is grounded once again in the possibility of keeping the work force at very low wage levels. Foreign capital, historically privileged fractions of domestic capital, and some emergent groups have become the main beneficiaries of the process, while a gigantic social debt keeps on accumulating. Paradoxically, the new channels responsible for the economic logic undermine the projects for political reform, which in turn are a necessary condition for a stable outcome to the crisis." Timossi Dolinsky, *Centroamérica,* pp. 111–112.

38. There are no reliable statistics on Central American migration, owing to the nature of this phenomenon. It is generally estimated that over 1.5 million people have migrated out of the region during the past decade and nearly 2 million have migrated within it; in other words, some 15 percent of the total population of Central America has been displaced. On this topic, see Sergio Aguayo, *El éxodo centroaméricano,* Colección Foro 2000 (Mexico: Secretaría de Educación Pública, 1985); Rodolfo Casillas R., "La migración centroaméricana de paso: un desafío a la política exterior de México," paper presented at the Seminar on International Migration in Mexico: Current Situation and Outlook, Cocoyoc, Morelos, Mexico, October 4–6, 1989; Manuel Angel Castillo G., "Contexto regional y migraciones a la frontera sur de México," paper presented to the Seminar on Information and Analysis of Migratory Labor along the Border and Undocumented Workers, Tapachula, Chiapas, April 2, 1990.

39. The situation is cause for debate and dispute in Mexico. For example, during the fourth session of the seminar on "Migration Policy Options," held by the Mexican Senate around a discussion of modifications in the abovementioned law, researcher Rodolfo Casillas R. of the Colegio de México pointed out that even though Mexico is cited as a transit point for narcotics traffic and undocumented workers, which "has created a series of international pressures, especially from the United States," it is unacceptable for the two activities—which are not sociologically comparable—to be equated by that country. And he added, "It is my hypothesis that in 1987, Mexico began to close its borders

in coordination of some type with U.S. migration policy." On the other hand, there have been numerous denunciations of abuses against undocumented workers on Mexican territory. In the above-mentioned seminar, Deputy Minister for Domestic Affairs Miguel Limón Rojas acknowledged that migration toward the United States represents "a very arduous pilgrimage that exposes a person to not one, but numerous situations of extortion and exploitation, evoking images of the greatest cruelty and human misery, which we intend to prevent." Aurelio Ramos M., "No hay deportaciones irregulares ni canje de indocumentados por armas," *Excélsior,* 21 June 1990.

40. For example, on February 28, 1990, the Supreme Court of the United States reviewed the case of Mexican Verdugo Urquídez, kidnapped and imprisoned in San Diego, California, since 1986. Citing the Fourth Amendment, it held that the FBI, the DEA, and the U.S. armed forces may use force to apprehend suspected criminals in other countries when the national interest is threatened. The most notorious application of this ruling was the capture of General Manuel Antonio Noriega; to accomplish this, it was necessary to invade Panama. Rodolfo Medina, "La Cuarta Enmienda: ¿impunidad de la DEA?" *UnomásUno,* 18 May 1990.

41. The Bush-Bennett (antidrug) Plan, announced in September 1989 permits the search of homes without a warrant in cases where individuals are suspected of selling or using drugs. It even permits the declaration of a state of siege in the disadvantaged neighborhoods of several cities, while in other areas like Detroit, South Philadelphia, and New Orleans "vigilante patrols have been formed that grant themselves police powers and boast of their successful campaigns against organized crime and drug abuse." Manuel Lois Méndez, "EUA: narcotráfico y seguridad nacional," *UnomásUno,* 13 June 1990.

42. According to DEA reports, poppy growing in Guatemala rose from 810 hectares in 1988 to 1,370 in 1989, while marijuana cultivation went from 325 to 600 hectares in the same period. This rapid growth can be partly explained by the participation of government sectors and the army. Among these figures is Lt. Col. Hugo Morán Carranza, accused of drug trafficking by the U.S. government; despite this, Morán continued to enjoy the protection of President Cerezo, who made him director of the Free Trade Zone in Santo Tomás de Castilla, an appropriate site if he is indeed involved in the drug trade. Similar narcotics charges have been leveled against Carlos Alfredo Cabrera Hidalgo, brother of then Christian Democratic candidate Alfonso Cabrera, and Milton Cerezo, brother of the president—this time for facilitating the entry of illegal aliens into Guatemala. Guatemalan analysts conclude that this must be what is behind the recent conflicts between the Office of the President and the U.S. Embassy in that country. *Crónica Semanal* 118 (Guatemala, 23 March 1990), pp. 11–17.

43. According to an IPS cable dated July 3, 1990, "between 10,000 and 20,000 kilos of cocaine a year" pass through Costa Rican territory. In fact, Costa Rica's Congress is concerned about the implications of the narcotics traffic for the country. Their investigations have revealed connections between people in high political and government places and the drug traffickers, as in

the case of former Minister of Security Benjamín Piza and other officials of Luis Alberto Monge's administration (1982–1986). The scandal has even touched former president Daniel Oduber. *Excélsior,* 4 July 1990.

44. This was one of the most important results of the "civil war of 1948," which forced various political and economic transformations in Costa Rican democracy. EDUCA, Costa Rica, and Miguel Acuña, "Los hechos políticos del 48" (Costa Rica: Imprenta Lehmann).

45. See Centro de Estudios de la Realidad Guatemalteca (CERG), "Las selvas de El Petén y el pulmón boscoco mesoamericano," *Perspectiva Centroamericana* 9 (Mexico, December 1989).

46. The case is being reviewed because of an appeal filed before the Honduran Supreme Court, calling for the return of Matta Ballesteros to the country. As the appeal points out, his illegal handing over to U.S. authorities violates the country's constitution. *Excélsior,* 4 July 1990, IPS cable published in the third part of Section A.

47. A number of ideas expressed in the seminar "Central America at the Turn of the Century" are expressed here. The seminar was organized by the Instituto Matías Romero de Estudios Diplomáticos (IMRED) of the Ministry of Foreign Relations of Mexico and the Facultad Latinaméricano de Ciencias Sociales (FLACSO) and held in Mexico May 17–18, 1990. I am especially indebted to participants Rómulo Caballeros and Héctor Dada.

48. Among other benefits, the San José Pact provides that if the resources derived from oil credits are designated for priority projects, especially in the energy sector, payments corresponding to 30 percent of the oil bill may be deferred twenty years at a 2 percent annual interest rate.

49. In this regard, see *Relaciones Centroamérica-México 1978–1986* (PECA-CIDE, 1987).

CHAPTER 5

The Future of Mexican–U.S.– Central American Relations: Final Considerations

GILBERTO CASTAÑEDA,
H. RODRIGO JAUBERTH,
PEDRO VUSKOVIC,
AND JESÚS HERNÁNDEZ

THE COMMON THREAD OF THIS WORK is the exploration of the historic triangularity of relations between Central America, Mexico, and the United States. In our view, an understanding of this is essential for a grasp of the bilateral relations between the parties, particularly Central American–Mexican and Central American–U.S. relations.

The triangular nature of the relationship and close ties between Central America and Mexico have helped to offset the enormous influence exerted by the United States over Central America and Mexico.

The origins of this dynamic lie in Central America's historical importance for both Mexico and the United States. From the outset, both countries have had differing positions on the future of the region and relations between the nations that compose it. Mexico has sought to avoid being surrounded by countries unconditionally allied to the United States, while Washington has tried to cement its hegemony over the region. In the meantime, for the peoples of Central America, Mexico has been a crucial ally in their struggle for democracy and national sovereignty.

Nevertheless, since the 1980s there has been a growing trend toward a modification of the triangular relationship. The current warming in relations between Mexico and the United States, particularly in the economic sphere but also on a political level, is significant; so is the cooling in relations between Central America and Mexico insofar as Mexican participation in the search for a solution to the conflicts in Nicaragua, El Salvador, and Guatemala is concerned. Despite this, there has been some movement toward closer economic ties between Mexico and these countries, in terms of cooperation and technical assistance, though the foundations for this are rather precarious.

Three Key Periods in the Triangular Relationship

The history of Central American–Mexican–U.S. relations began with the independence of what was once the Viceroyalty of New Spain (1821). Since then, this history has been marked by the need—not always achievable—for close ties between Central America and Mexico, particularly among the countries' progressive political and social forces. Thus, from early on, Central Americans pursued by the powers of the moment sought political asylum in Mexico. Since then, to varying degrees, Mexico has also backed political enterprises in opposition to the regimes of the moment and supported the response by progressive forces in Central America to U.S. interventionism in those countries; hence, Mexico's support for the liberal Revolution of 1871 in Guatemala and its defense of the Nicaraguan government of José Santos Zelaya (also a liberal), subjected to U.S. harassment in the early twentieth century.

To this history, the 1970s added several new factors: greater upheaval in Central America, Mexico's newly active Third World diplomacy, and the obstacles to the exercise of U.S. hegemony. Beginning in 1977, three periods can be distinguished.

The first began in 1977. Its relevant features were Mexico's support for the signing of the Torrijos-Carter Treaties, its backing for the anti-Somoza struggle in Nicaragua (and to a lesser extent, the revolutionary struggle in El Salvador), and the worsening of its differences and tensions with the Guatemalan regime. This period culminated in the formation of the Contadora Group in January 1983.

This was a period of great social upheaval and confrontation in Central America. The economic concentration and political exclusion that had mired Central American society for decades had produced social crisis and armed revolutionary movements. This was the period that witnessed the triumph of the Nicaraguan Revolution and the worsening of the armed domestic conflicts in El Salvador and Guatemala.

At the same time, the United States was experiencing domestic and foreign difficulties that interfered with its ability to exert its hegemony and domination in the region. This was the result of its defeat in Vietnam, a series of scandals including Watergate and revelations about past activities of the Central Intelligence Agency (CIA), and an economic crisis that was already part of the worldwide process of economic reconversion.

Mexico, in contrast, saw its capacity for international action enhanced, particularly with the advent of the oil boom in the late 1970s. This allowed its government to intensify and expand the diplomatic initiatives it had been promoting since early in the decade—a diplomacy basically centered around joint political and diplomatic efforts with Third World countries, as exemplified in the initiative for a new, more just, and equitable international economic order. The new aspect of Mexico's diplomacy became its activism in Central America.

Nevertheless, from roughly 1983 to 1987, there was a substantial change in this situation, marking the second period in the recent history of the triangular relationship—a period characterized by U.S. belligerence in the region with the advent of the Reagan administration (1981–1989).

Also significant in this second period was the collaboration of Honduras and Costa Rica in the interventionist plans of the United States and the birth of the counterrevolutionary offensives in Nicaragua, El Salvador, and Guatemala. At the same time, there was an unusual increase in U.S. pressure and aggression against Mexico, which damaged that country's prospects for maintaining an active role in Central America. All this led to a pullback by several Latin American and European governments and political parties (particularly the Socialist International) that had once supported the processes of social change. The obstacles to the advancement of the Nicaraguan government's goals, the impasse in the struggle in El Salvador, and the waning of the conflict in Guatemala all occurred in this context.

At the same time, economic problems were worsening in Latin America, especially those connected with the external debt. These problems affected both Central America and Mexico and led to the implementation of structural adjustment policies dictated by the International Monetary Fund (IMF) and the World Bank. In the case of Mexico, the government devised a strategy linked primarily to the payment of the debt and closer ties to the United States and possibly Canada.

Thus, in the process, there was a regionalization of Central America's conflicts under U.S. hegemony and domination. The United States managed to involve Honduras and Costa Rica in its anti-Nicaraguan activities and in the formation of the so-called "Tegucigalpa Bloc" between these countries and El Salvador. The main objective of the alliance was to isolate and topple the Nicaraguan Revolution, while increasing support for the Salvadoran regime.

This process led to an erosion of the Mexican government's support for social change in the area and a search for an easing of regional tensions through the resolution of interstate conflicts, chiefly between Nicaragua and neighboring Honduras and Costa Rica. For this to occur, however, multilateral Latin American action via the Contadora Group was a must. The Contadora Group expanded into the Support Group (1985), which then turned into the Río Group (1988). Contadora had the backing of both Nicaragua and, in 1985, Guatemala—though for very different reasons and with very different objectives in each case.

At the same time, the United States consolidated its hegemony in the region. Bilateral Mexican-U.S. and Central American–U.S. relations became the relevant ones, and with this, the triangularity of the relationship was reduced to its earlier historical parameters, where Mexican–Central American relations had little relevance or influence.

Thus, in late 1987, the third period in the triangular relationship took form, extending to the present day. Since 1987, we have witnessed what could be termed the "Central Americanization" of the peace efforts via the Esquipulas II accords, signed by the presidents in Guatemala that August 7. A key objective of the Reagan administration at the time was to take control of the negotiations process, which it managed to do to some extent. With the presidential resolutions of Esquipulas III, signed in Costa Rica in January 1988, Mexico's—and with it Contadora's—exclusion from the peace negotiations was definitive.

Nevertheless, Contadora retained a presence, especially in the negotiations aimed at economic reactivation. In all this, its Commission to Support the Economic and Social Development of Central America (CADESCA) played a role. Through this commission, Contadora broadened Latin American participation in the search for a solution to Central America's economic and social woes, and to accomplish this it also encouraged the participation of the European Economic Community (EEC) countries. In the meantime, Mexico strengthened its bilateral relations with the countries of the area.

Furthermore, pressured by its domestic difficulties, Mexico turned inward. This was the start of the government's current policy of forging closer ties with the United States, which it considers a key factor in resolving its crisis. This was very much in line with government objectives concerning the renegotiation of the external debt and economic reconversion to permit the competitive insertion of the country into the new world market. Meanwhile, the popular and progressive organizations of Mexico saw their prospects for solidarity with the Central American peoples reduced; their monitoring of foreign policy and consequent pressure on the Mexican government also diminished. This was the outcome of Mexico's crisis, of the need to solve domestic problems and increase the participation of these groups in national politics.

The governments of the region, in turn, traveled down similar roads in their quest for a solution to the crisis. They nevertheless were subjected to even greater economic and political pressures than Mexico. This led to a consolidation of U.S. hegemony in the area, reinforced by a multitude of new factors—among them, the dynamic of the worldwide economic reconversion, the triumph of conservative positions in the region with the advent of the Reagan administration, the transformations that were taking place in Eastern Europe, the demands and constraints imposed by the war on drugs, and the need for democratization and legitimization through elections that have recently led the governments of the region to adopt uniformly conservative positions.

Thus, political and diplomatic ties between Central America and Mexico are currently weak and appear to be moving in an essentially economic direction. Moreover, they are no longer as important as they were in the late 1970s and early 1980s. Nonetheless, some of their basic features remain, especially in the areas of bilateral cooperation, Mexico's support for a solution to the economic problems of the area, and its contribution to the peace negotiations at the governmental level, particularly where El Salvador is concerned.

Prospects

In this context, the future of Central American–Mexican–U.S. relations is difficult to foretell. Under the present worldwide economic and political transformation, these relations may be altered by factors beyond the grasp of even the players involved. (These changes are discussed in Chapter 4, "The Context of Central America–Mexican–U.S. Relations.") Still, the greatest force in these relations is clearly the United States, given its global influence and its role as the dominant pole in Central American relations.

In our view, a number of issues will exert an external influence on Central America and the triangular relationship over the short term: (1) greater economic integration between Mexico and the United States and the trend toward the creation of a North American common market, with Canadian participation; (2) the Japanese role in Central American–Mexican–U.S. relations, which will vary depending on whether Japan joins a Pacific Rim Agreement with U.S. participation or an exclusively Asian agreement; (3) the drift toward a worsening of North-South conflicts, once East-West tensions have ended; (4) U.S. economic difficulties and the looming possibility of recession; (5) the outlook for progress toward South-South—especially Latin American—integration.

At the international level, the worldwide economic reconversion will lead to a greater interdependence of production processes among the countries at its center, plus a rapid and growing internationalization of capital and a greater subordination of peripheral economies to such processes. Technological innovation also threatens to widen the gulf that separates countries like those of Central America from the industrialized nations.

Latin America's importance to the world economy is diminishing, and it runs the risk of being left out of the principal international trade flows. At the same time, it is strongly attracted to the countries at the center of the world economy, even though they hinder the regional integration processes necessary for addressing the region's crisis. The recent "Enterprise for the Americas" initiative launched by President Bush is an example of this.

For the moment, it is clear that an easing of international political tensions will not necessarily lead to an easing of international economic tensions. On the contrary, North-South economic relations may become attenuated and even more inequitable because of a growing marginalization of the natural resources and labor markets of the Third World. While relations between the countries at the center of the international dynamic are becoming increasingly important, their ties with those on the periphery are generally losing relevance.

The United States, faced with major economic problems of its own and increasing competition from other wealthy countries, needs a continent that will serve its interests. The "Enterprise for the Americas" initiative is an example of the Bush administration's strategy in this regard, fostering neoliberal economic restructuring in Latin America.

In Central America, the social confrontation has grown increasingly complex. The future of the movements for social change in Central America under the impositions of the international context just described will depend greatly on the course that the Nicaraguan situation takes, the time involved, and the progress of the negotiation and peace processes in El Salvador and Guatemala. In the long term, the wars will only vanish in response to a change in the terms that ignited the struggle for social change in the area in the first place.

Three Scenarios

In our view, three scenarios for Central American–Mexican–U.S. relations emerge from this set of circumstances. They are, in order of greatest likelihood:

1. An increase in U.S. hegemony and domination in both Latin and Central America. The U.S. economic crisis and the intensification of

competition among the capitalist countries is pushing the United States toward a greater expansion. For historical and geographical reasons, Mexico, Central America, and Latin America in general appear to represent its most immediate opportunities. Thus, the formation of a North American economic bloc and the bolstering of conservative positions in Central America, above all in the economic sphere, would put the isthmus in the position of becoming an appendage of that bloc. In that case, Central American–Mexican and Central American–U.S. bilateral relations would be modified through a U.S.-Mexican–Central American intermediation that, strictly speaking, would no longer be triangular but linear. We must bear in mind that the viewpoint of the region's power sectors favors a dynamic of this sort and that exogenous forces exist that are contributing, albeit unwittingly, to the rupture of the triangularity as we have known it.

A more marked variation of this scenario is also possible. Though not inevitable and certainly less likely, it would consist of a drift toward a certain homogenization of the foreign policies of Mexico and the United States, at least as far as Central America is concerned. If this came to pass, it would be in the areas of issues like the external debt, drug trafficking, and Central American migration to Mexico and the United States. Mexico's participation in this regard would thus tend to become "depoliticized" and take on an economic bias—i e , there would be a special emphasis on trade. Of course, this is not a *fait accompli*. It is a debate of historic proportions that has been ongoing in Mexico and is beginning to emerge in Central America and the United States.

2. A second likely scenario is one that involves a significant presence of other foreign players, such as the EEC and Japan. This extracontinental presence could modify U.S. clout to some extent in its relations with Mexico and Central America. Indeed, it could mean greater room for negotiations with the United States—something that Mexico has sought in the past—and, hence, greater possibilities for self-determination. For Central America, it could lead to the promotion of more independent policies on regional integration, with significant economic and social implications.

A variation on this scenario might be progress in the South-South integration processes. In that event, the outlook would be greater room for negotiation and self-determination in Latin America and a strengthening of regional economic integration processes.

3. The third and final scenario would be the possibility of advances by the political and social forces in their quest for peace and development, democracy and sovereignty in Central America, accompanied by similar progress in Mexico and the United States. The coming together of forces of this type within the countries of the triangular relationship—

which for now appears unlikely—would undoubtedly have sweeping repercussions for the region and for inter-American relations in general. In this case, the outlook could be a defusing of the local and regional conflicts of the Isthmus, the result of an end to the armed domestic conflicts, economic reactivation, and the building and strengthening of democracy, among other things.

An unlikely, though desirable, possibility would be the consolidation of the democratic process in Nicaragua and respect for all political parties—including the Sandinistas—in the wake of Violeta Chamorro's election victory. So too would be a true reopening of dialogue and negotiation in El Salvador and Guatemala and real commitments that would lay the groundwork for democratization and finding solutions to the most pressing economic and social concerns of these countries. Equally desirable would be an end to U.S. intervention, progress in regional integration, equitable income distribution, and, above all, the right to exercise political freedoms. Processes like these would make it possible to anticipate changes in the current configuration of political and social forces in the area. New national and international scenarios would therefore also be possible—scenarios that would restore the traditional triangular relationship between Central America, Mexico, and the United States on more solid and permanent grounds.

Nonetheless, we believe that the first scenario is the one most likely to prevail in the short run. It may be somewhat mitigated by the presence of Europe and Japan and by an advance of the alternative political and social forces in the region. The triangularity might thus be restored through relations among the organizations of the respective societies. Otherwise, the continuation and strengthening of U.S hegemony and domination is the likely future.

Epilogue:
Commentary from
Regional Specialists

**David Ibarra, Consultant to the Economic Commission
on Latin America and the Caribbean, Mexico**

We are living in an era of great changes in foreign relations and the
international division of labor and power, but it is also an era where
the great ideological contrasts that marked the nineteenth and twentieth
centuries are eroding or disappearing—at least on the surface. While
everything in the real world is changing, in the world of ideas, the
differences over the forms and objectives of society are apparently
narrowing.

In Latin America, these changes have created enormous imbalances
in the economic, social, and political spheres that, far from being
resolved, have produced the worst crisis that this century has known.
Not only has there been a paralysis in development and an extension
or a deepening of poverty and inequality, but progress toward a
democratic modernization, postponed to a greater or lesser degree since
the time of the independence movements, has been placed in jeopardy.

Central America has experienced the alterations in its external
environment more deeply and intensely than any other area of Latin
America, and it is perhaps the region that has been least able to adjust
or adapt to them. In the first place, the advent of the anti-Sandinista
struggle in Nicaragua marked the turning point in the East-West
confrontation in Central America. From then on, a burgeoning political
crisis drew the rest of the region in and merged with economic crises
that extended to the whole of Latin America.

The political tensions spilled over into the economic arena, undermining the foundation of Central American development, and most of
all, delaying adjustment to the new international realities. Indeed, the
ideological divisions and the armed conflict directly eroded economic
and regional integration, not to mention joint programs for industrialization. The massive emigration within and away from Central America

upset the labor markets, and the proliferation of armed conflict destroyed the infrastructure or at the very least, stunted its normal growth. External aid, largely allocated for sustaining the armed conflict, temporarily financed the balance of payments disequilibria and, in so doing, paradoxically postponed the indispensable economic readjustment.

In the early 1980s, Mexican foreign policy tempered more extreme influences of other origins. Due to its domestic need for autonomy with respect to the United States, Mexico endeavored to halt the rise in East-West tensions that were advancing toward its borders. Thus, it maintained that the roots of Central America's problems were to be found more in the enormous social inequalities and the frustration of the just aspirations of the peoples of the region than in the ideological struggle between socialism and capitalism.

However, events of domestic and external origin soon altered this panorama completely. The cold war abruptly vanished; Mexico, weakened at first by its economic crisis, determined to form a free trade bloc with the United States and Canada. Central America's priority in the U.S. agenda fell concomitantly. The Central American governments decided to embrace the cause of peace and economic integration, as evidenced in the agreements of Esquipulas and Antigua, while elections were held in the region that in nearly all cases represented clear democratic progress.

As the 1990s open, Central America finds itself with some battles won—largely on the fronts of peace and democracy—but highly debilitated and facing serious economic problems, with foreign aid clearly on the decline. The United States has reaffirmed its regional hegemony, but paradoxically, because of this, Mexico's balancing influence could begin to make itself felt within prescribed limits.

The story of this complex interaction of forces and events, which transcends the boundaries of any analytical discipline, constitutes the key contribution of the chapters in this book. There are undeniable interdisciplinary achievements in this book that also represent a breath of fresh air in a world contaminated by the ideologically monist avalanche that has extended to every latitude.

Guadalupe Gonzalez G., Director of the Division of International Studies of the Center for Economic Research and Teaching (CIDE), Mexico

The book starts off with the premise that Central America's domestic and external reality cannot truly be understood without situating it within the subregional context. Mexico, Central America, and the United

States share a particular geopolitical space that determines not only their changing patterns of interaction but also the room available to maneuver domestically for the region's countries to undertake projects leading to social, political, and/or economic change.

In this shared space, as revealed by Jesús Hernández's historical essay, which introduces the reader to this collective effort, the three angles of the triangle have followed a pattern of mutual cyclical policies, successively alternating moments of indifference and oblivion with periods of intense activity involving both economic and military measures. Based on this situation of reciprocal influences derived from the existence of a geopolitical space shared by countries on different rungs of the world power scale, history shows how the absence of one of the players has had as great an impact as its active presence in determining the various options for development, political modernization, and regional stability that have confronted Central America at one time or another.

From the longest side of the triangle, the United States commenced a new cycle of activism in the region toward the late 1970s, with the implementation of an unconventional strategy to contain the social change promised by the triumph of the Sandinista revolution. At the opening of the 1990s, this U.S. activism in response to the "perceived crisis" in an area deemed "categorically imperative" to U.S. national security appears to be winding down with the dismantling of the cold war, the fall of the Sandinista government through the electoral process, and the redrawing of Panama's political map through direct military intervention.

In the 1980s the risks to Central America derived chiefly from the bellicose activities of the Reagan administration, the growing strategic and military presence of the United States, and the potential regionalization of the conflict. At the close of the twentieth century, paradoxically, the threat will come from a return to historical U.S. indifference toward the region. Central America's decline in the immediate priorities of U.S. foreign policy, within the framework of a worldwide reshuffling, implies reduced possibilities for the transfer of financial resources (both government and private) to the region—resources that are ever more necessary to reverse the erosion of these countries' economic situation and to stabilize the area.

From the shortest side of the triangle, Mexico has closely followed the cycles of involvement and indifference that have characterized U.S. policy toward Central America. This is no accident. Historically, relations between Mexico and Central America have been judged by the relationship of each with the United States. The high concentration of Mexico's and Central America's foreign relations with the United States partly explains why mutual Mexican–Central American relations have been marginal for both parties when conditions in the region have been normal or relatively stable. In contrast, from Mexico's standpoint as a country with influence in the region, the events south of its immediate geopolitical border tend to take on importance as a function of the way they are handled by the United States north of the border. The nature of U.S. policy toward Central America is a key element in Mexican perceptions of threats deriving from the processes of socio-political change in the region.

From the standpoint of the Central American countries, the historical determinant of their international relations is unquestionably their relationship with the United States. However, at different junctures characterized by internal crisis and conflict with that hegemonic power, the importance of relations with Mexico tends to increase as a political and economic counterweight to the United States, providing an opening for forces within the Central American political spectrum whose prospects for political participation in their respective countries are otherwise dwindling.

Following the historical logic, it is reasonable to anticipate a return to a Mexican position characterized by relative indifference toward the events in Central America, thus intensifying the strategic marginalization of this area. The authors of this volume are acutely aware of the first signs of this new cycle of indifference and withdrawal. What is more, they share the opinion that in the future, the Mexican–Central American side of the triangle will tend to be undermined and eventually break, as the process of Mexican–U.S.–Canadian economic integration advances. Nevertheless, there are reasons to believe that, despite the profound changes under way in U.S. and Mexican foreign policy, which point to differences between the two players on the Central American scene, these differences are not absolute, and the dynamic of intermittent and variable attention will persist. As the book clearly indicates, the factors that led to the outbreak of the crisis in Central America a decade ago are still present, and the causes of the economic, social, and political instability have yet to be resolved. A fragile balance has therefore been established in Central America that can lead at any time to instability and, hence, to a new cycle of attention and activism on the part of the other two sides of the regional triangle. This latent conflict is already having a direct domestic impact, both in Mexico and the United States; its most dramatic feature is the growing migration of Central Americans toward Mexico and the United States, situating the social agenda of human and workers' rights at the heart of the region's concerns. Furthermore, Mexico's diplomatic withdrawal does not apply to its immediate neighbors, Guatemala and Belize.

A study like this one offered by Rodrigo Jauberth, Gilberto Castañeda, Pedro Vuskovic, and Jesús Hernández has a sense of timeliness that transcends intellectual vogues. It is precisely now, when the foreign policy of the main regional players (the United States and Mexico) relegates the Central American situation to a secondary plane, that a more objective analysis can be undertaken of the critical moments of the past, as well as an evaluation of the multiplicity of factors that will shape a future whose outlook is uncertain.

**Adolfo Aguilar Zinser, Researcher at the Institute
of U.S. Studies of the National
Autonomous University of Mexico (UNAM)**

Relations between Mexico and Central America are historically characterized by an attitude of mutual ambivalence and distrust. Traditionally, Central American perceptions of Mexico have shown certain similarities with the apprehension Mexicans have towards the United States, their own northern neighbor. Mexico's rich and engaging culture, its social history, and its authoritarian yet stable political system have attracted the admiration of Central Americans; many have seen the postrevolutionary Mexican regime, including its one-party system, as a model of social change and political order. However, Central Americans have also resented what they perceived are Mexico's sporadic attempts to establish a base of influence in the region and to take unfair advantage of its southern neighbors. But these visible similarities are not the only—and certainly not the most important—element of the triangular relationship that exists between Mexico, the United States, and Central America.

In fact, history and current experiences show that interactions of Central America with its northern neighbors have not always included this triangular link. Such a phenomenon has not always been evident, but in all cases, one of the crucial motives of U.S. diplomacy in Central America has been to respond directly or indirectly, explicitly or implicitly, to Mexico's presence and potential influence in the region. The series of essays presented in this book by Rodrigo Jauberth, Jesús Hernández, Pedro Vuskovic, and Gilberto Castañeda has laid the historical and conceptual groundwork for an understanding of this triangle. Their combined studies have not only explicitly addressed the complex interactions between the foreign policies of Mexico and the United States, as expressed in Central America, they also trace and analyze the ways in which these interactions have in fact shaped events in the region.

Mexico has always seen Central America as a potential area of influence. However, with few exceptions (most notably, the period from 1978 to 1986), it has not really exercised an active policy in the region. At least two distinctive factors have inhibited Mexico's involvement in Central America. First and foremost is the determining role that relations with the United States have played in Mexico's diplomatic, political, and economic history. The North has absorbed most of Mexico's attention. Also, the United States has at all times manifested remarkable sensitivity to any real or perceived attempt on the part of Mexico to dominate in Central America and the Caribbean.

The second factor contributing to Mexico's detachment from Central America is the rift caused by the uneven political development that both Mexico and Central America have experienced, especially after the Mexican Revolution of 1910. With the notable exception of Costa Rica, all the other Central American republics have had a very slow political evolution. They have been dominated by small oligarchic elites, obsessed with the preservation of their wealth and privileges and lacking a sense of national purpose. This has been translated into the entrenchment of highly resilient military regimes, fiercely antidemocratic and insensitive to the needs of the greater population.

The close identification of these governments with the United States has equally contributed to keeping Mexico and Central America at a distance, if not always in a posture of open hostility, at least in an attitude of mutual disgust. For a long time, Mexico prided itself for not being like the pro-American dictatorships of Central America. The implicit U.S. ban on Mexico's involvement in Central America, together with the underlying antipathy that those regimes and Mexico have felt for one another, long shelved whatever historic motivation Mexico had about its adjoining region. The clearest manifestation of this mutual detachment is the negligible size of their economic exchanges.

Nonetheless, in spite of this government-to-government aloofness, cultural and social contacts between Central America and Mexico have always been intense. The rich confluence of the two societies is manifested in a diversity of migration flows. Over several decades, Central Americans have gone to Mexico to be educated in a wide variety of disciplines ranging from the social sciences, the arts, and medicine to the military, with Central American officers receiving training in Mexico's War College. Central Americans have traveled constantly to Mexico not only for higher education but also as refugees, with intellectuals, political leaders, and journalists, as well as workers, peasants, and Indian communities and their leaders escaping repression and political persecution. During the past years, many have also gone to Mexico in search of work or passing through the country on their way to the United States.

All of these Central American population movements toward Mexico have created a social network and a cultural identity that gives Mexico a considerable, albeit not highly visible, influence in Central America.

The empirical evidence and theoretical discussion presented here make this book a valuable contribution to the study of regional diplomacy and is particularly useful for an understanding of the future role of Mexico and the United States in consolidating peace and promoting the economic development of Central America.

Carlos M. Vilas, Researcher at the Center for Interdisciplinary Research of the Humanities, National Autonomous University of Mexico (UNAM)

This new book highlights several important aspects of how the Central American crisis meshed with the political dynamic of the United States and Mexico and was processed by each. I will refer very briefly to three of these aspects.

First, the authors point out the different approaches and focuses to the Central American crisis in Mexico and the United States. For Mexico, the crisis is foremost a product of underdevelopment, external dependence, and dictatorship. In particular, the inability to find institutional channels for their demands for a better life and for democratization led many Central Americans to seek alternative, even violent, solutions. This is an interpretation based on Mexico's own history—on its revolutionary past—and on the Latin-Americanism that for many decades governed its foreign policy.

For the United States, in contrast, Central America and the Caribbean Basin in general have always been but a chapter, and a brief one at that, in its confrontation with the Soviet Union—as these areas were in its relations with Great Britain and then Spain in the last century and Germany early in this century. From this perspective, the Central American crisis is chiefly the product of Soviet-Cuban expansionism in the region, which directly compromises the vital interests of the United States. Thus, the United States does not recognize the autonomy of the regional players, who additionally are perceived as terribly vulnerable to pressures from "the East." The analysis of the White House's ambiguity about the Arias Plan and later the regional peace process is highly illustrative of this clearly arrogant attitude toward the Central Americans. Finally, this U.S. approach is incompatible with the development of a policy toward the region and, hence, a regional approach to the crisis, to the extent that the crisis is the product or forms part of the context of the global East-West confrontation.

"We don't want another Cuba"; "we don't want another Vietnam." White House policy never went much beyond these clichés. Today, with the crisis solved by the regional protagonists themselves, support from the governments of Latin America and Europe, and the disappearance of the East-West confrontation, the absence of a policy (and even policies) toward the region is unquestionable and leads one of the authors of this volume to speak of a "malign neglect" on the part of the United States toward Central America. I don't know whether it's a matter of neglect, but it certainly is not benign.

Second, the book points out the different instances and approaches of the successive Mexican administrations toward Central America. The study particularly highlights the evolution from Mexico's initial direct and highly political and diplomatic involvement toward an indirect and progressively weaker relationship with a lower profile. The book discusses factors that, in the authors' view, were instrumental in effecting these modifications: the unfolding of the regional crisis itself, the development of the political and economic situation in Mexico, the evolution of Mexican-U.S. relations, and the unveiling of initiatives springing from Central America itself, among other things. It is important to note that since the late 1980s, Mexico's attention toward the region has been channelled chiefly through support for the regional mechanisms to deal with the crisis.

Third, the book can be considered a study of the room to maneuver available to the more politically and economically developed regional protagonists—the intermediate powers—for addressing and resolving regional crises. It is also a study of their relative autonomy, which varies at different times and in different situations, with respect to the hegemonic players on a world scale. Similarly, the book notes the potential of regional approaches for crisis management, as opposed to the rigidities and limitations of a global approach.

I believe that this volume places a useful tool in the hands of a broad but informed public to help understand a traumatic phase in the history of Central America and provide some insight as to how it will evolve.

**Fernando Carmona de la Peña, Researcher at the
Center for Economic Research, National Autonomous
University of Mexico (UNAM)**

There is an abundance of reports, articles, essays, and books that separately analyze relations between the United States and Mexico and/

or relations between that continental and world power and one or several of the Central American countries—just as in the past decade there has been no lack of studies emanating from these latter nations that examine this same contradictory and difficult relationship, often so full of conflict.

The majority of these works are the fruit of academic research or reflect the economic, political, or cultural interests of individual U.S. authors or diverse government or private institutions, universities, or journalistic enterprises, as well as international organizations and even other (especially European) countries.

The literature on Central America is already abundant. This is due to the crisis in this ever-troubled region of the Americas, which for over a century has been the object of U.S. intervention. The guerrilla movements in Guatemala, the civil war in El Salvador, the instability in Honduras, the spectacular victory of the Sandinista revolution in Nicaragua in July 1979, and the no-less-spectacular defeat of the FSLN in February 1990, the economic and political difficulties in Costa Rica, as well as the advent of the nationalistic regime of Gen. Omar Torrijos in Panama and the eventual U.S. invasion and military occupation of that country, and even the independence of Belize, are expressions of the protracted crisis that has given rise to numerous studies.

This book, however, has three essential characteristics that distinguish it and endow it with a particular importance: first, it is the fruit of a U.S.–Mexican–Central American interinstitutional effort; second, it is authored by Latin American researchers (one Mexican, two Central Americans, and one Chilean) from different disciplines in the social sciences; and third, it is the first work that conceives of the relationship between the United States and the Central American countries as a triangularity that necessarily includes Mexico.

The fact that this is an interinstitutional, interdisciplinary, and, at the same time, international work is revealing of a growing consciousness of the importance of getting at the roots of the crisis in Central America, one of the most troubled regions on Earth. This is a region that, with the end of the cold war, emerges as a part of Latin America whose underlying problems—underdevelopment and backwardness, undemocratic political systems, growing social inequalities, weak and vulnerable economies—cannot be attributed to the so-called "East-West" conflict, for decades the foundation of the aggressive foreign policy of the United States and the defensive foreign policy of governments like Mexico's.

This book, of course, is an example of the advances that the social sciences in Latin America have made in recent decades. Today, even countries like those of Central America have hundreds of economists, sociologists, historians, anthropologists, political scientists, and dozens and dozens of students of international relations. Similarly, there are numerous academic and government centers for research into these problems—Mexico, of course, possessing the greatest number.

With issues as complex and polemical as the triangularity between the United States, Mexico, and Central America, the authors have made a real advance in focusing the study from the angle of the historical roots and evolution of the foreign policy of these countries, based on the development of a national consciousness and the interests fundamental to each, which diverged from the very beginning. Specifically, from early on, Mexico's foreign policy was grounded in the principles of international law and peaceful coexistence: nonintervention; the right of peoples to self-determination; respect for the sovereignty of other nations; the juridical equality of states; and the peaceful and negotiated settlement of conflicts between nations. These principles became paramount in the twentieth century, especially after World War II, with the worldwide decolonization process and the intensification of international relations on every level. The analyses contained in this book clearly outline the reasons for the international conduct of successive Mexican governments over the years.

Mexico, like the countries of Central America, has been the victim of external aggression since its independence from Spain: filibusterism, military invasions, even attempts to establish a European "Empire" on its soil. Mexico's entire history reveals a common destiny with its neighbors, which has been the weak link in its relations with the United States even long before that country became a great world power.

Mexico's economic relations with the United States have become progressively more difficult and are now critical. Mexico's destiny will inevitably be linked with its neighbor to the North, but more and more, it will also be linked with its neighbors to the South, in defense of its sovereignty, independence, and liberty.

David Brooks, Director, Mexico-U.S. Dialogos, American Friends Service Committee; Primitivo Rodriguez, Director, Mexico-U.S. Border Program, American Friends Service Committee

According to a poll conducted by the *Los Angeles Times* in 1988, over 60 percent of working-age Mexicans would choose to live in the United States if they were given a "green card." Another poll, conducted at the end of 1990 by Miguel Bazanez, a Mexican expert on public opinion studies, indicated that slightly more than half of all Mexicans would favor the formation of a single country by the U.S. and Mexico if that would improve living standards.

Polls are debatable but they do demonstrate a previously undetected change in the perception of Mexicans regarding their own country and the U.S.: The possibility of work and a better life take precedence over nationalist attitudes. Although there appear to be no similar polls from ten or twenty years ago by which to establish a comparison, it still is legitimate to conclude that the results of both polls indicate some significant effects of the economic crisis that Mexico has been suffering since 1982.

The devastating decapitalization of Mexico, or for that matter of all of Latin America, due to capital flight and foreign debt servicing, has been translated into the denationalization of the economy and of public attitudes as well. The capability to maintain both rising living standards and expectation for a better life has been lost. Thus, along with the export of capital accompanied by economic crises and social uncertainty, there has been an unprecedented flight of workers and a "brain drain." In Central America foreign intervention, civil war, and political persecution intensified the economic collapse, causing the migration of over one million people to foreign countries.

The transnationalization of U.S. capital and production preceded the exodus of capital and people south of the Río Bravo. Initially, this seemed to favor the union and national interests of North American workers. This illusion began to dissolve as of the end of the 1960s, leaving behind a labor movement experiencing no growth, increasingly on the defensive, and still under the influence of antimilitant and interventionist attitudes acquired during the era of almost absolute North American capitalist hegemony and of the cold war.

The Bush-Salinas proposal to initiate talks on free trade as a first step towards an eventual formation of a "North American Common Market" represents the most sophisticated attempt to formalize the denationalization of capital and production in this region of the Western Hemisphere. If this initiative is implemented, it will lead to increased privileges for capital while creating obstacles and loss of protections for all workers, unionized or not.

In light of these new phenomena, any analysis of the future of U.S.–Mexico–Central America relations must include a number of key elements that were not fully addressed at the beginning of the last decade: (1) the reorganization of capital-labor relations; (2) the regionalization of social movements, such as labor, civil, and human rights efforts, and environmentalism; (3) the formation of coalitions of advocacy groups at a multinational level. These three elements will have a decisive influence on the policy formulations and electoral platforms in those countries linked by free trade agreements or common markets. In this way the process of transnationalization will be brought into the political/electoral realm.

In this context, the "Binational Exchange: Popular Perspectives on U.S.-Mexico Relations" annual meetings, initiated in 1988 by Professor John Coatsworth of the University of Chicago and the authors of these pages, have provided participants (trade union representatives, farm-worker leaders, immigrant rights defenders, environmentalists, and policy analysts) the opportunity to analyze the impact of Mexico-U.S. integration on workers and their communities as well as to explore strategies for cooperation and joint action. The "Exchanges" were proposed as a forum for representatives of diverse social constituencies directly affected by the unprecedented integration process of a developed country with a developing nation such as Mexico.

The last meeting in Austin, Texas, held in June 1990, was attended by twenty-two Mexican participants, including trade union and labor federation presidents, as well as renowned Cardenista leaders who joined over thirty U.S. participants, among them representatives of several national unions and the AFL-CIO.

The "Binational Exchange" has brought together people not only with different organizing and professional experience but also with diverse ideological viewpoints. Frank discussions of problems have been possible through a climate of respect and equality among participants which has, in turn, allowed for the recognition of common interests in, for example, labor, educational, and environmental areas. As a result, various organizations represented at the meetings have initiated plans for joint cooperation in the context of growing Mexico-U.S. integration.

In these meetings, Baldemar Velásquez, president of the Farm Labor Organizing Committee, has pointed out one of the fundamental challenges now confronting workers: the internationalization of their organizing efforts and of their struggles as the only effective response to the transnationalization of capital and production. Perspectives based on exclusively specific union or national interests no longer can serve to defend the freedoms, rights, and the standard of living of working people, be they U.S. citizens or Central American refugees. The Chicano movement's slogan, "We are a people without borders," resonates today more than ever, from Alaska to Tierra del Fuego.

Cameron Duncan, Greenpeace International

This volume provides a comprehensive and timely analysis of the relationship between economic structures and political turmoil in Mexico, Central America, and the United States. The authors make a good effort to strike a balance between internal responsibilities and external causes of crisis, past and present. But there is insufficient analysis of the fact that orthodox economic "adjustment" policies, often imposed by the multilateral financial institutions, have reinforced existing social inequalities, damaged environments, and ignored popular participation at the same time that they have failed to produce economic growth.

In Mexico and Central America, market-based development policies based on opening national economies to unrestricted foreign investment have undermined ecological sustainability. In their rush to expand exports in order to pay off heavy foreign debts, countries often resort to the easiest short-term approach—rapid exploitation of their natural resource base—and thus avoid difficult political decisions such as the redistribution of productive land. As a consequence, depletion rates of forests, soils, fisheries, and other critical resources far exceed renewal rates.

The stories of ecological disasters underlying export successes have become common. Timber exports have denuded mountains in Mexico and Honduras, causing soil degradation and diminishing water resources. Cotton, winter vegetables, cut flowers, and other cash crop exports in Nicaragua and El Salvador have produced alarming levels of toxic contamination from the abuse of agrochemicals. Costa Rican banana workers have been poisoned by overuse of chemical pesticides. The relationship between the environment and the economy in the current international context is not adequately addressed in this volume.

From an environmental perspective, the free trade agenda is basically about distributing resources: energy, agricultural and forest resources, environmental quality—even food. Establishment of a North American common market along the lines of the corporate model being pursued by the Bush, Salinas, and Mulroney administrations will weaken the ability of national governments to control the development of vital resources and to determine who will develop these resources and for what purposes. As an economic constitution for North America, it will enshrine the rules that have, over the past few hundred years, resulted in an enormous flow of resources from the South to the North—from people who have little to people who consume most of the world's production.

The other critical point which must be underlined is that the market-based corporate trade agenda will undermine any efforts in the direction of tougher environmental regulation. And it will limit the progress we have made in countries that have forged higher standards of environmental protection. It is not surprising that transnational corporations

are interested in constraining countries such as Mexico and Canada
that have valuable resources to export.

If popular groups are to successfully confront this corporate agenda,
we not only have to build our coalitions among national popular
movements, but build our relations internationally as well. We must
work to develop trade relations among our countries that are socially,
environmentally, and economically sustainable. By coordinating internationally our work on environmental, trade, development, and human
rights problems, we can build a future of social justice and harmony
between humans and nature.

Rev. Jesse Jackson, Founder of the Rainbow Coalition, Former Candidate for the Democratic Nomination for President

We should thank the authors of this book for enriching our understanding
of Mexico's relations with the United States and the rest of Latin America.
In foreign policy terms, they propose a basis of cooperation around
fundamental principles of self-determination and negotiated solutions
to conflicts. These suggestions should be considered seriously.

This book also does a fine job of illuminating the changing international economic environment and the adjustments that Mexico and
other countries in the Americas are making to it. Perhaps the single
most important issue in the remaking of hemispheric economic relations
right now is the U.S.-Mexico Free Trade Agreement, with the likely
participation of Canada.

As the authors point out, we already trade extensively. We are Mexico's
largest trading partner; Mexico is our third largest, behind only Canada
and Japan. In 1989, trade between Mexico and the United States surpassed
$51 billion dollars. In this context the Bush administration's proposal
to negotiate a free trade zone with Mexico has an instant appeal. At
a time when protectionist barriers seem to be rising elsewhere, the
United States, Canada, and Mexico would constitute a common market
larger than Europe's.

The administration claims that a Free Trade Agreement would help
the development of Mexico's economy, providing the United States with
a richer market for exports, and helping to slow the flow of migrants
and drugs into this country. All these are worthy goals. But we should
make sure that the kind of Free Trade Agreement that the Bush
administration wants to make will actually achieve them, and whether
other goals may be sacrificed.

If care is not taken, such an agreement might hurt workers in both
countries. U.S. multinationals would go south to take advantage of 75–

cent-an-hour labor. Mexico's government would confront a powerful lobby demanding a continuation of low wages and lax environmental, health and safety, and consumer protection regulation. Mexican peasants drawn toward the northern part of their country by the opportunity to work are unlikely to long accept legal 75–cent-an-hour wages if they can find illegal $3.00–an-hour work in the United States. We can do better and reach an agreement that truly benefits the people of both countries, rather than a handful of corporations. We must reach an agreement that treats our neighbor as a friend and partner.

The European Economic Community (EEC) offers an example. As an integral part of their common market, the Europeans are negotiating a social charter, agreeing on basic minimum levels for wages and working conditions, social benefits, and environment and consumer regulation, that they will all observe. At the same time, the EEC is offering aid and assistance to poorer members like Spain and Portugal.

We cannot just declare free trade. Already on the Mexican border, we allow U.S. companies to establish plants in Mexico. The result is investment designed solely to exploit cheap labor and lax environmental laws. We import foods and goods made with poisons that we have banned, by labor paid less than we would allow, working in conditions below what we would accept. Mexicans get jobs without much hope, as well as a despoiled environment. We lose jobs and import the poisons we ban. Working people in neither country benefit.

Instead, we should carefully seek to negotiate a minimal social compact with Mexico: minimum wages and conditions, health and safety, environmental, consumer protection, and child labor laws. At the same time, we should offer to help relieve Mexico of its inordinate burden of debt. Together these measures would enable trade barriers to come down without undermining labor in the North or exploiting workers in the South.

If, as this book implies, U.S.-Mexico relations will determine U.S. policy toward all of Latin America, then what is at stake with a Free Trade Agreement is whether we share the best of our societies or the worst of our public policies. Already, Bush administration policymakers are talking about further trade agreements with other countries and regions in Latin America.

We are at a crossroads. As presently proposed, Mexico and the rest of Latin America would get little in the way of the economic development that the United States has enjoyed through such agreements. Rather, they would get our plant closings and hostility to unions, and we would get low wages and unemployment. Everyone would end up with environmental degradation.

What *should* we share? Both sides of any border will benefit if we can share strong unions and farmers' organizations, and if those groups play an active role in setting policy on trade, investment and debt, fair labor practices, and safeguards on the health of workers and communities. Nobody would deny that there are majority constituencies for these policies on both sides of all borders.

To achieve this, however, working people must begin to meet together, to talk together, to work together across national boundaries. Worker cooperation and coordination must flow as freely as capital across state borders. We can grow together or decline apart.

About the Book and Authors

Although relations with Central America dominated U.S. foreign policy with its southern neighbors during the 1980s, relations with Mexico will likely shape U.S. foreign policy in the next decade. This book examines the troubled nature of the triangular link between Mexico, Central America, and the United States in order to understand the implications of U.S. policy for peace and development in the Western Hemisphere.

The book begins with an analysis of Mexico's foreign policy and its historical role in seeking diplomatic solutions to volatile situations in Central America. The authors then assess the probable impact on the region of increased economic integration, particularly the U.S.-Mexico free trade agreement, especially important in light of Mexico's enormous debt and immigration issues. Special attention is also given to diplomatic aspects of the relationship, with a focus on the process of negotiations to resolve conflicts in Central America. A lengthy epilogue offers critical commentary on key issues discussed in the text by such prominent figures as Jesse Jackson, Carlos Vilas, David Ibarra, and Guadalupe Gonzales.

H. Rodrigo Jauberth is research coordinator of Central America studies at CIDE, Costa Rica; **Gilberto Castañeda** is research associate of Central America studies at CIDE, Guatemala; **Jesús Hernández** is research associate of U.S.-Mexican studies at the Universidad Nacional Autonoma de Mexico; **Pedro Vuskovic** is research coordinator of economic studies at Coordinadora Regional de Investigaciones Económicas y Sociales (CRIES) in Nicaragua.

Index